Habakkuk

Hope for a Leader in Troubled Times

CLINTON'S BIBLICAL LEADERSHIP COMMENTARY SERIES

J. Robert Clinton, D. Miss., Ph.D.

BARNABAS PUBLISHERS

Copyright © J. Robert Clinton, August 2002

All Rights Reserved

No Part of this publication may be reproduced, stored in a retrieval system, or transmitted in any form or by any means - electronic, mechanical, photocopy, recording, or any other - except for brief quotations embodied in a critical article or printed reviews, without prior permission of the publisher.

Barnabas Publishers
P.O. Box 6006
Altadena, CA 91003-6006
ISBN No. 1-932814-10-8

Printed in the United States of America

Series & Title Cover Design: D.M. Battermann, R&D Design Servies
Book Design & Layout: D.M. & R.D. Battermann, R&D Design Services

Habakkuk

CLINTON'S BIBLICAL LEADERSHIP COMMENTARY SERIES

Hope for a Leader in Troubled Times

J. Robert Clinton, D. Miss., PhD.

ISBN No 0-9710454-4-5

Copyright © J. Robert Clinton August 2002

Table of Contents

Contents	Page
Abbreviations	v
List of Tables	vi
List of Figures	vii
Introduction to Clinton's Leadership Commentary Series	viii
Preface	x
General Reflection on Habakkuk	1
Overview	3
Leadership Topics and Leadership Lessons	5
1. BIOGRAPHICAL GENRE	5
2. FAITH (Prayer)	5
3. COMPLEX SITUATIONS	6
4. BROADER PERSPECTIVE	7
5. TRANSPARENCY	8
6. FUTURE PERFECT THINKING	8
7. WORSHIP/ CELEBRATION/INSPIRATIONAL LEADERSHIP	8
Habakkuk Commentary	9
For Further Study	21

Leadership Articles[1] (bold faced items appear in other commentaries as well): 22

1	Babylonians, The	24
2	Babylonians—Power Encounter	27
3	Bible Translations And Hebrew Poetic Format	31
4	**Biblical Framework—The Redemptive Drama**	34
5	**Daniel—Power Encounters**	50
6	**Figures and Idioms in the Bible**	52
7	**Future Perfect Paradigm**	59
8	Getting God's Perspective, A Leader's Necessity	64
9	God's Judgment on the Babylonians	68
10	**God The Promise Keeper**	73
11	**God's Shaping Processes with Leaders**	76
12	**God's Timing and Leadership**	80
13	Habakkuk, Celebration—A Leadership Function	86
14	Habakkuk, Contextual Flow—Understanding the Argument	90

---

[1] Articles listed with numbers are included with this commentary. Some articles, without numbers occur in other commentaries.

15	Habakkuk, Crucial Faith Words	93
16	Habakkuk, Four Shaping Activities	95
17	Habakkuk, God's Timing	100
18	Habakkuk, Important Ideas to Communicate	103
19	Habakkuk, Important Words to Study	108
20	Habakkuk, Judgment and Revelation	117
21	Habakkuk, Left Hand of God	120
22	Habakkuk, Regaining Hope Via a God-Ordained Paradigm Shift	124
23	Hebrew Poetry	129
24	**Isolation Processing—Learning Deep Lessons from God**	136
25	**Leaders, Intercession Hints from Habakkuk**	143
26	**Leadership Eras In The Bible, Six Identified**	149
27	**Leadership Functions, 3 High Level Generic Properties.**	153
28	**Left Hand of God, The**	156
29	**Macro Lessons—Defined**	160
30	**Macro Lessons: List of 41 Across Six Leadership Eras**	163
31	Needed, Sons of Issachar	166
32	Paradigms And Paradigm Shifts	171
33	**Promises of God**	176
34	**Prophecy Overview**	179
35	**Prophetic Crises—Three Major Biblical Times**	185
36	**Six Biblical Leadership Eras, Approaching the Bible with Leadership Eyes**	192
37	Spiritual Disciplines—and On-going Leadership	207
38	Spiritual Leadership—Prolonging the Life of God in a Work	213
39	Structural Time—Simplified Overview	220
40	Transparency With God	227
	Glossary of Leadership Terms	231
	Bibliography	241

Abbreviations

Bible Books

Genesis	Ge	Nahum	Na
Exodus	Ex	Habakkuk	Hab
Leviticus	Lev	Zephaniah	Zep
Numbers	Nu	Haggai	Hag
Deuteronomy	Dt	Zechariah	Zec
Joshua	Jos	Malachi	Mal
Judges	Jdg	Matthew	Mt
Ruth	Ru	Mark	Mk
1 Samuel	1Sa	Luke	Lk
2 Samuel	2Sa	John	Jn
1 Kings	1Ki	Acts	Ac
2 Kings	2Ki	Romans	Ro
1 Chronicles	1Ch	1 Corinthians	1Co
2 Chronicles	2Ch	2 Corinthians	2Co
Ezra	Ezr	Galatians	Gal
Nehemiah	Ne	Ephesians	Eph
Esther	Est	Philippians	Php
Job	Job	Colossians	Col
Psalms	Ps	1 Thessalonians	1Th
Proverbs	Pr	2 Thessalonians	2Th
Ecclesiastes	Ecc	1 Timothy	1Ti
Song of Songs	SS	2 Timothy	2Ti
Isaiah	Isa	Titus	Tit
Jeremiah	Jer	Philemon	Phm
Lamentations	La	Hebrews	Heb
Ezekiel	Eze	James	Jas
Daniel	Da	1 Peter	1Pe
Hosea	Hos	2 Peter	2Pe
Joel	Joel	1 John	1Jn
Amos	Am	2 John	2Jn
Obadiah	Ob	3 John	3Jn
Jonah	Jnh	Jude	Jude
Micah	Mic	Revelation	Rev

Other

BAS	Basic English Version
CEV	Contemporary English Version
fn	footnote(s)
KJV	King James Version of the Bible
NEB	New English Bible
NLT	New Living Translation
N.T.	New Testament
O.T.	Old Testament
Phillips	The New Testament in Modern English, J.B. Phillips
TEV	Today's English Version (also called Good News Bible)
Vs	verse(s)

List of Tables

	Page
Hab 1-1. Main Old Testament References to Chaldeans or Babylonians	24
Hab 2-1. Elements of Power Encounter Seen In Daniel	30
Hab 3-1. Bibles and Poetic Format	31
Hab 3-2. Some Help In Noting Parallelism In Printed Poetic Format	32
Hab 4-1. Bible Books Related To Chapters of the Redemptive Drama	48
Hab 5-1. Elements of Power Encounter Seen In Daniel	50
Hab 5-2. Giftedness and Overall Results	51
Hab 6-1. 11 Figures in the Bible Defined	53
Hab 6-2. 13 Patterned Idioms	54
Hab 6-3. 15 Body Language Idioms	56
Hab 6-4. 14 Miscellaneous Idioms	57
Hab 7-1. Biblical Leaders And The Future Perfect Paradigm	60
Hab 7-2. 5 Stages Leading to the Future Perfect Paradigm	61
Hab 8-1. Other Perspective Macros Seen in Habakkuk	66
Hab 9-1. Habakkuk's Prophecy of Judgment on Babylon	68
Hab 10-1. God The Promise Keeper—Examples	74
Hab 11-1. Early Shaping Processes Identified and Defined	77
Hab 11-2. Middle Ministry Shaping Processes—Identified, Defined	78
Hab 11-3. Latter Ministry Shaping Processes—Identified and Defined	78
Hab 12-1. 13 Bible Characters and God's Timing	81
Hab 13-1. Biblical Leaders and Instances of Celebration	88
Hab 15-1. The Just Shall Live By Faith—4 Occurrences	93
Hab 16-1. 4 Process Items Seen in the Book of Habakkuk	96
Hab 16-2. Macro Lessons Possibly Learned by Habakkuk	98
Hab 17-1. Some Examples of the Timing Macro Lesson	101
Hab 18-1. 8 Key Ideas From the Book of Habakkuk	104
Hab 19-1. Statement Of The General Language Laws	110
Hab 19-2. The General Language Laws Related As To Focus	112
Hab 19-3. Habakkuk 1:5 Look (KJV Behold)	113
Hab 19-4. Habakkuk 1:5 Look Very Carefully (KJV Regard)	113
Hab 19-5. Habakkuk 1:5 Astonish (KJV wonder marvelously)	114
Hab 19-6. Habakkuk 1:5 Emphatic Superlative (KJV working a work)	115
Hab 19-7. Habakkuk 1:5 Believe (KJV believe)	115
Hab 19-8. Some Other Words in Habakkuk For Word Study	116
Hab 21-1. Some Occurrences of the Left Hand of God	120
Hab 22-1. Hope Macro Lesson And Related Information	125
Hab 23-1. Basic Procedure—Analyzing Extended Hebrew Poetry	133
Hab 24-1. Isolation Results	137
Hab 24-2. Common Happenings in Isolation	137
Hab 24-3. Job and Type I Isolation	138
Hab 24-4. Moses and Type II Isolation	138
Hab 24-5. Elijah's Type I Isolation Experience, 1Ki 17:1-6—Some Observations	139
Hab 24-6. Elijah's Type II Isolation Experience	139
Hab 24-7. Nine Observations from Paul's Isolation Experiences	140
Hab 25-1. 5 Prayer Observations Seen in Habakkuk	143
Hab 26-1. Basic Questions To Ask About Leadership Eras	150
Hab 26-2. Six Leadership Eras in the Bible—Brief Characterizations	151
Hab 27-1. Typical Task-Oriented Leadership Functions	154
Hab 27-2. Typical Relational-Oriented Leadership Functions	154

Hab 27-3. Typical Inspirational Leadership Functions	154
Hab 28-1. Some Occurrences of the Left Hand of God	157
Hab 28-2. God's Left Hand Working Through Cyrus	158
Hab 29-1. Leadership Eras and Number of Macro Lessons	161
Hab 29-2. Top Three Macro Lessons in O.T. Leadership Eras	161
Hab 29-3. Top Three Macro Lessons in N.T. Leadership Eras	162
Hab 31-1. Mintzberg's Five Structural Elements	167
Hab 31-2. Examples: Mintzberg's Structural Elements	168
Hab 32-1. 10 Examples of Biblical Paradigm shifts	172
Hab 32-3. Needed Paradigm Shifts to Impact the Post-Modern Era	174
Hab 33-1. God The Promise Keeper—Examples	178
Hab 34-1 Eight Guidelines for Interpreting Prophecy—Basic Hermeneutics	180
Hab 34-2. Two Special Prophecy Observations About Fulfillment	183
Hab 35-1. The Restoration Era Crises And Related Biblical Material	188
Hab 35-2. The Restoration Era Crises And Related Biblical Material	189
Hab 36-1. Six Leadership Eras Outlined	193
Hab 36-2. Six Leadership Eras in the Bible—Definitive Characteristics	194
Hab 36-3. Seven Leadership Genre—Sources for Leadership Findings	194
Hab 36-4. Six Leadership Eras, On-Going Impact Items, Follow-Up	200
Hab 36-5. Transitions Along the Biblical Leadership Time-Line	203
Hab 36-6. Moses' Transition/ Lessons/ Implications	204
Hab 36-7. Jesus' Transition/ Lessons/ Implications	204
Hab 37-1. Abstinence Disciplines Defined	209
Hab 37-2. Abstinence Disciplines—Some purposes	209
Hab 37-3. Abstinence Disciplines—Applicational Ideas	210
Hab 38-1. Three Important Macro Lessons From the Kingdom Era	216
Hab 38-2. Spiritual Leaders Who Prolonged God's Work	217
Hab 39-1. List of Macro Lessons A Leader Needs	220
Hab 39-2. 5 Structural Time Paradigms Usefulness For Perspective	222
Hab 39-3. 12 Structural Time Stages Described	223

List of Figures and Charts

Chart Hab 4-1 The History Books—Major Content	42
Chart Hab 4-2 Differences in Palestine—Close of O.T., Beginning of N.T.	43
Hab 4-1. Overview of Redemptive Drama Time Line	35
Hab 6-1. 11 Common Figures of Speech	53
Hab 7-1. The Future Perfect Paradigm on a Continuum	60
Hab 11-1. Some Major Shaping Processes Across The Time-Line	77
Hab 13-1. Spiritual Disciplines Categorized	87
Hab 19-1. Overall Scheme of Hermeneutical System	110
Hab 22-1. Three High Level Leadership Functions	127
Hab 23-1 Tree Diagram Giving Overview of 3 Types of Parallelisms	130
Hab 24-1. Three Types of Isolations	136
Hab 24-2. Isolation Sovereignty Continuum	137
Hab 26-1. Tree Diagram Categorizing the Basics of Leadership	150
Hab 27-1. Three High Level Leadership Functions	153
Hab 29-1. Leadership Truth Continuum/Where Macro Lessons Occur	160
Hab 34-1. 3 Types of Prophetic Genre Concerning Jesus Christ	181
Chart Hab 35-1 The History Books—Major Content	186
Hab 36-1. Leadership Eras— Rough Chronological Length In Years	201
Hab 36-2. Overview Time-Line of Biblical Leadership	202
Hab 36-3. Two Major Transitions—National Transition and Great Divide	203
Hab 38-1. Simplified Prophets' Chart	214
Hab 39-1 Clinton's Basic Modality Cycle	225

Introduction

This leadership commentary on Habakkuk is part of a series, **Clinton's Leadership Commentary Series.** For the past 13 years I have been researching leadership concepts in the Bible. As a result of that I have identified the 25 most helpful Bible books that contribute to an understanding of leadership. I have done ten of these commentaries to date and am continuing on the rest. I originally published eight of those leadership commentaries in a draft manuscript for use in classes. But it became clear that I would need to break that large work (735 pages) into smaller works. The commentary series does that. Titus was the first in the series. Haggai was the second of the series that is being done as an individual work. And Habakkuk is the third.

This is a leadership commentary, not an exegetical commentary. That means I have worked with the text to see what implications of leadership are suggested by it.

A given commentary in the series is made up of an *Overview Section*, which seeks to analyze the book as a whole for historical background, plan, theme, and fit into the Bible as a whole. In addition, I identify, up front, the basic leadership topics that are dealt with in the book. Then I educe leadership observations, guidelines, principles, and values for each of these leadership topics. This *Overview Section* primes the reader to look with leadership eyes.

Then I have the *Commentary Proper*. I use my own translation of the text. I give commentary on various aspects of the text. A given context, paragraph size, will usually have 3 to 4 comments dealing with some suggestions about leadership things.

The *Commentary Proper* suggests *Leadership Concepts* and connects you to leadership articles that further explain these leadership concepts. The emphasis on the comments is not exegetical though I do make those kinds of comments when they are helpful for my leadership purposes.

The *Leadership Articles* (in Habakkuk, there are 40 totaling 208 pages) in the series carry much of what I have learned about leadership in my 38 years of ministry. In one sense, these articles and others in the series are my legacy. I plan to publish all of the articles of the total series in a separate work, **Clinton's Encyclopedia of Biblical Leadership Insights,** which will be updated periodically as the series expands. I think a leader at almost any level of leadership can be helped greatly by getting leadership perspectives from these articles.

I also include a *Glossary* which lists all the leadership concepts labeled in the comments.

Other books in the series, to be released over the next five years, include:

1,2 Timothy--Apostolic Leadership Picking Up the Mantle
1,2 Corinthians--Problematic Apostolic Leadership

Daniel--A Model Leader in Tough times
Philemon--A Study in Leadership Style
Philippians--A Study in Modeling
John--Jesus' Incarnational Leadership (John)

All of the above were previously done in the large manuscript and used in classes. Now I will break these out as individual commentaries in the series. And then I will do other books anticipated in the series over the next five years. Some of these will be done as I can get to them:

Jonah—Seeing God's Perspective--A Crucial Paradigm Shift
Nehemiah—Focused Leadership
Malachi—Renewal Lessons Needed to Face Nominality Head-On

And my long-term thinking includes developing the following:

Acts—Apostolic Leadership in Transition Times
Deuteronomy--A Study in Moses' Inspirational Leadership
Numbers--Moses, Spiritual Authority, and Maintenance Leadership
Mark--Jesus' Power Ministry
Joshua--Courageous Leadership
Mathew--A Study in Leadership Selection and Development (Matthew)
1,2 Samuel--3 Leaders Compared and Contrasted (1,2 Samuel)

I (Bobby) have already done a study of each book in the Bible from a leadership standpoint and have identified and written up a number of leadership topics for each book. This analysis is captured in my book, **The Bible and Leadership Values**.

In an age of relativity, we believe the Bible speaks loudly concerning leadership concepts offering suggestions, guidelines, and even absolutes. We, as Christian leaders, desperately need this leadership help as we seek to influence our followers toward God's purposes for them.

J. Robert Clinton
November 2002

Preface

Every Scripture inspired of God is profitable for leadership insights (doctrine), pointing out of leadership errors (reproof), suggesting what to do about leadership errors (correction), for highlighting how to model a righteous life (instruction in righteousness) in order that God's leader (Timothy) may be well equipped to lead God's people (the special good work given in the book Timothy to the young leader Timothy) .
(2 Timothy 3:16,17—Clinton paraphrase--slanted toward Timothy's leadership situation)

The Bible--a Major Source of Leadership Values and Principles

No more wonderful source of leadership values and principles exists than the Bible. It is filled with influential people and the results of their influence--both good and bad. Yet it remains so little used to expose leadership values and principles. What is needed to break this *leadership barrier*? Three things:

1. A conviction that the Bible is authoritative and can give leadership insights;
2. Leadership perspectives to stimulate our findings in the Bible--we are blind in general to leadership ideas and hence do not see them in the Bible;
3. A willful decision to study and use the Bible as a source of leadership insights.

These three assumptions underlie the writing of my leadership commentary series. **Habakkuk** is one of a series of books intended to help leaders cross the *leadership barrier*.

Leadership Framework

Perhaps it might be helpful to put the notion of leadership insights from Habakkuk in the bigger picture of leadership in the Bible. Three major leadership elements give us our most general framework (cross-culturally applicable as well) for categorizing leadership insights. The study of leadership involves:

1. **THE LEADERSHIP BASAL ELEMENTS** (The *What* of Leadership)
   a. leaders
   b. followers
   c. situations

2. **LEADERSHIP INFLUENCE MEANS** (The *How* of Leadership)
   a. individual means
   b. corporate means

3. **LEADERSHIP VALUE BASES** (The *Why* of Leadership)
   a. cultural
   b. theological

Preface

It is these elements that enable us to analyze leadership throughout the whole Bible. Using these major notions we recognize that leadership at different times in the Bible operates sufficiently different so as to suggest leadership eras--that is, time periods within which leadership follows more closely certain commonalties than in the time preceding it and following it. This allows us to identify six such eras in the Bible.

Six Bible Leadership Eras

The six leadership eras include,

1. **Patriarchal Era**

2. **Pre-Kingdom Era**
   A. Desert Years
   B. The War Years
   C. The Tribal Years

3. **Kingdom Era**
   A. United Kingdom
   B. Divided Kingdom
   C. Southern Kingdom

4. **Post-Kingdom Era**
   A. Exilic
   B. A Foothold Back in the Land

5. **Pre-Church Era**
6. **Church Era**

For each of these major eras we are dealing with some fundamental leadership questions. We ask ourselves these major questions about every leadership era.[1] Usually the answers are sufficiently diverse as to justify identification of a unique leadership era.

Where does Habakkuk fit?

The book of Habakkuk obviously fits in the third leadership era, *The Kingdom Era*. In fact, it occurs in part c of that leadership era—*Southern Kingdom*. It is a time of difficulty for leadership. The northern kingdom has already been destroyed by the Assyrian empire. And the Southern Kingdom is going downhill fast. God has warned

---

[1] The six questions we use to help us differentiate between leadership eras includes: 1. What is the major leadership focus? 2. What are the influence means used? 3. What are the basic leadership functions? 4. What are the characteristics of the followers? 5. What was the existing cultural forms of leadership? 6. Other? See **Article**, *36. Six Biblical Leadership Eras, Approaching the Bible with Leadership Eyes*.

Preface

repeatedly that if the Southern Kingdom, Judah, did not repent and turn to Him that He would destroy it. Habakkuk lives in this time and he is in a crisis in his life and ministry. He sees injustice and ungodliness all around him. He is beginning to doubt God, His character and His working. The book exposes his innermost feelings in this faith crisis situation. He voices his honest complaint to God and waits for God's answer. God's answer shocks Him and forces him to ask another question of God. God's next answer is so overwhelming that Habakkuk responds with awe, fear and joy in God's future work.

And so God meets Habakkuk in his situation and shows us as leaders today how to trust in God in our own situations.

What does Habakkuk say?

Before we can look at leadership insights from Habakkuk we need to be sure that we understand why Habakkuk is in the Scriptures and what it is saying in general. Having done our homework, hermeneutically speaking, we are free then to go beyond and look for other interpretative insights--such as leadership insights. But we must remember, always, first of all to interpret in light of the historical times, purpose of, theme of, and structure of the book.

One way of analyzing the structure, that is, the way the author of Habakkuk organizes his material to accomplish his purposes would be:

Structure
- I. (1:1-2:1)   Habakkuk's Honest Struggle With Faith
- II. (2:2-2:20)   Habakkuk's Faith-Wait Response
- III. (3:1-19)   Habakkuk's Response of True Faith

The overall thematic intent of this short epistle could be represented by a subject, which permeates all of what God is doing through Habakkuk's leadership.

Theme   **HABAKKUK'S STRUGGLE OF FAITH**
- involved his honest questioning of God,
- was met by God's own explanation, and
- resulted in a joyous acceptance by faith of that which God was doing.

The heart of it is how God gives hope to a leader in the midst of trying times.

It is always difficult to synthesize statements of purpose when the author does not directly and explicitly give them. But it seems reasonable to imply that the following are some of the purposes of this small three-chapter book in the Old Testament.

- to teach God's people to trust unconditionally in God's complex workings in history to bring about his just purposes,
- to reveal how God matures a leader in faith,
- to highlight the need always for a person of God to live by faith in God,
- to indicate that when God uses nations in history for His purposes He is still true to His nature.

Preface

Having done our overview of the book, hermeneutically speaking we can look into how God shaped this prophetic leader in a critical time in his life. And we see how a leader who trusts God in difficult times is renewed with hope.

General Reflection—Habakkuk

With this back ground in mind, we can now proceed to the leadership commentary including its *General Reflection*, *Leadership Lessons*, *Commentary notes*, *Articles*, and *Glossary*.

Today, we live in the church leadership era.[1] It is difficult to place ourselves back hundreds of years into the 3rd leadership era—Kingdom Leadership.[2] So most modern day pastors and parachurch leaders do not bother to go back and study this period of time in the Bible. Judah, the Southern Kingdom, is on a rapidly destructive path. The Northern Kingdom has already felt the discipline of God's left hand (the Assyrians). Now it is Judah's turn. The Northern Kingdom had no godly leaders in its history. It self-destructed in a relatively short time. The Southern Kingdom, which from time-to-time had spiritual leaders who instituted renewal reforms, has lasted longer.[3] But the basic pattern has been set. The Southern Kingdom is deteriorating in its obedience to God and His on-going efforts to renew it through prophetic voices. Habakkuk sees the sinful times and recognizes the destructive path. But where is God in this. That is Habakkuk's cry. And God meets him.

All leaders at one time or other will face a faith crisis such as Habakkuk did. The shaping activity of God to instill faith in a leader is very instructive. The leadership lessons from Habakkuk should have widespread acceptance from leaders today. Essentially, we live in a world, which offers little or no hope. Hope[4] is what we need. Habakkuk tells us how to get hope in the midst of hopeless times. The basic answer, that the "just shall live by faith" still rings true today.[5]

Suggested Approach for Studying Habakkuk

Read through the overview to get a general feeling of what Habakkuk is about. Note particularly the *Theme* of the book and its *Plan* for developing that theme, i.e. the outline for developing that theme. Then note the various purposes that we suggest that the book of Habakkuk is seeking to accomplish. Then read through each of the leadership findings that we suggest are in the book. This is all preparation for the first reading of the text.

---

[1] See **Articles**, *26. Leadership Eras In The Bible, Six Identified; 36. Six Biblical Leadership Eras, Approaching the Bible with Leadership Eyes.* This is probably an important pre-requisite for you before approaching the commentary.

[2] See **Article**, *4. Biblical Framework—The Redemptive Drama.* This is another important pre-requisite giving important background information setting the situation in which Habakkuk's incident happens. See also **Article**, *35. Prophetic Crises, 3 Major Biblical Times*, which pinpoints the crisis Habakkuk was facing.

[3] See **Articles**, *38. Spiritual Leadership—Prolonging the Life of God in a Work; Structural Time—A Simplified Overview.*

[4] See **Article**, *22. Habakkuk, Regaining Hope Via a God-Ordained Paradigm Shift.*

[5] See **Article**, *15. Habakkuk, The Crucial Faith Words.*

General Reflection—Habakkuk page 2

Read the text itself, all three chapters at one sitting, without referring to any of the commentary notes. Just see if you can *see what of the overview information* and the *leadership lessons* are suggested to you as you read the text.

Then reread the text, probably a chapter at a time and note the comments we give.[6] From time-to-time, go back and read a leadership lesson again when it is brought to your mind as you read the text and the commentary. Also feel free to stop and go to the **Glossary** for explanation of leadership terms suggested by the commentary. And do the same thing with the **Articles**. These articles capture what we have learned about leadership over the years as we have observed it, researched it, and taught it. It is these articles that will enlighten your leadership understanding. Obviously because of the unique time in which Habakkuk ministered, there will be some unusual leadership articles.

We have provided some *note space* at the conclusion of the Habakkuk commentary where you can jot down ideas for future study. Have fun as you work through Habakkuk, and by all means learn something about *celebration and inspirational leadership* and *how a leader's faith in God is restored*. See the philosophy of history and be comforted to know that God is working today just as in Habakkuk's day to oversee history toward its just conclusion. May your perspective be broadened, just as Habakkuk's was.

Read through the overview, which follows. It gives a summarized version of the hermeneutical background studies for Habakkuk.

---

[6] From time-to-time in the comments, I will use the abbreviation SRN. SRN stands for Strong's Reference Number. Strong, in his exhaustive concordance, labeled each word in the Old Testament (dominantly Hebrew words but also some Aramaic/ Chaldean) and New Testament (Greek Works mostly) with an identifying number. He then constructed an Old Testament and New Testament lexicon (dictionary). If you have a **Strong's Exhaustive Concordance** with lexicon, you can look up the words I refer to. Many modern day reference works (lexicons and word studies and Bible Dictionaries and encyclopedias) use this Strong's Reference Number.

BOOK	**HABAKKUK**	**Author:** Habakkuk

Characters   Habakkuk

Who To/For   For Judah

Literature Type   Extended Hebrew Poetry; dialogue, Habakkuk and God.

Story Line   Habakkuk is in a crisis in his life and ministry. He sees injustice and ungodliness all around him. He is beginning to doubt God, His character and His working. The book exposes his innermost feelings in this faith crisis situation. He voices his honest complaint to God and waits for God's answer. God's answer shocks Him and forces him to ask another question of God. God's next answer is so overwhelming that Habakkuk responds with awe, fear and joy in God's future work.

Structure
- I. (1:1-2:1)   Habakkuk's Honest Struggle With Faith
- II. (2:2-2:20)   Habakkuk's Faith-Wait Response
- III. (3:1-19)   Habakkuk's Response of True Faith

Theme   **HABAKKUK'S STRUGGLE OF FAITH**
- involved his honest questioning of God,
- was met by God's own explanation, and
- resulted in a joyous acceptance by faith of that which God was doing.

Key Words   Habakkuk 2:4 the basic answer to the faith crisis.

Key Events   Habakkuk's open challenge to God, God's answer (the Babylonian captivity), Habakkuk's incredulous response to that, God's response (justice for Babylon), Habakkuk's surrender (the faith song).

Purposes
- to teach God's people to trust unconditionally in God's complex workings in history to bring about his just purposes,
- to reveal how God matures a leader in faith,
- to highlight the need always for a person of God to live by faith in God,
- to indicate that when God uses nations in history for His purposes He is still true to His nature.

Why Important   All leaders must eventually learn to walk by faith, that is, trust in an unseen God's dealings with their own life, ministry, events around them, and the world whether or not they can understand the complexity or see what God is doing. God's people must also learn this lesson. Habakkuk reveals several processes whereby God teaches this valuable Biblical lesson. Like Jonah and Job the book focuses not on ministry to others but on God's dealing with His leader. When there is increasing deterioration in the society, as was the

Habakkuk —Overview   page 4

case during Habakkuk's time, ungodliness will abound. And there will be unjust things going on with no apparent repercussions. It is in the midst of these things that we need to see a bigger perspective. We need to see the present happenings in terms of the larger picture, the history leading up to it and that, which is to come. God frequently does just that. He meets a leader in a crisis situation by broadening perspective. And we are thankful for just such processing, for otherwise we, like Habakkuk would be ready to give up.

Where It Fits   Habakkuk's ministry most likely takes place in Chapter 2, The Destruction of A Nation[7] and in the single kingdom phase of Kingdom leadership.[8] He probably overlapped with Jeremiah's ministry. And if he did see the prophecy fulfilled (3:16) then he probably ministered in the latter part of the single kingdom era.

---

[7] See **Article**, *4. Biblical Framework—The Redemptive Drama*.

[8] See **Article**, *36. Six Biblical Leadership Eras, Approaching the Bible with Leadership Eyes*. This is probably an important pre-requisite for you before approaching the commentary.

Habakkuk Leadership Lessons

Leadership Lessons

1. **BIOGRAPHICAL GENRE.**[9] Habakkuk is a biographical snapshot of a pivotal point, a critical moment in the life of a leader. Its processing includes crisis, isolation, a paradigm shift, as well as a faith challenge. Habakkuk responds positively to this shaping work of God. Lessons include principles on prayer, faith, solitude and a philosophy of God's working in history. If we are willing to draw out some implications we can suggest a number of things about Habakkuk. He was a poet. The entire book was written in Hebrew poetry. He was a sensitive man. He was a man of emotion. He was a musician. He saw the importance of getting truth from God and putting it into a form that could impact others—a song. He was a prophet—needed to speak into unjust situations around him. He obviously had a deep life of communion with God. He was a practical theologian, one who knew the character of God (holiness, justice).

Leadership Principles/ Values Suggested by this concept:
   a. God uses critical incidents in a leader's life to shape that leader for God's purposes.
   b. Some critical incidents are pivotal in the life and ministry of a leader. That leader can see this critical incident either as a springboard for further ministry for God or a point of turning away From God.
   c. The difference between leaders and followers is perspective. The difference between leaders and effective leaders is better perspective. God uses paradigm shifts in a leader's life to give better perspective.
   d. God's perspective on history includes His working to bring about a just solution to unjust situations.
   e. God can use ungodly nations to accomplish his judgments.
   f. Faith often matures because of isolation experiences.
   g. A successful response to a faith challenge includes a "trust" response to God and His accomplishment of His word as well as a joyful response to it—no matter what the consequences of it are personally.

See **Articles**, *11. God's Shaping Processes with Leaders*; *16. Habakkuk, Four Shaping Activities; Paradigm Shifts*; *22. Habakkuk, Regaining Hope Via a God-Ordained Paradigm Shift, Leadership Genre—Seven Types.*

2. **FAITH (Prayer).** Leaders serve an unseen God who has revealed Himself and intervened in history. A basic lesson that all leaders must learn is the one Habakkuk learned here (2:4). Leaders must believe that God is, that He is trustworthy, and that He is a rewarder of them that seek Him (Hebrews 11:6). Habakkuk faced his doubts with God and persevered through till he got God's answer to his questions. He got God's perspective on his situation and more. And then he learned the important lesson of being satisfied with God's answer. Three stages of faith are seen in this book. Chapter 1 gives Stage 1, Confused Faith. It reveals a leader doubting God and God's activity in his situation. Chapter 2 shows Stage 2, Confronting faith, in which Habakkuk now sees God

---

[9] Biographical genre is the major source of leadership information in the Old Testament. The other six leadership genre include: Direct Leadership Contexts; Indirect Leadership Contexts; Leadership Acts; Parabolic Passages; Books As A Whole; Macro Lessons.

Habakkuk — Leadership Lessons   page 6

in his situation but does not like what God is doing. Chapter 3 shows Stage 3, Conquering Faith, in which Habakkuk resolves his issues with God and joyously accepts God's future workings. It is the highest stage of faith—trusting God to work what He says He will do and being satisfied with it.

<u>Leadership Principles/ Values or other Statements Suggested by this concept:</u>
  a. Descriptors of faith as seen illustrated in Habakkuk's critical incident:
     (1) True faith searches honestly.
     (2) True faith is matured in solitude.
     (3) True faith is marked by stability.
     (4) True faith is manifested in surrender.
     (5) True faith is satisfied with God's solution.
  b. Prayer hints seen in Habakkuk's testimony:
     (1) A proper understanding of God's holiness causes one to have a burden to pray about social injustices.
     (2) God's answer to prayer may be difficult to discern in the pressure of complex ministry circumstances.
     (3) A leader should not be afraid to tell God exactly how he/she feels in any situation. A simple honest talk with God will do much to relax the heart.
     (4) Prayer should be a dialog and not just a monologue.
     (5) Sometimes it will take a concentrated time (in a special place) of solitude to discern God's working and to stabilize one's faith on some issue.
  c. A leader must expect faith to be tested.
  d. A leader should learn to be honest with God about doubts.
  e. A leader should not be satisfied with anything less than God's convincing answer to his/her personal problems of faith.
  f. Faith and righteousness are intertwined (2:4).
  g. Persevering (stable) faith ultimately results in a heart of joy in the midst of any circumstances.
  h. The main thing about a leader's faith is the object of that faith.

See **Articles**, *15. Habakkuk, The Crucial Faith Words; Habakkuk, 18. Important Ideas to Communicate; 25. Leaders, Intercession Hints from Habakkuk.*

3. COMPLEX SITUATIONS. All leaders will at some time or times in their ministry see situations, which apparently deny God's existence or love or intervening care (1:2-4). This is particularly true of urban ministries. Their belief in the character and promises of God will be tested. Learn vicariously from Habakkuk's experience. Be forewarned and determine now to go deep in faith in your response to God. A most important lesson to learn vicariously is that you will need breakthroughs on perspective in order to understand your ministry situation. Habakkuk certainly illustrates the complexity macro lesson, which is seen increasingly through the six leadership eras. A <u>macro-lesson</u> is a high level generalization of a leadership observation (suggestion, guideline, requirement, value), stated as a lesson, which repeatedly occurs throughout different leadership eras, and thus has potential as a leadership absolute. The complexity macro lesson, which summarizes all of the other macro lessons is stated succinctly.

Habakkuk — Leadership Lessons   page 7

Leadership is complex, problematic, difficult and fraught with risk—which is why leadership is needed.

Leadership Principles/ Values Suggested by this concept:
 a. All ministry situations involve complexity for which God's perspective is needed.
 b. Frequently, to get necessary perspective, God must take a leader through a paradigm shift so that the new perspective can be grasped.

See **Articles**, *17. Habakkuk, God's Timing; 28. Left Hand of God, The; 21. Habakkuk, Left Hand of God.*

4. BROADER PERSPECTIVE. Often God's solution to a perplexed leader is to give that leader a broader perspective, that is, a much larger context in which to evaluate the present perplexing situation. The difference in leaders and followers is perspective. Leaders have a broader view on what is happening and what God wants to do. The difference in leaders and effective leaders is better perspective. Sensitivity to God, intimacy with God, and dependence upon God will lead to broader perspective. Leaders who seek God for broader perspective will find Him (2:1; 3:1-15). The broader perspective needed by all leaders is how God is working in history. A leader must learn to perceive his/her own ministry situation and time in terms of the broader working of God in history.

Leadership Principles/ Values Suggested by this concept:
Some general principles seen about God's working in history as seen in Habakkuk include:
 a. God is an absolutely just God. The WOE of chapter 2 repeated 5 times emphatically underscores this. It is a repeated word of judgment. Sin will always be punished because God is absolutely just.
 b. God is controlling history (2:13).
 c. God will ultimately and totally reveal Himself over all the earth (2:14).
 d. God is all knowing. His revelation of future things is absolutely correct. The five woes were actually fulfilled in history. God is the promise keeper.
 e. God is all powerful. Who can control nations and manipulate them as God does? (see also Isa 40:15).
 f. God is a holy God (2:20 in his holy temple).

Some general principles seen on perspective include:
 a. Frequently, to get necessary perspective, God must take a leader through a paradigm shift so that the new perspective can be grasped.
 b. Need is a critical determining factor prompting a leader to seek new perspective and willingness to go through a paradigm shift.

See **Articles**, *39. Structural Time—Simplified Overview; 34. Prophecy Overview; 38. Spiritual Leadership—Prolonging the Life of God in a Work; 17. Habakkuk, God's Timing; 35. Prophetic Crises—Three Major Biblical Times*

Habakkuk —Leadership Lessons   page 8

5. **TRANSPARENCY.** Honest reflection and transparency with God is the starting point for seeking perspective. Leadership, which has learned to be transparent in interiority will be more likely to be transparent in exteriority and thus increase its impact upon followers. See *interiority, exteriority*, **Glossary**.

Leadership Principles/ Values Suggested by this concept:
   a. Transparency in interiority (one's inner life with God) is the starting point for developing transparency in exteriority (one's exemplary living before others).
   b. Modeling that involves transparency will impact others.

6. **FUTURE PERFECT THINKING.** If we believe God for future happenings, then we should act upon that belief. Habakkuk's response, one of the most beautiful in the scriptures (3:16-19), is an illustration of future perfect thinking. The book of Habakkuk illustrates three important macro lessons beside the previously mentioned complexity macro lesson. A <u>macro-lesson</u> is a high level generalization of a leadership observation (suggestion, guideline, requirement, value), stated as a lesson, which repeatedly occurs throughout different leadership eras, and thus has potential as a leadership absolute. The three other important macro lessons seen in Habakkuk include: (1) the future perfect macro lesson, (2) the perspective macro lesson, and (3) the hope macro lesson.
The future perfect macro: *A primary function of all leadership is to walk by faith with a future perfect paradigm so as to inspire followers with certainty of God's accomplishment of ultimate purposes.* The perspective macro: *Leaders must know the value of perspective and interpret present happenings in terms of God's broader purposes.* The hope macro: *A primary function of all leadership is to inspire followers with hope in God and in what God is doing.* Habakkuk's final song certainly does that.

See *future perfect*, **Glossary**. See **Articles**, *29. Macro Lesson Defined; 30. Macro Lessons: List of 41 Across Six Leadership Eras; 7. Future Perfect Paradigm.*

7. **WORSHIP/ CELEBRATION/INSPIRATIONAL LEADERSHIP**
Habakkuk's response in chapter 3 is a song of worship. First he sings of trust in God to do what He has revealed. Then his song is one of pure joy as he trusts God no matter what the future will bring. Habakkuk's worship attests to his patient waiting for God's working of retribution upon the Babylonians.

Leadership Principles/ Values Suggested by this concept:
   a. Leaders must design and use public celebrations as a major means of inspiring hope in followers.
   b. Music is a most appropriate means for capturing truth, which celebrates and inspires.

Articles, *27. Leadership Functions, 3 High Level Generic Properties; 13. Habakkuk, Celebration—A Leadership Function.*

Habakkuk

CLINTON'S BIBLICAL LEADERSHIP COMMENTARY SERIES

Hope for a Leader in Troubled Times

Verse By Verse Commentary

Habakkuk 1:1-4

I. (ch 1:1-2:1) Habakkuk's Honest Struggle With Faith

1   This is the word from God which Habakkuk the prophet received.[1]

Habakkuk Speaks—Are You There, O God[2]

2   O Jehovah, how long shall I beg for your help,[3]
      When will you listen?
   I cry out unto you about violence,
      And you will not deliver.[4]

3   Why do you tolerate the iniquity I see,
         And cause me to experience such injustice?
   For destruction and violence are before me,
      And there is strife,
      And criminal activity all about.
4   Therefore, the law is not enforced,
      And justice does not happen.
      For evil people outnumber the righteous.
   Therefore justice is distorted.[5]

---

[1] This reflective testimony of a critical time in the life of a prophet, reveals God meeting a leader who honestly faces things, which seem to deny the reality of God. The prophetic message of the book is probably not as important as the example of God's shaping a leader. Habakkuk's transparency is significant. Habakkuk experiences a paradigm shift to get God's perspective. See *Habakkuk's dilemma*, **Glossary**. See **Articles**, *8. Getting God's Perspective, A Leader's Necessity; 40. Transparency With God*.

[2] See the **Article**, *14. Habakkuk, Contextual Flow—Understanding the Argument*. That article traces the dialogue between Habakkuk and God. I have inserted hints of that back and forth interplay with these italic headings.

[3] Significantly, the entire book of Habakkuk is in Hebrew Poetic format. Poetry is the language of the heart. Habakkuk is deeply affected, emotionally, by his situation and what he hears from God. He closes by worshipfully singing his poetic response to God. See *celebration*, **Glossary**. See **Articles**, *23. Hebrew Poetry; 13. Habakkuk, Celebration—A Leadership Function*. Some English Bibles translate in part or whole using poetic format. See **Article**, *3. Bible Translations and Hebrew Poetry*.

[4] The thrust of stanza 1 (verse 2) is an honest cry from Habakkuk. "I pray for help. You do not hear! I plead because of the violence I see. Yet you do not do anything!" This reaction by Habakkuk to his situation is faced by many today in our own world. We see things like violent criminal activity going on. Where is God? Leaders who are pursuing ministry in difficult situations and are thoughtfully analyzing what is going on around them will be faced with the Habakkuk dilemma. See *Habakkuk dilemma*, **Glossary**.

[5] The thrust of the second stanza (verses 3,4) is that God is allowing the sinful conditions. And the criminal activity and destruction and violence are so impactful that no one is upholding the law and hence there is no justice. In such situations, and I see this in various urban/inner city ministry, it is very easy to question the reality of God. Habakkuk is honest with God. This is a crisis for Habakkuk. See *Crisis Process Item*, **Glossary**. This concept of a leader being honest with God about doubting God is one of the most important ideas of the book. See **Articles**, *40. Transparency With God; Habakkuk, 16. Four Shaping Activities; 18. Habakkuk, Important Ideas to Communicate*.

Habakkuk 1:5-9

God Speaks—I Am Doing Something About This[6]

5   Look[7] among the nations;[8] look very carefully,
      There is something that will astonish you,
   For I am really doing something[9] even as you speak,[10]
      Which, you won't believe, even when told.
6   Consider: I am raising up the Babylonians,[11]
      That ruthless and unruly nation,
      That marches all over the land,
      To possess homes and cities that are not theirs.
7   They are fierce and dreaded,
    They are a law unto themselves.[12]
8   Their cavalry troops are swifter than leopards,
      And are more ferocious than the evening wolves.
    Their cavalry troops gallop rapidly on.
      Indeed, their horsemen cover ground rapidly.
    They move swiftly as an eagle that swoops to devour.
9   There whole army moves forward, eager to destroy.
    Like a desert wind their hordes break through.
      And they gather captives countless as the sand.

---

[6] Habakkuk does not tell how God spoke. All we know is that God broke in with this startling revelation. In chapter 2, Habakkuk isolates himself to talk to God and hear from God. But here it is in the midst of the daily grind that God speaks.

[7] This is the first of many words that need special study. See **Article**, *19. Habakkuk, Important Words to Study*.

[8] This is a call for leaders to know the times in which they live from a perspective of, "What is God doing in the nations and in the situations all around us?" Note 1Ch 12:32 *And of the children of **Issachar**, which were men that had understanding of the times, to know what Israel ought to do.* See **Article**, *31. Needed, Sons of Issachar*.

[9] This is a Hebrew idiom, the *repetitive superlative*. It uses repeated words for emphasis. Literally, I am working (SRN 6466) a work (6467). I have captured the idiom by using *I am really doing something*. See **Article**, *6. Figures and Idioms*.

[10] This delay to prayers being answered illustrates need to see the timing of God. In fact, God was answering Habakkuk's prayer. See **Articles**, *17. Habakkuk and God's Timing; 12. God's TimingAnd Leadership; 29. Macro Lesson Defined; 30. Macro Lessons: List of 41 Across Six Leadership Eras*.

[11] This illustrates God's sovereign work through nations not having allegiance to Himself. They don't know that God is using them for His purposes. Most Babylonians would not even know that they were being used by God. Some did. See the case of Nebuzaradan in Jeremiah 39: 1 The word that came to Jeremiah from the LORD, after that Nebuzaradan the captain of the guard had let him go from Ramah, when he had taken him being bound in chains among all that were carried away captive of Jerusalem and Judah, which were carried away captive unto Babylon.2 And the captain of the guard took Jeremiah, and said unto him, *The LORD thy God hath pronounced this evil upon this place*. See *left hand sensitivity*, **Glossary**. See **Articles**, *28. The Left Hand of God; 1. The Babylonians*.

[12] Just because a nation has power to do what it wants does not justify its doing what it wants. See also verse 11. Verses 8,9 point out that the Babylonians had military power. Though Babylon was being used by God, nevertheless they would be held accountable for their abuses. See the five woes of chapter 2 of Habakkuk.

Habakkuk 1:10-15

10 At kings they scoff;[13]
   And of rulers they make sport.
   They are not dismayed by fortified cities.
   They raise siege-works and capture them.[14]
11 Then they sweep by like the wind, and go on,
   guilty men, whose own might is their god.

Habakkuk Speaks Referring to God's Traits[15]

12 Aren't you from everlasting,[16]
   O Jehovah, my God, my Holy One?
   Surely we must not die.
   O Jehovah, have you ordained them for judgment?
   And you, Rock, have you established them for correction?[17]

13 Your pure eyes should not behold evil,
   You cannot look on wrongdoing,
   Why do you look on faithless men, and are silent,
   When the wicked devour a people more righteous than themselves?[18]
14 For you make men like the fish of the sea,[19]
   like crawling things that have no ruler.
15 He brings all of them up with a hook.
   He drags them out with his net,
   He gathers them in his seine.
   So he rejoices and exults.

---

[13] The book of Jeremiah aptly illustrates what these arrogant Babylonian leaders thought about the rulers of the Southern Kingdom of Judah. See Jer 52:10,11 And the king of Babylon slew the sons of Zedekiah before his **eyes**: he slew also all the princes of Judah in Riblah. Then he put out the **eyes** of Zedekiah; and the king of Babylon bound him in chains, and carried him to Babylon, and put him in prison till the day of his death.

[14] See Jeremiah 19:19; 21:4;9; 39:1; 52:4,5.

[15] Habakkuk has gone through a major paradigm shift, now believing God is working. But unfairly. The Babylonians are more unrighteous as a nation than are the Israelites. So Habakkuk pleads with God to correct this apparent unfairness. Note, however, that Israel has far more revelation for which it is being judged than the Babylonians. This whole prayer illustrates the prayer macro lesson. See *paradigm shift*, **Glossary**. See **Articles**, 29. *Macro Lesson Defined; 30. Macro Lessons— List of 41 Across Six Leadership Eras; 32. Paradigms and Paradigm Shifts; 20. Habakkuk, Judgment and Revelation.*

[16] It is interesting to note that a number of Bible leaders, when they intercede with God concerning their ministries, will base their intercession on God's character, God's past works or God's promises. See **Article**, *25. Leaders—Intercession Hints*.

[17] These are not questions looking for an answer. Habakkuk is really saying, "How can you use these Babylonians?" And he is doing it emphatically—note the repetition.

[18] Generally, this is the crux of all left hand operations. How can God use nations that do not follow Him at all to correct situations in the world, especially those dealing with followers of God? See **Article**, *28. Left Hand of God.*

[19] In Verses 14,15,16,17 the Hebrew poetry develops an extended metaphor to graphically emphasize what he is saying in his two questions of verse 13. In fact, in these stanzas and especially the stanzas of chapter 2 Habakkuk uses a great deal of figurative language. See *metaphor*, **Glossary**. See **Article**, *6. Figures and Idioms in the Bible*.

Habakkuk 1:16-2:2

16 Therefore he sacrifices to his net,
   And burns incense to his seine,
   For by them he lives in luxury,
   And his food is rich.
17 Is he then to keep on emptying his net,
   And mercilessly slaying nations forever?

II. (2:2-2:20) Habakkuk's Faith-Wait Response

2:1 I will doggedly set myself to wait for God's answer,
    And station myself on the watch tower,
    And watch carefully to perceive, what He will communicate to me.
    And then I will have an answer to my complaint.[20]

2   And Jehovah answered me.[21]

---

[20] The sense of this stanza (the four lines of verse 1) seems to be that Habakkuk will isolate himself until he perceives God's reply to his complaint that God is unfair using the wicked Babylonians to bring about judgment on Judah. Lines 1 and 2 seem to indicate that Habakkuk will go into the outlying fields where observation towers were set up with sentries to watch for enemies attacking. Lines 3,4 seem to indicate that he will persistently wait till he can perceive what God is saying. Habakkuk is hoping for some restorative word (answer SRN 07725) to his complaint (SRN 08433) to God (the word complaint connotes rebuke). How much time is involved in this is uncertain. But that Habakkuk is getting away from his normal way of life in order to especially hear from God is indicated. This is at the core of the shaping activity identified in leadership emergence theory as isolation processing. 90% of leaders go through some form of isolation processing in their lifetime of ministry. It is well that leaders learn as much about isolation as they can. Forewarned is forearmed. See *isolation processing*, **Glossary**. See **Article**, *24. Isolation Processing—Learning Deep Lessons From God*.

[21] What we don't know here are the details—How long was Habakkuk in isolation? How did God speak? Was it through meditation about the current situation? Did Habakkuk actually study into Babylonian history and current happenings and then draw some conclusions? Or what this a special word of revelation either verbal or in the heart? What we do know is that God answered! In isolation processing, frequently the leader is subjected to the silence of God. And then finally in the midst of the isolation, God speaks.

God Speaks with Authoritative Judgment

>   Write down the revelation.[22]
>   Record it plainly upon tablets.
>   So that a messenger may run with it.
> 3 Trust me, the prophetic word will come true, in its time.
>   At its destined time it will happen.
>   It will not fail to happen.
>   It will surely come.
>   It will be right on time.
>
> 4 Consider carefully the message:
>   Those who are evil will not survive,
>   But those who are righteous will live
>   because they trust in God.[23]
>
> 5 Moreover wine is treacherous;
>   The arrogant man is restless.
>   His greed is as big as death itself,
>   Like death he never has enough.
>   He conquers for himself all nations,
>   And collects as his own all his captives.
> 6 Shall not all these conquered people finally take up their taunt against him?
>   In scoffing derision of him, They will say:

---

[22] It is clear that this revelation from God is not for Habakkuk alone. Habakkuk is becoming aware that his own problem is bigger than himself. God is using this incident to explain more of Himself and His workings in history. Two books in Scripture especially show how God is working in history. Daniel is the most comprehensive. But Habakkuk shows the same thing on a smaller scale and in terms of one leader's understanding of what is going on in his ministry. God is working in history and the book of Habakkuk has as one of its major purposes to teach God's people to trust unconditionally in God's complex workings in history to bring about his just purposes. At least 4 values are implied about God and history: (1) God is controlling history to cause it to work to an absolutely just conclusion. (2) God can use any group of people as instruments to suit His purposes. (3) God is concerned about an individual (Habakkuk) in the course of history. (4) History cannot be rightly interpreted until all the data is in. We have but a partial picture from a limited perspective. Wait till the whole show is over. All the data is not in. Time is involved. See **Article**, *8. Getting God's Perspective, A Leader's Necessity*.

[23] This is probably the most important faith lesson in the book of Habakkuk. The Babylonians will not survive. But those, like Habakkuk himself, who learn to trust God shall live. This is quoted three times in the New Testament: Romans 1:17; Gal 3:11; and Heb 10:38. In each of those cases it is used in relationship to some aspect of being made right with God as opposed to some sort of earning one's righteousness before God. Seemingly, here in Habakkuk, it is talking about those who belong to God trusting in God for their future. See **Article**, *15. Habakkuk, Crucial Faith Words*.

Habakkuk 2:7-11

A miserable future is yours! You are doomed! (**Woe 1**)[24]
You who amass stolen goods—for how long?
And load yourself with pledges.
7   Will not your debtors suddenly arise in rebellion?
They will awake and make you tremble?
Then you will become their victim.
8   Because you have plundered many nations.
All the remnant of these peoples will return cruelty to you,
Because you murdered many and brought violence to the land,
to the cities and all who lived there.

9   A miserable future is yours! You are doomed! (**Woe 2**)
You who gets evil gain for his house,
to set his nest on high.
to be safe from the reach of harm.[25]
10 You have brought dishonor to your family,
by cutting off many peoples.
You have forfeited your life,
11 (Your own house condemns you)
the stone will cry out from the wall,
and the beam from the woodwork will echo back.

---

[24] I have taken a whole line to translate one word that the KJV translates as *woe* (*hoy* SRN 01945). This one word, *hoy*, is an interjection—that is, a word of exclamation. It is a word of passion, grief, despair. It is usually a lamentation. It occurs some 48 times in the prophets. At least six usages refer to mourning for the dead. But the large majority (40+) involve negative warning or threats of God's physical chastisement. That is the sense it is used here in Habakkuk 2. Five times God repeats this word, *hoy*. See verses 6, 9, 12, 15, 19. And each time it marks a stanza which describes judgment. It takes more than one English word to capture the connotation of this small word. The denotation is simply that of grief, despair, deep passion. I have captured the connotation that associates with the word as well as the passionate denotation by several words—"a miserable future is yours! You are doomed!" Various translations use the following to try to catch the meaning: Both the **Good News Bible** and **The Learning Bible** use, *You are doomed!*; the **New English Bible** uses *Woe Betide*!; The **New Testament in Basic English** uses *A Curse on Him!* God is answering Habakkuk's rebuke, his complaint, (see line 4 of stanza 1, verse 1 of this chapter). How can Habakkuk handle the news that God will use the Babylonians, a more wicked nation than Judah, to bring judgment on Judah. Because he knows that in the end God will bring judgment on the Babylonians—a very severe judgment. Ultimately there will be justice. The hoys pile up. The repetition is emphatic. Babylon will be judged. God's justice, will reveal his glory throughout the world. Habakkuk is learning about a philosophy of history, from God's perspective. See **Article**, *9. God's Judgment on the Babylonians*.

[25] The idea of *nest on high* and to be *safe from the reach of harm* imply that the Babylonians who relied on their might as their god thought they could build a safe and secure place. But see Daniel 5, final judgment, and Daniel 6 where the Medo-Persian empire sieged and broke through this fortified city via the water system (drained it and went under the wall). See **Article**, *1. The Babylonians; 9. God's Judgment on the Babylonians*.

12 A miserable future is yours! You are doomed! (**Woe 3**)
   You who builds a town on crime and violence,
   And founds a city by violent deeds of injustice.
13 Consider carefully, is it not from the all powerful Lord,
   That judgment comes upon evil people,
   And nations come to nothing?
14 For the earth will be filled,
   With the knowledge of the glory of Jehovah,
   As the waters cover the sea.

15 A miserable future is yours! You are doomed! (**Woe 4**)
   You who make your neighbors drink, of the cup of wrath,
   And makes them drunk,
   to gaze upon their shame!
16 Now you will be disgraced, instead of praised,
   Drink yourself, and stagger!
   The cup in Jehovah's right hand will come around to you,
   And instead of honor you will be disgraced!
17 You will be repaid for the violence done to Lebanon,
   For your needless destruction of animals,
   For the murders of people of the world,
   And for destruction of cities people in them.[26]

18 What use is an idol,[27]
   Made by a human being,
   It's only a metal image, a source of lies.
   For the workman trusts in his own creation,
   when he makes dumb idols!
19 A miserable future is yours! You are doomed! (**Woe 5**)
   You who says to a wooden thing, Awake!
   To a dumb stone, Arise!
   Can this give revelation?
   Consider carefully, it is overlaid with gold and silver,
   There is no breath at all in it.

---

[26] The Babylonians have shown violence in many ways: to animals, murdering of people—men, women, and children. Destruction of cities that took years to build. None of these details have escaped God's awareness. They will be judged.

[27] The fifth woe is climactic. Of all the things the Babylonians will be judged for, the most important and final one is their rejection of God. They have served idols, which they themselves have made. And so here in this stanza (verses 18, 19, 20) we have a power encounter between the living God and the gods of the Babylonians, represented by their idols. See also the Daniel commentary where the power encounter is graphically demonstrated in chapter 5 by the handwriting on the wall. God's power was shown in the destruction of Babylon. See **Article**, *5. Daniel—Power Encounters; 2. Babylonians—Power Encounter*.

Habakkuk 2:20-3:2

20 **BUT** Jehovah is in his holy temple;
   Let all the earth keep silence before him.[28]

III. (3:1-19) Habakkuk's Response of True Faith

Habakkuk responds by remembering God's miraculous interventions in the past.

1 A prayer of Habakkuk the prophet, set to Shigionoth.[29]

2 O Jehovah, I have heard[30] of your doings,[31]

---

[28] Note the final parallelism in verse 20. These two lines are antithetical to all the previous lines in the stanza. In contrast to these idols, which are powerless there is God who is ruling. He has the final word. All others are silent before Him who rules throughout the whole earth. And that means Habakkuk too. God is telling Habakkuk, "Rest assured! I know what I am doing. I will have ultimate justice throughout all the earth. None will be able to speak saying I have not ruled powerfully and justly." Habakkuk has his answer to his questions of the stanza in 2:1. How will he now respond?

[29] Verse 1 is significant for several reasons. One reason concerns the note of celebration. Habakkuk thought this experience with God worthy of celebrating it publicly with others. Celebration is a very important leadership function that falls under the notion of inspirational leadership. There are three major overall high level leadership functions that a leader must make sure happens in his/her ministry: Task Oriented Leadership; Relational Oriented Leadership; Inspirational Oriented Leadership. Celebration falls under inspirational leadership. One thing that inspires people is public celebration which rejoices in who God is and what He will do. Habakkuk does that. That is what chapter 3 is all about. When celebration includes personal testimony it carries an additional impact. Habakkuk does that. When a leader shares personally with his/her followers what God means to him/her, there will be impact. Followers will be inspired. A second reason verse 1 is important is that it connects Habakkuk, a prophet, to the temple institution. (see also postscript following verse 19—To the choirmaster: with stringed instrument). Not much is known about Habakkuk, except that he was a prophet and ministered to the southern kingdom. Here we have indications that he may have served in the temple, perhaps as a priest or a worship leader. Certainly we get the idea that he was connected with the public ministry of the temple as well as being a prophet who spoke into situations. And we recognize his creative talent. See **Article,** *27. Leadership Functions, 3 High Level Generic Properties;13. Habakkuk, Celebration—A Leadership Function.*

[30] The word Habakkuk uses for hearing (SRN 8085) means not just to hear but perceive in order to obey or what was said. It is a hearing that implies responding.

[31] Doings (SRN 8088) is roughly akin to our modern use of *track record*. Habakkuk is saying, "I have heard of your fame, what you have done in the past. I am awe struck by your track record." He then goes on to allude to many things he had heard of God's track record. The majority of chapter 3 contains his references to God's track record. Some of the allusions are difficult to follow. I have chosen to translate them more or less literally even if I am not sure what they are referring to. But even though we may not know for certain the actual things Habakkuk is referring to we do know that Habakkuk is impressed with God and what God has done in the past. And he is counting on this same God to fulfill what He has promised in Chapter 2—the five *Woes*.

Habakkuk 3:3-6

> And I am awestruck by what you have done, O Jehovah.
> Now do again in our day,
> The great things you did in the past;[32]
> Be merciful, even in the midst of your anger.[33]

3   God came from Teman,[34]
    And the Holy One from Mount Paran.
    His splendor covers the heavens,
    And the earth was full of his praise. SELAH
4   His brightness was like the sunrise,
    sun rays flashed from his hand,
    hiding his mighty power.
5   Before him went plagues,
    And fever followed close behind.
6   He stood and measured the earth.
    He looked and shook the nations.
    Then the ancient mountains crumbled,
    The age-old hills collapsed.
    His ways are eternal.

---

[32] These words illustrate Habakkuk's positive response to the faith challenge that God is giving him in this critical incident in his life. Habakkuk is about to recite a lot of things God has done in the past. And here he is saying, "I believe you can again do these things." The book of Habakkuk has some important principles about faith—the most important being Habakkuk 2:4. But there are some 9 other principles worth noting. We as leaders need these principles in our own ministry. (1) Expect your faith to be tested in regards to your prayer life (1:1,2). (2) One should be absolutely honest with God about his/her doubts (1:1-4). (3) In regards to your struggles of faith, expect God to meet with you with a convincing solution deep in your heart (3:2). (4) Do not be satisfied with anything less than God's convincing answer to your personal problem of faith (2;1). (5) Faith and righteousness are intertwined (2:4). 6. A leader can trust God to work out the course of history to bring about absolute justice (Gen 18:25; Hab 2;14). (7) True faith is not incompatible with honest doubt or honest fears (1:1-4; 3:2,16). 8. Persevering faith ultimately results in a heart of joy in the midst of any circumstances (3:17-19; see also the book of Philippians). (9) The main thing about faith is the object of our faith. Trust **GOD**. Not **TRUST** God. See *faith challenge*, **Glossary**. See **Article**, *16. Four Shaping Activities in Habakkuk's Life*.

[33] Habakkuk realizes that God has answered his prayer about injustice seen in Stanza 1 of Chapter 1. In answering, God has revealed that he will bring about a terrible judgment. Answers to prayer do not always come in the forms that leaders expect them. Habakkuk wants things to be made right. God is going to do that. But the price will be high. And Habakkuk like many other O.T. leaders who have gone before him (see especially Abraham, Moses, Samuel, and Daniel) adds a plea of intercession for mercy in the midst of the judgment. Habakkuk illustrates the prayer macro lesson. See **Articles**, *29. Macro Lesson Defined; 30. Macro Lessons— List of 41 Across Six Leadership Eras; 32. Paradigms and Paradigm Shifts; 20. Habakkuk, Judgment and Revelation; 25. Leaders, intercession Hints from Habakkuk.*

[34] I will not comment on the allusions to God's working (very difficult material to translate and understand), which occur in verses 3-15. But I will include them so you can get the sense of how Habakkuk realized that God's power would back up his claims.

Habakkuk 3:7-16

7 I saw the tents of Cushan and Midian ripped apart,
  These desert people were afraid.
8 Were you mad at the rivers, Jehovah?
  Were you angry against the sea?
  Did you rage against the sea?
  When you did ride upon your horses,
  Upon your chariot of victory?
9 You got ready to use your bow,
  and put the arrows to the string. SELAH
  You split the earth apart with rivers.
10 The mountains saw you, and writhed,
  the raging waters swept on,
  ocean waves roared and rose high.

11 The sun and moon stood still,
  at the lightning-like speed of your arrows,
  at the flash of your glittering spear.
12 You angrily marched across the earth,
  You furiously trampled the nations.
13 You went forth to save your people,
  To save your anointed one.
14 You struck down the leader of the warriors,
  who came like a whirlwind to scatter us.
  Gloating as if they could get away with it in secret.
15 You trampled the sea with your horses,
  The surging of mighty waters.

Habakkuk's final fearful and joyful response to God's meeting him.[35]

16 I hear your message, and I am weak with fear,
  My lips quiver fearfully.
  My bones feel like they are giving way.
  I stumble as I walk.
  I will quietly wait for the day of judgment,
  When disaster will come upon the people who invade us.[36]

---

[35] These are probably the most significant stanzas of the book. Habakkuk in his crisis moment of not seeing God in his situation has responded to God's revelation about what He is doing. This final response is inspirational. Habakkuk has responded positively to all four shaping activities of God: (1) the crisis shaping, (2) the isolation, (3) the paradigm shift and (4) the faith challenge. See **Articles**, *16. Habakkuk, four Shaping Activities; 22. Habakkuk, Regaining Hope Via a god-Ordained Paradigm Shift.*

[36] Responding to God's Word does not necessarily mean an easy path is ahead. Habakkuk recognizes that what lies ahead is going to be tough. He fears it deeply. But he has stilled his heart to respond to God in the things that will come.

Habakkuk 3:17-19

17 Though the fig tree quits blossoming,
   There is no fruit on the vines,
   The olive trees do not produce,
   The fields yield no food,
   The flock be cut off from the fold,
   And there be no herd in the stalls,[37]
18 Yet I will rejoice[38] in Jehovah,
   I will joy in the God of my salvation.
19 Jehovah, the Master, is my strength.
   He makes my feet like hinds' feet.
   He makes me tread upon my high places.[39]

To the choirmaster: with stringed instrument.

---

[37] These lines of this stanza (verse 17) show that Habakkuk understands the ramifications of God's revelation. Prosperity as it has been known in Judah will be gone forever. This is the functional equivalent of all our retirement plans and savings being lost. Our jobs gone. The basis for our living, destroyed.

[38] *Yet I will rejoice* translates one Hebrew word (SRN 05937). That word carries with it the sense of rejoicing but also of exulting and doing so triumphantly. Note, Habakkuk's triumphant rejoicing is not in the circumstances but in God: Jehovah the eternal one (SRN 3068); Elohim—the God who delivers (SRN 0430; 03468); Jehovah Master (Adonai) (SRN 3068; SRN 0136). A leader's view of God is the most important thing about that leader. Habakkuk now has a good view of God.

[39] This is one of the beautiful similes in Scripture (used three times: once in 2 Sa 22:34 and once in Psa 18—both relating to the same incident in David's life and here relating to Habakkuk). It is a picture of a deer climbing a steep mountainside and deftly picking out the safe places to tread as it negotiates the difficult terrain to get to the top. Most likely we are seeing that Habakkuk was familiar with the Psalms. This is probably a quote by Habakkuk making that simile his own. The simile being interpreted means that God will safely and surely lead him through very dangerous situations. It is a beautiful way to express his faith in God in terms of what he will face as God works out the future. And it is a beautiful note on which to end the book. I am reminded of Dr. G. Allen Fleece's quote, "It is always God's way to end victoriously." See *capture*; *simile*; **Glossary**. See **Article**, *6. Figures and Idioms in the Bible*.

For Further Study

For Further Leadership Study
1. Study in depth the biographical analysis of Habakkuk's pivotal point.
2. Note the dialogic nature of prayer that develops interiority.

Special Comments
This is one of the special books in the Old Testament which focuses on God's development of a leader (see Job, Jonah). In Seeing the processes--crisis, isolation, paradigm shift, faith challenge-- we learn not only what God was doing with Habakkuk but we can also see how He matures leaders.

Habakkuk

CLINTON'S BIBLICAL LEADERSHIP COMMENTARY SERIES

Hope for a Leader in Troubled Times

Commentary Articles

Leadership Articles[1] (bold faced articles appear in other commentaries as well).

1. *Babylonians, The*
2. *Babylonians—Power Encounter*
3. *Bible Translations And Hebrew Poetic Format*
4. ***Biblical Framework—The Redemptive Drama***
5. ***Daniel—Power Encounters***
6. ***Figures and Idioms in the Bible***
7. ***Future Perfect Paradigm***
8. *Getting God's Perspective, A Leader's Necessity*
9. *God's Judgment on the Babylonians*
10. ***God The Promise Keeper***
11. ***God's Shaping Processes with Leaders***
12. ***God's Timing and Leadership***
13. *Habakkuk, Celebration—A Leadership Function*
14. *Habakkuk, Contextual Flow—Understanding the Argument*
15. *Habakkuk, Crucial Faith Words*
16. *Habakkuk, Four Shaping Activities*
17. *Habakkuk, God's Timing*
18. *Habakkuk, Important Ideas to Communicate*
19. *Habakkuk, Important Words to Study*
20. *Habakkuk, Judgment and Revelation*
21. *Habakkuk, Left Hand of God*
22. *Habakkuk, Regaining Hope Via a God-Ordained Paradigm Shift*
23. *Hebrew Poetry*
24. ***Isolation Processing —Learning Deep Lessons from God***
25. *Leaders, Intercession Hints from Habakkuk*
26. ***Leadership Eras In The Bible, Six Identified***
27. *Leadership Functions, 3 High Level Generic Properties.*
28. ***Left Hand of God, The***
29. ***Macro Lessons—Defined***
30. ***Macro Lessons: List of 41 Across Six Leadership Eras***
31. *Needed, Sons of Issachar*
32. ***Paradigms And Paradigm Shifts***
33. ***Promises of God***
34. ***Prophecy Overview***
35. ***Prophetic Crises—Three Major Biblical Times***
36. ***Six Biblical Leadership Eras, Approaching the Bible with Leadership Eyes***
37. *Spiritual Disciplines—and On-going Leadership*
38. *Spiritual Leadership—Prolonging the Life of God in a Work*
39. *Structural Time—Simplified Overview*
40. *Transparency With God*

---

[1] Articles listed with numbers are included with this commentary. Some articles, without numbers occur in other commentaries.

Article 1

1. Babylonians, The

Introduction

The Chaldeans are the villains of the book of Habakkuk. The prophet Habakkuk was shocked when God told him He would use the Chaldeans to punish Judah. Who were they? How long did their empire last? What was its extent? And how did Habakkuk know about them?

Bible References to the Chaldeans (Babylonians).

Table Hab 1-1 lists the main Old Testament references to the Chaldeans or Babylon or related words built on their stems.

Table Hab 1-1. Main Old Testament References to Chaldeans or Babylonians

When Mentioned	Where Mentioned	Number of Times
Before the Divided Kingdom	Gen Josh	Chaldea* 3 Babylon* 1
During the Divided Kingdom	Isaiah	Chaldea* 7 Babylon* 16
	Jeremiah	Chaldea* 47 Babylon* 178
	Ezekiel[2]	Chaldea* 1 Babylon* 22
	1,2 Kings	Chaldea* 8 Babylon* 34
	1,2 Chronicles	Chaldea* 1 Babylon* 9
After the Exile	Daniel	Chaldea* 11 Babylon* 19
	Ezra	Chaldea* 8 Babylon* 22
	Nehemiah	Chaldea* 1 Babylon* 2
	Esther	Chaldea* 0 Babylon* 1

---

[2] Ezekiel spans both the divided kingdom and after the exile. The majority of his references occur before the exile.

1. The Babylonians

Some observations can be drawn from this table:

1. The large majority of the references occur in the book of Jeremiah. 1,2 Kings and Ezekiel are second to Jeremiah. And most of these references are dealing with the time of the Babylonian invasion into Palestine and other southern kingdoms.
2. Though Babylon (or the early Chaldean locals) exists in the earliest of Biblical times, it does not become prominent until after Isaiah's writings about it in Isaiah 39.
3. After the exile the references start diminishing. The implications of this are that the Babylonian empire was relatively short lived, probably less than 100 years.

Without going into a technical history of this empire, I will mention some prominent things mentioned in the Bible about the Babylonians.

Isaiah

1. Isaiah prophesies that Babylon will someday capture Judah.

In Isaiah 39 an envoy from Babylon visits the southern Kingdom. Hezekiah was sick. They visited and brought greetings to Hezekiah. Hezekiah showed them around his holdings. Evidently this was a *flesh act*[3] as Isaiah rebuked Hezekiah for showing them everything and prophesied that they would some day capture all that had been shown and that descendants of Hezekiah would be taken away in captivity (Daniel and his friends).

2. Isaiah also has strong judgmental prophecies about Babylon.

Isaiah 13, 14 give these judgmental prophecies. Several isolated statements about these judgmental prophecies being fulfilled also occur in Isaiah 47, 48.

Jeremiah

1. Sees Left Hand of God[4]

Jeremiah recognized that God was going to use the Babylonian forces to destroy Jerusalem. That is, he saw the *Left Hand of God* in the Babylonian siege.

2. Jeremiah Protected

Jeremiah was recognized by the Babylonians as having encouraged Judah to surrender and submit to the Babylonians. One of the Babylonian Army Commanders also recognized being the Left Hand of God. See the case of Nebuzaradan in Jeremiah 39:1.2

> 1 The word that came to Jeremiah from the LORD, after that Nebuzaradan the captain of the guard had let him go from Ramah, when he had taken him being bound in chains among all that were carried away captive of Jerusalem and Judah, which were carried away captive unto Babylon.2 And the captain of the guard took Jeremiah, and said unto him, *The LORD thy God hath pronounced this evil upon this place*.

3. Jeremiah Also Predicted Judgment on Babylon

Jeremiah prophesied strong judgment to come upon Babylon. See Jeremiah 50,51.

---

[3] A <u>flesh act</u> is a process item identified in leadership emergence theory in which a person goes ahead of God in guidance, making some decision without checking it out with God ahead of time. *See flesh act, process items*, **Glossary**.

[4] The *Left Hand of God* refers to God's use of non-believers to accomplish His purposes. See **Article**, 21. *Habakkuk, Left Hand of God*.

1. The Babylonians

So then Habakkuk, Isaiah and Jeremiah, though all recognizing that Babylon was being used of God (Left Hand of God), also saw that God would bring judgment on Babylon later.

What We Can Learn About the Babylonians From Habakkuk

From Habakkuk 2:4 we learn that the Chaldeans were full of arrogance and pride and were self-dependent. God says they shall not live. From chapter 1 of Habakkuk, we learn a number of characteristics about the Chaldeans.

From chapter 1 we have these descriptors of the Chaldeans:

1. They were ruthless.
2. Their armies were massive and mobile.
3. They has specialized attack units, Cavalry Units which were very fast.
4. They captured cities and confiscated properties.
5. They were fierce. Surrounding nations feared them.
6. They were a law unto themselves.
7. They were adept at besieging fortified cities.
8. They operated on the principle that might is right.
9. Might was their god.
10. They were merciless in their destruction of nations.

From chapter 2 we have these descriptors of the Chaldeans:

1. They are proud and will not survive.
2. They are arrogant.
3. The are restless. That is they are not satisfied with what they have.
5. They are greedy.
6. They make slaves of captured people.
7. They ransacked and looted the conquered nations.
8. They murdered many.
9. They were violent to peoples conquered.
10. They were self-reliant and felt secure in their defensive preparations in their homeland.
11. They brought dishonor to their country.
12. They destroyed cities.
13. They destroyed animals needlessly.
14. They were idolaters.

Closure

Is it no wonder that Habakkuk was shocked that God would use such a ruthless bunch to destroy Judah? The five woes of chapter 2 comforted Habakkuk. He knew God would judge the actions of the Babylonian armies and rulers. And he was assured from God that total justice would eventually be done. The Chaldeans were mighty. And their empire was magnificent. But it was for a relatively short time. God did bring judgment on them. They were destroyed.[5] Nevertheless, it is very challenging to one's understanding of God to see that God would use such a group of people as these Chaldeans.

---

[5] Daniel lets us see this happen. See Daniel Chapter 5.

Article 2

2. Babylonians—Power Encounter

Introduction

Frequently a ministry breakthrough involves power ministry in which God intervenes miraculously to authenticate His reality, power, and superiority. One such example of power ministry was coded by Tippett as a power encounter.[6]

Definition A <u>power encounter</u> identifies a situation in which the power of God is tested over against some other god's power.

A sterling Biblical example of a power encounters include the classic example of Elijah on Mt. Carmel, 1 Kings 18:17-40.[7]

While Habakkuk basically deals with God's shaping activity with the prophet Habakkuk, there is the prediction of a power encounter between God and the Babylonians. And that power encounter is worth noting since it was predicted years before it actually happened.

The Prediction in Habakkuk

In the book of Habakkuk, 2:18-20, we have the actual prediction of the power encounter as God reveals to the prophet Habakkuk the judgmental woes He will bring on Babylon in the future. Habakkuk has already learned to his dismay, that God is going to use the Babylon army to punish the southern Kingdom of Judah for its evil ways. Habakkuk has questioned how God can do this. God has assured the troubled prophet that He will also take care of the Babylonians. In chapter 2 he gives 5 judgmental woes that will accomplish justice as far as the Babylonians are concerned. Read carefully the 5th woe given below.

Habakkuk Chapter 2
18 What use is an idol,
    Made by a human being,
    It's only a metal image, a source of lies.
    For the workman trusts in his own creation,
    when he makes dumb idols!
19 A miserable future is yours! You are doomed! (**Woe 5**)[8]

---

[6] <u>Power encounter</u> is a phrase that was first defined by a missiologist A. R. Tippett, Professor of Anthropology at the School of World Mission of Fuller Theological Seminary. It identifies a situation in which the power of God is tested over against some other god's power. Tippet first observed this in field studies in the southwest Pacific islands. Later he saw the same concept in the Scriptures. See his classic, **Solomon Island Christianity**. I studied under Tippett in 1978.

[7] I cover more thoroughly the definition and examples in the **Article**, 5. *Daniel—Power Encounters*.

[8] I have taken a whole line to translate one word that the KJV translates as *woe* (*hoy* SRN 01945). This one word, *hoy*, is an interjection—that is, a word of exclamation. It is a word of passion, grief, despair. It is usually a lamentation. It occurs some 48 times in the prophets. At least six usages refer to mourning for the dead. But the large majority (40+) involve negative warning or threats of God's physical chastisement. That is the sense it is used here in Habakkuk 2. Five times God repeats this word, *hoy*. See verses 6, 9, 12, 15, 19. And each time it marks a stanza which describes judgment. It takes more than one English word to

> You who says to a wooden thing, Awake!
> To a dumb stone, Arise!
> Can this give revelation?
> Consider carefully, it is overlaid with gold and silver,
> There is no breath at all in it.

The five woes given in chapter 2 are a list idiom in which the final item is the one being highlighted. That is, the fifth woe is climactic. All are important. But the 5th is the most important. Of all the things the Babylonians will be judged for, the most important and final one is their rejection of God. They have served idols, which they themselves have made. And so here in this stanza (verses 18, 19, 20) we have a power encounter between the living God and the gods of the Babylonians, represented by their idols.

God has enumerated a list of evil things the Babylonians have done and for which he is going to bring judgment. The first four woes all empathetically describe the evil practices for which God is going to judge the Babylonians. The climactic item is their worship of idols. God is going to take the Babylonians down and thus show His superiority over these idols. How did it work out?

The Fulfillment of it in Daniel

It is clear right from the beginning of the book of Daniel that there will be a power encounter—at least in retrospect, after reading Daniel 5.

Daniel Chapter 1

1 During the third year that Jehoiakim ruled as king of Judah, King Nebuchadnezzar of Babylon attacked Jerusalem and surrounded it. 2 And the Lord gave him victory over Jehoiakim king of Judah. He captured and took back with him to the temple of his gods in Babylon, some of the sacred articles of the house of God, which he put in the treasure house of his god.

Notice in verse 1 who is behind this downfall of Judah. The *Lord gave*. Just as God had told Habakkuk He would use the Babylonians to punish Judah, He did so. It was not military prowess by Nebuchadnezzar that brought about this victory. It was ultimately the Lord's doing. And He had his purposes in it. This is the *Left Hand of God*[9] openly at work. It was God who gave them up to the Babylonians. Daniel had to grapple with this apparent rejection of the people of God by God just as Habakkuk had to.

Notice in verse 2 that the stage is set for the power encounter, which will come later (in chapter 5). Sacred articles taken from the house of God are put into Nebuchadnezzar's treasure house of his god (idols). And then in chapter 5 Belshazzar misuses these sacred articles in a drunken orgy. Note here that these articles are put in Nebuchadnezzar's temple.

---

capture the connotation of this small word. The denotation is simply that of grief, despair, deep passion. I have captured the connotation that associates with the word as well as the passionate denotation by several words—"a miserable future is yours! You are doomed!" God is answering Habakkuk's rebuke, his complaint. How can Habakkuk handle the news that God will use the Babylonians, a more wicked nation than Judah, to bring judgment on Judah? Because he knows that in the end God will bring judgment on the Babylonians—a very severe judgment. Ultimately there will be justice. The hoys pile up. The repetition is emphatic. Babylon will be judged. God's justice, will reveal his glory throughout the world. Habakkuk is learning about a philosophy of history, from God's perspective. See **Article**, 9. *God's Judgment on the Babylonians*.

[9] The *Left Hand of God* refers to God's use of non-believers to accomplish His purposes. See **Article**, 21. *Habakkuk, Left Hand of God*.

2. Babylonians—Power Encounter

This sets the stage for the power encounter in chapter 5 between Belshazzar's god and the Most High.

Daniel Chapter 5—Fulfillment Realized

1 King Belshazzar threw a great banquet for a thousand of his noblemen. They drank wine together. 2 While drinking the wine, Belshazzar gave the command to bring the gold and silver vessels, which his father Nebuchadnezzar had taken from the temple which had been in Jerusalem. He wanted to drink from them along with his lords, his wives, and his concubines. 3 So they brought the gold vessels that had been taken from the temple of the house of God which used to be in Jerusalem. The king and his lords, his wives, and his concubines drank from them. 4 They drank wine, and praised the gods of gold and silver, bronze and iron, wood and stone. 5 Suddenly the fingers of a man's hand appeared and wrote on the plaster of the palace wall. And the king saw the hand as it was writing. 6 Then the king turned pale with fear. His legs began to give way beneath him. 7 He cried loudly to bring in the astrologers, the sorcerers, and the seers. The king spoke, saying to these wise men of Babylon, "Whoever reads this writing, and tells me its interpretation, shall be clothed with purple and have a chain of gold around his neck; and he shall be the third ruler in the kingdom." 8 No one could read the writing, or make known to the king its interpretation. 9 Then King Belshazzar paled even more and became more visibly distressed. His nobles, also, were shaken.

The story goes on. Daniel is called in when the king's wise men cannot understand the writing. Daniel, represented the Most High God interprets the writing, which is a final pronouncement of judgment—Habakkuk's woe 5 is happening before our very eyes as we read this story.

Note the climactic verses of this chapter. Daniel is rewarded. Then in one simple sentence Woe 5 is completely fulfilled.

Daniel 5

29 Then Belshazzar gave the command, and they clothed Daniel with purple and put the gold chain of honor around his neck. They proclaimed him to be the third ruler in the kingdom. 30 That very night Belshazzar, king of the Chaldeans, was slain. 31 And Darius the Mede, at 62 years of age, took over the kingdom.

This whole chapter illustrates the notion of a power encounter. A classic power encounter has several elements:

a) A crisis between people representing god and other people is seen.
b) There must be recognition that the issue is one of power confrontation in the supernatural realm.
c) There must be public recognition of the pre-encounter terms (If...Then...).
d) There is an actual crisis/ confrontation event. The more public, usually the better will be the aftermath.
e) There must be confirmation that God has done the delivering as the power encounter resolves.
f) Celebration to bring closure and insure continuation of God's purpose in the power event.

2. Babylonians—Power Encounter

Not all of these elements are actually seen in all power encounters but the most important one is in all: God is seen to be the most powerful.

In chapter 1 it was noted that these sacred Hebrew objects were taken from Jerusalem and put in the temple of Nebuchadnezzar. From that short account it may appear that Nebuchadnezzar's gods were more powerful. But it was further stated that it was God who did this. Now in this chapter God is seen to be more powerful than these Babylonian gods. When Belshazzar uses these sacred objects to praise his gods, he has gone too far. God intervenes. And Daniel will represent God and explain his intervention. Table Hab 2-1 below shows the aspects of the power encounter seen in Daniel 5. Two checks means openly seen. One check means implied.

Table Hab 2-1. Elements of Power Encounter Seen In Daniel

Power Encounter Element	Dan 5
a) A crisis between people representing god and other people must be differentiated clearly.	√√
b) There must be recognition that the issue is one of power confrontation in the supernatural realm.	√
c) There must be public recognition of the pre-encounter terms (If...Then...).	√
d) There is an actual crisis/confrontation event (the more public usually the better will be the aftermath).	√√
e) There must be confirmation that God has done the delivering as the power encounter resolves.	√√

Closure

The amazing thing about this power encounter is that it was predicted to Habakkuk many years before it happened. Habakkuk ends his book by giving a testimony, which essentially trusts God to bring about His purposes—one of which was to carry out the punishment of the Babylonians. And it happened just as God predicted. Habakkuk's trust was vindicated.

The end result for us, observers of this power encounter in the Scripture, is a simple one. Our faith should be increased to believe God is who He says He is and will do what He says He will do. Habakkuk believed. He never saw it fulfilled. But it happened. Be encouraged dear leader. You serve a God who will accomplish His purposes.

Article 3

3. Bible Translations And Hebrew Poetic Format

Introduction

In another article[10] I have mentioned that more than 1/3 of the Old Testament is in *Hebrew Poetic* format. Some Bibles, particularly some of the later versions, have recognized the importance of showing the *Hebrew Poetry* as poetry. They have attempted to display phrases, couplets, and stanzas of Hebrew Poetry so that the English reader is made aware of it.

Comparison of Bibles and Indications of Hebrew Poetry Format

In the study of Hebrew Poetry, the first step is to recognize it. Then one must identify and label lines. And finally there is the analysis of relationships between lines. A good start on this procedure is to get a Bible, which already has identified Hebrew Poetry and printed it so you can recognize it.[11] Table Hab 3-1 lists a number of Bibles and comparatively displays how (or how not) they picture **Hebrew Poetry**.

Table Hab 3-1. Bibles and Poetic Format

None	Some	All
KJV	ASV (Job, Psa, Prov, SOS, Lam, few others)	RSV
LB	NBV (Psa, SOS, Lam, Joel, few others)	NRSV
AB	PB (Job, Psa, Prov, Ecc, Isa, Jer, Lam, Eze, some Dan, Hos, Joel, Amos, Obad, Mic, Nah, Hab, Zeph, Hag, Zech, Mal)	NEB
	GNB (almost all passages, just a few scattered minor passages; Proverbs is not poetic format)	TLB[12]

---

[10] See **Article**, *23. Hebrew Poetry and Habakkuk* included in this commentary.

[11] Sometimes even though the Bible prints in poetic format, you will find yourself disagreeing with the identification of lines. The poetic formats of the different Bible versions do not necessarily agree with each other. Nor will you.

[12] **The Learning Bible—Contemporary English Version**, prints all Hebrew Poetry in poetic format. However, be warned it will also do reduction statements of couplets, so that frequently you don't have all the lines of the stanza. Instead you have the meaning of the couplet(s) given in a reduction statement.

3. Bible Translations And Hebrew Poetic Format

Key To Abbreviations Used in Table Hab 3-1

KJV	= King James Version
LB	= Living Bible
AB	= Amplified Bible
ASV	= American Standard Version
NBV	= New Berkley Version
PB	= Paragraph Bible
GNB	= Good New Bible (Today's English Version)
RSV	= Revised Standard Version
NRSV	= New Revised Standard Version
NEB	= New English Bible
TLB	= The Learning Bible (Contemporary English Version)

There are perhaps other versions, which also print in poetic format. These given represent the Bibles, which I regularly use in my own personal study of Hebrew Poetry.

Some Help In Noting Parallelism in Printed Poetic format

Most Bibles use some basic scheme to standardize their printing format. Some capitalize the first word of a phrase. Some capitalize only the first word of the phrase of an extended unit. Some indent to indicate the second line of a couplet. Some give spaces between stanzas. It is helpful to recognize some of these methods. The following table relates what I have found concerning printed formats. The RSV and NRSV has been the most helpful in this regard. Unfortunately none of these Bibles actually gives a key to their own printing of Hebrew Poetry format.

Table Hab 3-2. Some Help In Noting Parallelism In Printed Poetic Format

Bible	Phrases	Couplets	Extended Parallelism	Stanzas
RSV (NRSV)	Begins a new phrase of couplet at left margin. 2nd phrase of couplet is indented. Any related phrase beyond couplet is also indented. Continuations of a phrase are indented more than a new phrase	First phrase always begins at far left. 2nd phrase is indented about 3 spaces.	1st word of phrase of a series of related parallel phrases is capitalized. Each succeeding phrase is lower case and indented 3 spaces. These sub-units almost always yield a major idea for the entire unit.	Spaces (also in prophets, it gives some titles summarizing the unit)
GNB	Like RSV	Like RSV	Like RSV	Like RSV
ASV	Starts each phrase with a capital letter at left margin	Usually terminates with a period or its equivalent	None	None
PB	Like ASV	Like ASV	Not clear	Spaces or indents

3. Bible Translations And Hebrew Poetic Format

Table Hab 3-2 continued

NEB	Each line is a phrase	Simple couplets done like ASV	Not clear; do some indenting	Spaces
NBV	Like RSV except 2nd line not indented	1st phrase of couplet is capitalized	Like RSV except succeeding lines not indented	Spaces and indents 1st line of stanza
TLB	Like RSV	Like RSV; 1st word of 2nd phrase of couplet is also capitalized	Not clear.	Spaces between stanzas; also some topic headings at beginning of stanza

Conclusion

From a comparative study of Bibles, which print in Hebrew Poetry format, you will see that identification of lines and phrases is not an exact thing. You will frequently have to modify that given in one of these Bibles to show what you are seeing in lines and relationships between the lines.

Article 4

4. Biblical Framework—The Redemptive Drama

Introduction
In each of the overviews on the various individual books in the leadership commentary series I have a section called **Where It Fits**. In that section, I try to deal with the application of my first general hermeneutical principle,[13]

Language Principle 1 Book and Books
In The Spirit, Prayerfully Study The Book As A Whole In Terms Of Its Relationship To Other Books In The Bible (i.e. the Bible as a whole) **TO INCLUDE**:
  a. its place in the progress of redemption (both as to the progress of revelation, what God has said, and also the notion of what God has done in redemptive history)
  b. its overall contribution to the whole or Bible literature (i.e. *its purposes — why is it in the Bible?*) and
  c. its abiding contribution to present time.

I seek to find **Where It Fits** using two basic overall frameworks:

1. *The Unfolding Drama of Redemption*—that is, telling the story of what God has said and done in the Bible.[14]

2. *The Leadership Framework.* Since this is a leadership commentary series, I want to trace the contribution of a book to leadership. The leadership era it fits in helps inform us as to how to interpret its leadership findings.

This article is concerned with the first of these two frameworks: *The Unfolding Drama of Redemption.* I have previously dealt with the second framework in several articles.[15]

I will first introduce the overall framework with a diagram. Then I will give a brief synopsis for each chapter of the redemptive drama. Finally, I will list the Bible books in terms of the chapters of the redemptive drama.

---

[13] See Appendix G in **Having A Ministry That Lasts** for the whole hermeneutical system I use.

[14] I am deeply indebted to a teaching mentor of mine, James M. (Buck) hatch who introduced me to this framework in his course, Progress of Redemption, given at Columbia Bible College. I have used his teaching and adapted it in my own study of each book in the Bible in terms of the Bible story as a whole. I have also written in depth on this in my handbook, **The Bible and Leadership Values**. This article is a condensed version of that larger explanation.

[15] See **Articles**, 36. *Six Biblical Leadership Eras--Overviewed;* 29. *Macro Lesson Defined;* 30. *Macro Lessons--List of 41 Across Six Leadership Eras.*

4. Biblical Framework—The Redemptive Drama   page 35

Overall Framework—Redemptive Drama Pictured

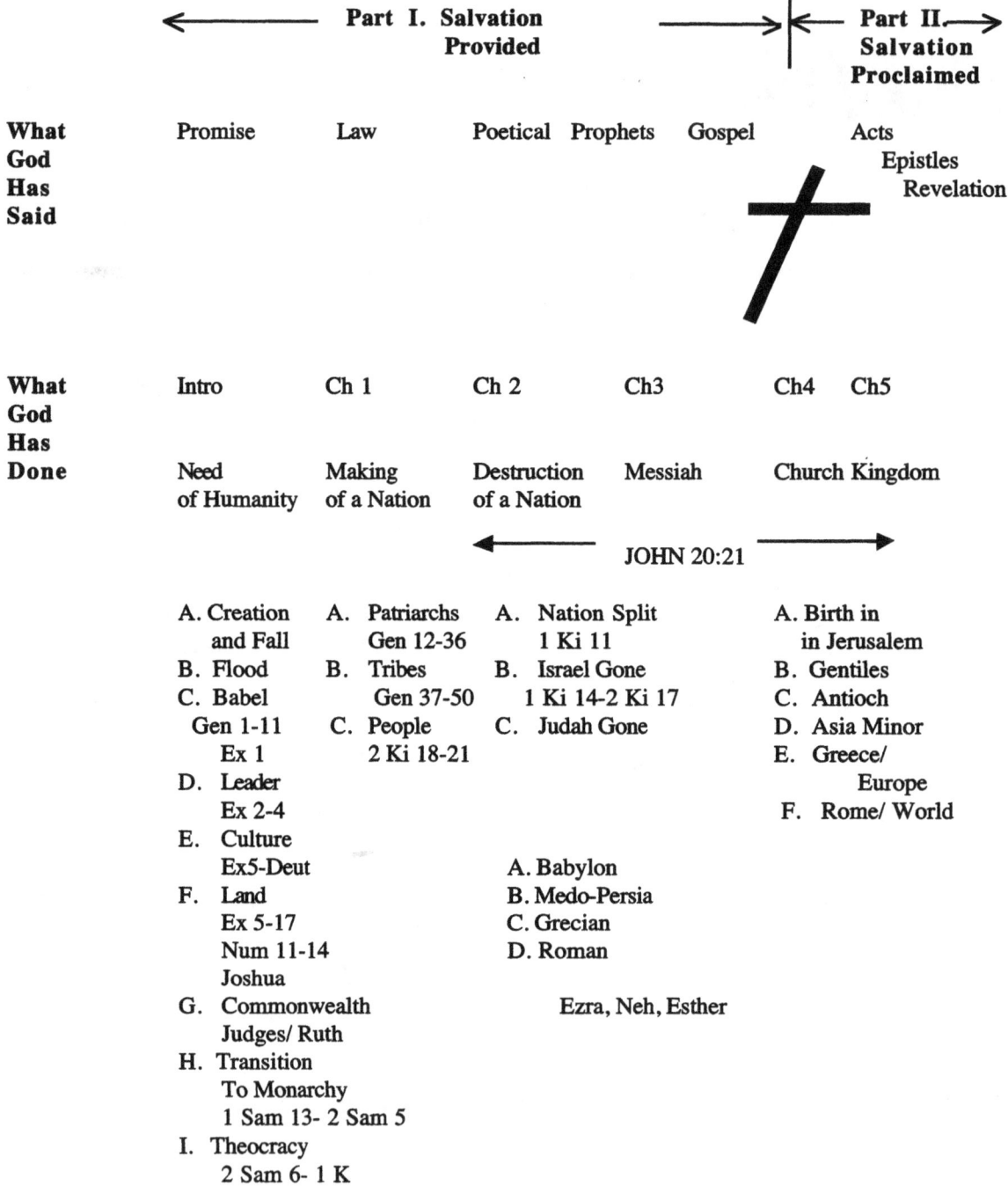

Figure Hab 4-1. Overview of Redemptive Drama Time Line

The **Time-Line of the Redemptive Story** contains six sections,

> Introduction,
> Chapter 1. The Making of A Nation,
> Chapter 2. The Destruction of A Nation,
> Chapter 3. Messiah,
> Chapter 4. The Church, and

4. Biblical Framework—The Redemptive Drama

Chapter 5. The Kingdom.

This story is briefly explained in a Running Capsule of the Redemptive Story. The story traces **what God does** and **what He says** throughout the Bible. And it shows that there is a progressive revelation of God throughout the whole drama. The Bible is unified around this salvation history. Once this is recognized then the notion of intentional selection becomes important. Each book in the Bible is there for a purpose and contributes something to this salvation story.

It is this framework, which provides the macro context for studying each book of the Bible. Where is the book in the progress of redemption time-line? What does it contribute to it? Why is it there? What would we miss if it were left out? Understanding each book in terms of its own purpose is a preliminary first step that must be done before we can interpret it for leadership findings.

The Running Capsule for the Redemptive Story

I will first give an overview and then give more detail from each part of the redemptive drama.

Overall

At the center of the Biblical revelation is the concept of a God who has intervened in human history. He created the human race. He has revealed himself to that race. That race rebelled against His desires. In its fallen state it continually rebels against His wishes and desires and for the potential that it could accomplish.

So He started again and selected specifically a people through whom He could reveal Himself to the world. God moves unswervingly toward His purpose which is to redeem people and relate to them. He moves toward His purposes whether or not the people He has chosen follow them or not. They can willingly be a part in which they enjoy the blessings of God or they can be by-passed and He will find other ways to accomplish His purposes. He patiently works with them to include them in His purposes. But when all is said and done He moves on with or without them.

All the time He is increasingly revealing more of Himself and His purposes to His people. They come to know Him as a mighty God, all powerful and controlling, yet allowing human beings their choices. He is a holy God, that is, a being of perfection. He reveals His purposes as that of having a Holy people following Him. People who are becoming Holy as He is holy. They learn that to fall short of His demands or standards is to sin against Him and is deserving of retribution if justice is to be satisfied.

Part I of the redemption drama, **SALVATION PROVIDED**, is His selection of a people, which will prove foundational to accomplishing His purposes. Out of that people will come one who is central in the decrees of God. Not an afterthought but mysteriously beyond our thinking, known to God. Look at Revelation 13:8, the Lamb slain before the foundation of the world. In terms of what we know of God today, we see this Part I as revealing to us, God the Father, that is, the God who is source of all that we are and to whom we relate, infinite, eternal, powerful, a spirit.

God protects that line through which He will come over a period of many years and in times of failure on their part to know Him and obey Him as they should.

His incarnation into the world begins Part II of the Redemptive Drama, **SALVATION PROCLAIMED**. Galatians 4:4, in God's time. That incarnate God, manifest in the flesh, to communicate directly with the human race, to be a part of it, to share in its joys

4. Biblical Framework—The Redemptive Drama

and sorrows, finally pays the supreme price of rejection, by a world who wanted to call its own shots, the death of the Cross, perfection paying the perfect price to satisfy God's Holy just demands. The great dilemma was solved, how God could be absolutely just and yet lovingly receive to Himself, those for whom justice demanded the harsh penalty of death. That time in which Jesus lived and walked and taught and did so many things to reveal God to us is the time, as we now know it of God the Son, God revealed to a human race as one of that race. Having accomplished the first portion of His work, the Cross, He ascended to heaven and will yet come again. Having ascended, He sent the Holy Spirit into the world, the intimation of what is to come, the Spirit who indwells those people He has chosen.

In the meantime while we wait we are involved in Part II **Salvation Proclaimed**, which shows that this message was more than just for the Jews but for a whole world. And that is what we are about today, the proclamation of that reconciling message, that God has provided a way in which sinful human beings can be rightly related to Him and progress to live a satisfying and fruitful life, in harmony with His purposes. And as they live this purposeful life, demonstrating the power and presence of God in their time on earth, they know that God is going to make all things right someday—there is a justice coming; the Lord Jesus, now a risen Savior, a life-giving Spirit will return to claim His own. There will be a time of His reigning on earth and then there will be eternity. And we who have been called out, as a people to His name, will reign with Him for all eternity. In terms of what we know today, this is the Age of God, the Spirit.

Introduction

Genesis tells us of many beginnings. It tells of the beginning of the creation, the human race, of sin in the world, of the spread of the race, of judgment on the race and a new beginning for the race. It does not satisfy all our questions. We would ask more and want more. But it does give us the backdrop for the salvation story. Humanity is in need. It can not get along with itself. It has alienated itself from God. Left to itself it will be destructive at best. There is a need. And the salvation story, which begins in Genesis chapter 12 will give God's response to meet that need.

Chapter 1. The Making of a Nation

God's basic plan is to choose a people and to reveal Himself and His plans for reconciling the world to Himself through that nation. Chapter 1 tells of the story of God's building of the nation.

If I were to pick out the most important events in the making of a nation, Chapter 1 of the redemptive drama I would say the following would certainly be a part of it.

1. The call of Abraham—the Abrahamic Promise
2. The renewal of the covenant with Isaac
3. The renewal of the covenant with Jacob
4. The deliverance of Jacob and sons through Joseph
5. The call of Moses
6. The power encounters in Egypt and the Exodus
7. The Red Sea deliverance
8. The Spies in the Land/corporate failure of a faith check
9. The Giving of the 10 Commandments/covenant
10. Moses' failure—striking the rock
11. Moses' outstanding leadership in the desert years with a rebellious followership and his transition of Joshua into leadership
12. Crossing of Jordan
13. Circumcision at Gilgal
14. Joshua meets the Captain of the Hosts
15. Capture of Jericho

4. Biblical Framework—The Redemptive Drama

16. Failure at Ai
17. Success at Ai
18. Gibeonite deception
19. Capture of Land (lack of total obedience)
20. Repetitive Failure—moving from dependence to independence. The Cycle of the Judges (need for centralized influence)
21. Samuel's unifying influence
22. Saul's anointing and failure
23. David's anointing and success
24. David's failure and discipline
25. David's preparation for building the temple

Lets examine some of the Bible books, which present these events.

From Genesis

From the introduction we know that humanity is not in good shape and is in need of intervention by God. And God has a plan thought out in eternity past.

God chooses one man, Abraham, and Promises (*The First Great Revelation—The Promise*) to make of him a great nation and to give them land and to bless the world through his offspring. (Gen 12:1-3, 7; 15:4,18, et al) Now God plans to use the nation He will bring forth to be a channel of redemption and revelation of Himself. So He begins to build a nation. For a nation you need people (including numbers) a coherent culture, a land, and a leader.

God begins to work on these things—the people first (the land has people on it who will be judged eventually when they are too evil to be redeemed). From this one man, who exemplifies faith in God's promise, comes a son, Isaac. Isaac has two sons, one of whom, Jacob, becomes the successor of the family line through which God will work—the 12 heads of the tribes: Reuben, Simeon, Levi, Judah, Zebulun, Issachar, Dan, Gad, Asher, Naphtali, Joseph, Benjamin.

Joseph, a son of Jacob's old age and his favorite, is sold into slavery by his jealous brothers (Acts 7:9). Because the patriarchs were jealous of Joseph they sold him as a slave into Egypt. But God was with him and rescued him from all his troubles. He gave Joseph wisdom and enabled him to gain the goodwill of Pharaoh king of Egypt; so he made him ruler over Egypt and all his palace.) Joseph, a person of proven integrity, rises to power through a series of providential appointments in which he shows wisdom from God upon several occasions. God gives some dreams to Pharaoh, the ruler of Egypt, which predict some good years followed by famine years. Joseph gives a wise plan to Pharaoh on how to prepare for it. He is put in charge and is right on target to protect his own family when the famine hits. The family comes to Egypt and rides through the famine years. It stays and expands in the land. Joseph, never losing sight of God's promise, exacts a promise from his brothers and fellow Israelites that they will take him back into the land when God takes them back. That is how Genesis ends.

From Exodus

Exodus opens many years later. There are many Israelite descendants, so many in fact, that the Egyptian King is fearful of them so he subjugates them. They are slaves and being ill-treated. Persecution takes the form of enforced labor and attempts to cut down the population (executing the boy babies).

4. Biblical Framework—The Redemptive Drama

God, having fulfilled the first part of his plan, getting a people, now works on the second part—getting a leader. Moses, an Israelite baby is preserved providentially and taken into the palace and educated as an Egyptian royal class person. As he reaches adulthood he recognizes that his people by blood relationship are in great bondage. So he wants to free them. His first attempt to help them is a disaster. He kills an Egyptian and has to flee Egypt. He goes to Midian, settles down, marries a Midianite woman, and has a family. After forty years, God selects him via a miraculous revelation, to go back to Egypt to lead God's people out of Egypt and into the promised land. Moses goes back and after 10 major confrontations with the Egyptian ruler (in which God-given power is seen—Moses certainly has spiritual authority) the people are freed to leave. But on the way the Egyptian ruler has second thoughts and pursues with his military. The military should overtake the Israelites who will be trapped by the Red Sea. God miraculously intervenes and they escape across the Red Sea on dry ground. The sea moves back as the military forces start to cross and they are wiped out. This is the heart of *the Exodus*.

From Exodus and Leviticus

God next begins to build the people culturally into what He will need. He gives them the LAW, the second great revelation and reveals more of Himself, His standards, and His purposes. The tabernacle, which He gives the plans for reveals more of who God is in terms of access and revelation. The rest of EXODUS is given to that, revealing who God is as is the whole of LEVITICUS. It is especially in Leviticus that the holiness of God is developed—an understanding of sin and its implications; what atonement is (that is, being made right with God by making up for wrong against Him).

From Numbers

After disobedience and a lack of faith prevent the people from going in to the land (see NUMBERS) they wander for 40 years in the Sinai desert until the older rebellious people die off. During the desert years they learn to trust in God's provision. God reveals Himself primarily through his leader Moses. Near the end of the 40 years they are again ready to go into the land. God has a people, a culture, a leader, Moses, and a leader to take his place, Joshua. Moses prepares them for that push into the land by giving them a series of addresses (DEUTERONOMY—second law). These messages, his final words to them, reflect warnings drawn from their desert experience, remind them of standards of obedience which reflects what they have learned of God, and gives encouragement in the form of expectations as they enter the land. He closes his final words to them with songs of warning and blessing that portend the future. And thus we are ready for the third part of God's plan to build Himself a people—getting them into the land.

From Joshua

Joshua transitions into leadership with some sterling miraculous interventions by God, which give him the spiritual authority he will need to follow Moses (a hard act to follow) as leader. Joshua seizes Jericho, after following a supernaturally revealed plan for its capture. He proceeds after an unexpected failure, which teaches an important corporate lesson on obedience, to the people, to split the land in two militarily and then begins to mop up in the north and south. The land is allotted. Each tribe has a portion, just as Moses had planned. They decentralize and begin to settle into their spots—with much trouble. After having been so long in a centralized authoritarian mode, they enjoy being decentralized and having autonomy. But this decentralization eventually leads to spiritual deterioration. This brings us up into the times of the judges.

From Judges

For a long period of time, longer than we in the United States have been a nation, the twelve tribes live scattered. There is frequent civil war in specific locales and much

4. Biblical Framework—The Redemptive Drama   page 40

fighting with various surrounding nations and peoples who were not totally destroyed when the land was taken.

In short there is an oft repeated cycle: the people deteriorate spiritually getting far from God, God brings judgment upon them, they finally recognize that their problem is relationship with God—they repent and cry out for God's help. He sends along leaders, very charismatic who usually lead a volunteer army to defeat their enemies. There are at least 13 of these including: Othniel, Ehud, Shamgar, Deborah (Barak), Gideon, Abimelech, Tola, Jair, Jephthah, Ibzan, Elon, Abdon, and Samson. Some of these are more well known than others. Gideon and Samson for example. These are evil times and few there are who follow God.

In a section of the Judges (Judges 2:7) the writer sums it up well, "After Joshua had dismissed the Israelites, they went to take possession of the land, each to his own inheritance. The people served the Lord through out the lifetime of Joshua and of the elders who outlived him and who had seen all the great things the Lord had done for Israel." And then again in the closing portion a repeated phrase haunts us—Judges 21:25, "In those days Israel had no king; everyone did as he saw fit." These are the pre-kingdom years. Corporately the people are negatively prepared for the kingdom, which will come.

From Ruth
There is a spark of life during those dreadful times. Ruth introduces us to that life by showing that there were some people of integrity who honored the Lord. This little romantic book shows how God provides and also allows us to see how the line through which the redeemer will later arise progresses.

The Judges and Ruth are pre-kingdom times. They prepared the Israelites to want a centralized structure after so much independence and autonomy. The Israelites were dependent upon voluntary armies raised up in times of crisis. Many times, other of the tribes than the one threatened, were not interested in their local squabbles and would not fight for them. Thus the entire commonwealth of tribes comes to the place where it needs, wants, and will accept a kingdom. Again God steps in and provides a transition leader—Samuel.

From 1 Samuel
The first thirteen chapters show how Samuel was providentially raised up as a leader. His ministry as judge was not just a momentary deliverance but a continual one. He visited the different tribes and judged them—that is, established law and justice for them. Samuel paves the way for a centralized kingdom. Crises around the people spur the need; Samuel's own sons are not able to replace him. The people demand a king—showing their need for one but also showing that they basically did not trust the unseen King. God gives them one king, Saul, who outwardly is what they would expect. But he fails repeatedly to follow God. His kingdom is spiritually bankrupt. God replaces him with David, whom God describes as *a man after my own heart*. The last part of 1 Samuel describes Saul's fall and David's early pre-kingdom years, in which David is gaining military expertise as a guerrilla warfare leader with a para-military band.

From 2 Samuel and 1 Chronicles and the Psalms
2 Samuel and 1 Chronicles give David's story—one written earlier to it and one written later. David is a long time in getting the kingdom as Saul's descendants try to hold on to the kingdom. After seven years of civil war, David is ruling a smaller part of Israel, the kingdom is united. God gives a covenant to David concerning his descendants. The poetical literature, particularly the Psalms, emerge more solidly from this era. David is an

4. Biblical Framework—The Redemptive Drama

artistic person who spends time alone with God in worship. Many of the Psalms come out of those times alone with God, many spurred on by crises in David's kingdom. The kingdom is established under David and expands. In mid-life David has a major sin which tarnishes his lifetime. He has one of his military leaders killed in order that he might take his wife for himself. It and failure to manage his family well lead to a rebellion by one of his sons Absalom. David is deposed briefly but comes back winning a strategic battle. He is reinstated. Most of the rest of his kingdom is downhill. David's son, Solomon, after some manipulation and political intrigue succeeds David.

A number of the Psalms are ascribed to David. They reveal something of the personal touch—what that great leader was feeling during some of the more important times of his kingdom. They particularly show his need for God and why God calls him a "man after my own heart."

From Proverbs and Ecclesiastes

Solomon has the best start of any king in all the history of Israel. There is peace in the land. The borders have expanded almost to the full extent of God's promise. There is money and resources in the kingdom as well as a good military. Times are stable. Solomon builds the temple for God—a symbol of the centralized importance of religious worship in the capital. Solomon's early years are characterized by splendor. Most likely during the early and middle part of his reign many of the Proverbs were collected. These sayings embody truth that has been learned over the years (times of the Judges, times of the kingdom) about how to live harmoniously with others. Toward the end of his reign, he slips and falls away from following God. In this latter part of his reign, he writes Ecclesiastes which sums up much that he has learned over his lifetime. Its cynical tone shows need for an intimate relationship with God that is missing.

The nation is there. There are people. They know of God and his desires for them. There is a land. But they continually fail to live up to what God wants. During the reigns of David and Solomon the kingdom reaches its zenith. And thus ends Chapter 1, the making of a nation. In it all, God is seen to weave His purpose all around a people who frequently rebel against Him. They freely choose to live as they do, whether following after God or not. But even so He manages to move unswervingly forward to His purposes.

Chapter 2. The Destruction of a Nation

The story-line of chapter 2 hinges around the following major events:
1. Solomon goes away from the Lord, great warning—had the best start of any king yet did not finish well.
2. Rehoboam (1 Kings 12) makes unwise decision to increase taxes and demands on people—kingdom splits as prophecy said. 10 tribes go with the northern kingdom, Judah with the southern.
3. The northern kingdom under Jereboam quickly departs from God. Jereboam is used as the model of an evil king to whom all evil kings are likened; He had a good start also—God would have blessed him.
4. The southern kingdom generally is bad with an occasional good Kings and partially good kings: Asa, Jehoshaphat, Joash, Amaziah, Uzziah, Jotham, Hezekiah, Josiah. But the trend was always downward. The extended length of life of the southern kingdom, more than the northern kingdom, is directly attributed to the spiritual life of the better kings. Spiritual leadership does make a difference.
5. During both the northern and southern kingdoms God sent prophets to try and correct them—first the oral prophets (many—but the two most noted were Elijah and Elisha) and then the prophets who wrote.

4. Biblical Framework—The Redemptive Drama

Now in order to understand this long period of history you should know several things:
1. The History books that give background information about the times.
2. The Bible Time-Line, need to know when the books were written.
3. Need to know the writing prophets: northern or southern kingdom, which crisis, direct or special.

The History Books

The history books covering the time of the destruction of a nation include 1, 2 Samuel, 1,2 Kings, and 1,2 Chronicles. The following chart helps identify the focus of each of these books as to major content.

Chart Hab 4-1 The History Books—Major Content

1 Samuel	2 Samuel / 1 Chronicles	1,2 Kings / 2 Chronicles
Samuel, Saul, David	David	1,2 Kings: Solomon to Zedekiah 2 Chronicles exclusively on line of Judah

There are four categories of prophetical books. Prophetical books deal with three major crises: the Assyrian crisis which wiped out the northern kingdom; the Bablonian crisis, which wiped out the southern kingdom; the return to the land after being exiled. There are also prophetical books not specifically dealing with these crises but associated with the time of them. The prophetical books dealing with these issues are:

A. Northern—Assyrian Crisis
   Jonah, Amos, Hosea, Nahum, Micah
B. Southern—Babylonian Crisis
   Joel, Isaiah, Micah, Zephaniah, Jeremiah, Lamentations, Habakkuk, Obadiah
C. In Exile
   Ezekiel, Daniel, Esther
D. Return From Exile
   Nehemiah, Ezra, Haggai, Zechariah, Malachi

In addition, to knowing the crises you must know that prophets wrote:

A. Direct to the Issue of the Crisis either Assyrian, Babylonian, or Return To The Land
   Amos, Hosea, Joel, Micah, Isaiah, Jeremiah, Ezekiel, Haggai, Zechariah, Malachi
B. Special
   Jonah, Nahum, Habakkuk, Obadiah, Zephaniah, Daniel.

The special prophets, though usually associated with one of the crisis times, wrote to deal with unique issues not necessarily related directly to the crisis. The following list gives the special prophets and their main thrust.

1. Jonah—a paradigm shift, pointing out God's desire for the nation to be missionary minded and reach out to surrounding nations.
2. Nahum—vindicate God, judgment on Assyria.

4. Biblical Framework—The Redemptive Drama

3. Habakkuk—faith crisis for Habakkuk, vindicate God, judgment on Babylon.
4. Obadiah—vindicate God, judgment on Edom for treatment of Judah.
5. Zephaniah—show about judgment, the Day of the Lord.
6. Daniel—give hope, show that God is indeed ruling even in the times of the exile and beyond, gives God's plan for the ages.

<u>The Destruction of A Nation—The Return From Exile</u> (see page 32)

Several Bible books are associated with the return to the land from the exile. After a period of about 70 years (during which time Daniel ministered) Cyrus made a decree which allowed some Jews (those that wanted to) to return to the land. Some went back under Zerrubabel, a political ruler like a governor. A priest, Joshua, also provided religious leadership to the first group that went back. This group of people started to rebuild the temple but became discouraged due to opposition and lack of resources. They stopped building the temple. Two prophets, after several years, 10-15, addressed the situation. These two, Haggai and Zechariah, were able to encourage the leadership and the people to finish the temple.

Another thirty or forty years goes by and then we have the events of the book of Esther, back in the land. Her book describes the attempt to eradicate the Jewish exiles—a plot which failed due to God's sovereign intervention via Esther, the queen of the land and a Jewish descendant going incognito, and her relative Mordecai.

Still another period of time passes, 20 or so years and a priest, Ezra, directs another group to return to the land. The spiritual situation has deteriorated. He brings renewal.

Another kind of leader arrives on the scene some 10-15 years later. Nehemiah, a lay leader, and one adept at organizing and moving to accomplish a task, rebuilds the wall around Jerusalem. He too has to instigate renewal.

Finally, after another period of 30 or so years we have the book of Malachi, which again speaks to renewal of the people. The Old Testament closes with this final book.

A recurring emphasis occurs during the period of the return. People are motivated to accomplish a task for God. They start out, become discouraged, and stop. They must be renewed. God raises up leadership to bring renewal.

<u>Preparation for the Coming of Messiah—The Inter-Testamental Period</u>

I do not deal with this in detail, that is, in terms of the various historical eras.[16] Some 400+ years elapse between the close of the Old Testament and the Beginning of the New Testament. There are significant differences in the Promised Land. The following chart highlights these differences.[17]

Chart Hab 4-2 Differences in Palestine—Close of O.T., Beginning of N.T.

The End of the Old Testament	The Beginning of the New Testament
1. Palestine was part of a Persian satrapy, since Persian, an eastern nation was the greatest governmental power in the world at the time.	1. Palestine was a Roman province, since the entire world had come under the sway of the western Nation of Rome.

---

[16] In **Leadership Perspectives**, I do deal more in a detailed way with the various historical sub-phases of this period of history. A number of books in the Catholic canon occur during this period of time.

[17] These notes are adapted from material studied with Frank Sells at Columbia Bible College in his Old Testament survey course.

4. Biblical Framework—The Redemptive Drama

2. The population was sparse.	2. One of the most dense parts of the Roman empire.
3. The cities of Palestine as a whole were heaps of rubbish.	3. There was general prosperity throughout Palestine.
4. The temple of Zerubbabel was a significant structure.	4. The temple of Herod the Great was a magnificent building.
5. There were no Pharisees or Sadducees, although the tendencies from which they developed were present.	5. The Pharisees and Sadducees were much in evidence and strong in power.
6. There were no synagogues in Palestine.	6. Synagogues were located everywhere in the Holy Land. There was no hamlet or village so small or destitute as to lack a synagogue.
7. There was little extra-biblical tradition among the Jews.	7. There was a great mass of tradition, among both the Jews of Palestine and those of the dispersion.
8. The Jews were guilty of much intermarriage with the surrounding nations.	8. There was almost no intermarriage between Jews and non-Jews.
9. Palestine was under the rule of a Hebrew.	9. Palestine was under the rule of an Edomite vice-king, Herod the Great.
10. The Hebrew governor was regarded by the Jews as their spiritual leader.	10. The scribes and priest were regarded by the Jews as their spiritual leaders.

In addition to differences, there were some similarities between end of O.T. times and beginning of N.T. times.

1. **Freedom from idolatry**. God had used the Babylonian Captivity to free His people from their oft-repeated tendency to idolatry.
2. **Israel in two great divisions**, the Jews of the Homeland (Isolation) and the Jews of the Dispersion (who were scattered throughout the world). In the time of Malachi a relatively small proportion of God's chosen people was located in Palestine, while by far the larger part was still in exile. Although Palestine was much more thickly populated in the time of Christ than in the time of Malachi, the same general situation prevailed as to the two-fold division of Israel into Palestinian Jews and Jews of the Diaspora (Dispersion), with a far greater number in exile than in the land of Canaan.
3. **Externalism and dead orthodoxy**. A comparison of Malachi (the last prophetical book of the Old Testament) and Nehemiah (the last historical book of the Old Testament) with the Gospels indicates that the outward conformity of the Pharisees to the law which they inwardly revolted from, was but an advanced step of the hypocritical conformity which had marked many Israelites at the end of Old Testament days.

It was during the inter-testamental period that these changes occurred. Daniel had foretold of the various empires that would emerge after Babylon: the Medo-Persian, the Grecian, and the Roman. Each of these were used by God to prepare the way for the coming of Messiah, the next chapter in the redemptive drama.

Galatians 4:4 states that Messiah came at the "fullness of time." That is, the time was ready. Some have suggested a fivefold preparation for Christ's Coming.

4. Biblical Framework—The Redemptive Drama

1. Religious Preparation—both negative and positive
2. Political Preparation—world at peace
3. Cultural Preparation—lack of meaning; cultural vehicle through which to spread the Gospel
4. The Social Preparation—great needs; life under bondage
5. The Moral Preparation

Chapter 3. Messiah

At the right moment in time—Jesus was born. His miraculous birth attested to his uniqueness.

He was the fulfillment of the Old Testament as to many of its prophecies, types, symbols. He was the seed of the woman who dealt a fatal blow to the seed of the serpent (Genesis 3:15); he was the tabernacle who lived among us (Exodus 25-40); he was the arch type of the brazen serpent, lifted up that people might look, see and be healed (Numbers 21); he was the arch types of the Levitical offerings, the perfect sacrifice (Leviticus 1-5); he was that prophet like unto Moses (Deuteronomy 18); he was the ultimate fulfillment of the Davidic covenant (2 Samuel 7); he was the Messianic Sufferer (Psalm 22); he was the one who was anointed to preach good news to the poor, to proclaim freedom for the captives, and release from darkness those who are prisoners, to proclaim the year of the Lord's favor (Isaiah 61:1ff) and the Suffering Servant (Isaiah 53); he was the righteous branch from David's line (Jeremiah 23); he was the one shepherd, the servant David, the prince of Ezekiel (Ezekiel 37); he was the one greater than Jonah, the sign after three days he arose (Jonah 21); he was the proper leader coming out of obscure Bethlehem (Micah 5:2); and we could go on.

Matthew showed he was the Messiah King, rejected. Mark showed him to be vested with divine power, a person of action and authority. Luke showed him to be the perfect representative of the human race: one of courage, ability, social interests, sympathy, broad acceptance. And John showed him to be Immanuel, God with us, revealing God to us and acting to demonstrate grace and truth, the heartbeat of the divine ministry philosophy.

The bottom line of the story line is given in a quote taken from John, "He was in the world, and though the world was made through him, the world did not recognize him. He came unto his own, but his own did not receive him. Yet to all who received him, to those who believed in his name, he gave the right to become children of God, children born not of natural descent, nor of human source but born of God. The Word became flesh and made his dwelling among us. We have seen his glory, the glory of the One and Only, who came from the Father, full of grace and truth." (John 1:10-14).

The story of this chapter of the redemptive drama ends abruptly. But there is a postscript. Each of the Gospel stories and the Acts tell us of Jesus Christ's resurrection. After His death He arose and was seen for a period of about 40 days upon various occasions. During those days He gave the marching orders for the movement He had begun. The great commissions repeated five times, Matthew 28:19,20, Luke 24:46,47, Mark 16:15, John 20:21, and Acts 1:8. Each of these carry the main thrust which is to go into the world and tell the Good News of salvation, that people can be reconciled to God. Each also carries some special connotation. It is these marching orders, which set the stage for Chapter 4, The Church, in the redemptive story.

Chapter 4. The Church

The essence of the story line of chapter 4, is contained in the book of Acts. Its central thematic message is the essence of the story line.

4. Biblical Framework—The Redemptive Drama

Theme: **The Growth Of The Church**
- which spreads from Jerusalem to Judea to Samaria and the uttermost parts of the earth,
- is seen to be of God,
- takes place as Spirit directed people present a salvation centered in Jesus Christ, and
- occurs among all peoples, Jews and Gentiles.

This basic phenomenon reoccurs as the Gospel spreads across cultural barriers throughout the world. Though the message of the book of Acts covers only up through the first two thirds of the first century its basic essence reoccurs throughout the church age until the present time in which we live.

About half of the book of Acts tells of the formation of the church in Jerusalem and its early expansion to Jews, Samaritans, and finally to Gentiles. The latter half of the book traces the breakout of the Gospel to Gentiles in Asia and Europe. The structure of the book highlighted by the linguistic discourse markers (the Word of the Lord grew) carries the notion of a God-given church expanding.

Structure: There are seven divisions in Acts each concluding with a summary verse. The summary verses: 2:47b, 6:7, 9:31, 12:24, 16:5, 19:20, 28:30,31

I.	(ch 1-2:47)	The Birth of the Church in Jerusalem
II.	(ch 3-6:7)	The Infancy of the Church in Jerusalem
III.	(ch 6:8-9:31)	The Spread of the Church into Judea, Galilee, Samaria
IV.	(ch 9:32-12:24)	The Church Doors Open to the Gentiles
V.	(ch 13-16:5)	The Church Spreads to Asia Minor
VI.	(ch 16:6-19:20)	The Church Gains a Foothold in Europe
VII.	(ch 19:21-28)	The Travels of the Church's First Missionary To Rome (The Church on Trial in its Representative Paul)

As to details there are many important pivotal events in the Acts, many of which have similarly reoccurred in the expansion of the Gospel around the world and throughout church history. Acts begins with Jesus' post resurrection ministry to the disciples and his Ascension to heaven. Then the disciples are gathered at Jerusalem praying when the Pentecost event, the giving of the Holy Spirit to the church, as promised in Luke's version of the Great Commission, happens and Peter gives a great public sermon which launches the church.

Early church life is described. Peter and John imbued with power heal a lame man at the temple gate and are put in prison. They are threatened and released. An incident with Ananias and Sapphira shows the power and presence of the Holy Spirit.

Stephen an early church servant has a strong witness and is martyred for it. General persecution on the church breaks out. The believers are scattered and preach the gospel where ever they go. Phillip, another early church servant leads an Ethiopian palace administrator to Christ and has ministry in Samaria.

Saul, the persecutor of Christians, is saved on the road to Damascus. Peter demonstrates Godly power in several miraculous events. Peter is divinely chosen to preach

4. Biblical Framework—The Redemptive Drama

the Gospel to a Gentile, Cornelius. Herod kills James and imprisons Peter. Peter is miraculously delivered.

The story line now switches to follow the missionary efforts of Barnabas and Paul (formerly Saul) to Cyprus and Asian minor. It then goes on to follow Paul's efforts which go further into Asia minor and Greece. Paul makes a return visit to Jerusalem where he is accused by the Jewish opposition in Jerusalem. Eventually after several delays and hearings he is ordered to Rome. The book ends with the exciting journey to Rome, including a shipwreck.

The books of the New Testament were written to various groups during the church chapter. Many were written by Paul. These generally were letters to the various churches which had resulted from his missionary efforts. Each was contextually specific—written at a certain time, written at a certain stage of Paul's own development as a leader, and dealing with a specific situation—either an individual in a church or to a corporate group, some church at a location or in a general region.

Other New Testament books were not written by Paul. The book of Hebrews, author uncertain, John's three letters, Jude's one letter and Peter's two letters all are of a general nature. With the exception of possibly 2nd and 3rd John, these letters were written to believer's in general in scattered regions—probably Asia minor.

All of these, Paul's letters, and the general books, deal with the church. They give us insights into church problems, church situations at that time, and the essence of what the church is and how Christians ought to live. These New Testament books are filled with leadership information. Each of them represents a major leadership act of a leader seeking to influence followers of Christ. Many of them have actual details that reflect leadership values, leadership problem solving, and leadership issues. All of them have important modeling data.

We would have an unfinished story if we were left only with *just these* New Testament books. We would have a task. And men and women would be out and about the world attempting to fulfill that task. But where is it leading. What about those Old Testament prophecies yet to be fulfilled about *that day*. Our story is incomplete. We need to know how this redemptive drama is going to end. And so the Revelation.

Chapter 5. The Kingdom

The final book of the Bible is aptly named. The Revelation (unveiling, revealing, making clear) of Jesus Christ (the unveiling of Jesus Christ) brings closure to the redemptive drama. This final book in the Bible has among others these purposes:

1. to reveal future purposes of Jesus Christ and graphically show the power He will unleash in accomplishing His purposes, which include bringing about justice and bringing in His reign,
2. to show those purposes and power to be in harmony with His divine attributes, and
3. to bring a fitting climax to the redemptive story developed throughout Scripture.

The theme statement of the book of Revelation highlights the fitting climax of the redemptive drama.

4. Biblical Framework—The Redemptive Drama

Theme: **God's Ultimate Purposes For His Redemptive Program**
- center in the Person of His Son,
- involve His churches,
- will take place in a context of persecution and struggle—as described cryptically by many visions,
- will focus on the triumph of Jesus and his judgment of all things in harmony with his divine attributes, and
- will be realized in final victory for His people and ultimate justice accomplished in the world.

God's intent from the first of Genesis on has been to bless His people with His eternal presence. Ezekiel closes his book with that thought in mind. Numerous of the prophets point to a future day in which things would be made right and God would dwell with His people. The plan has had many twists and turns but through it all God has sovereignly moved on to His purpose.

Some have followed hard after God and were included in His purposes. Others refused to follow God. They were cast aside. God moved on.

In the New Testament God prepares a way where He can reveal Himself in justice and love and reconcile all people unto Himself. The Cross climaxes all of God's preparation to bless the world. The message of the Cross is seen to be for all. The church goes out into all the world. It has its problems. But always it seeks to be part of God's future purposes looking forward to Christ's return. Were there no Revelation, the Redemptive Story would be incomplete. The Revelation brings to a fitting climax all of God's working to bless the world. There is an ultimate purpose in history! Justice is meted out! And then a final blessing—God's eternal presence of with His people.

Suggested Chronological Writing of New Testament Books

When we study a given book of the bible we should know where it occurs in the redemptive drama. We should be familiar with what God has revealed to that point in time and what God has done redemptively up to that time. Table Hab 4-1 below list each book of the Bible in terms of the Chapter in the redemptive story in which it falls. I have attempted to list each book in chronological order though there is not scholarly consensus on when some of these books were written.

Table Hab 4-1. Bible Books Related To Chapters of the Redemptive Drama

The Bible Books: Chapter 1. The Making of a Nation

Exodus	Joshua	2 Samuel	Ecclesiastes
Leviticus	Judges	1 Chronicles	Song of Songs
Numbers	Ruth	Psalms	
Deuteronomy	1 Samuel	Proverbs	

The Bible Books: Chapter 2. The Destruction of a Nation

1,2 Kings	Hosea	Zephaniah	Daniel	Nehemiah
2 Chronicles	Micah	Jeremiah	Haggai	Malachi
Jonah	Isaiah	Lamentations	Zechariah	
Joel	Nahum	Obadiah	Esther	
Amos	Habakkuk	Ezekiel	Ezra	

The Bible Books: Chapter 3. Messiah

Matthew	Mark	Luke	John

4. Biblical Framework—The Redemptive Drama

The Bible Books: Chapter 4. The Church

James	2 Corinthians	Colossians	Titus	2 John
Acts	Galatians	Philemon	2 Timothy	3 John
1 Thessalonians	Romans	1 Peter	Hebrews	
2 Thessalonians	Ephesians	2 Peter	Jude	
1 Corinthians	Philippians	1 Timothy	1 John	

The Bible Book   Chapter 5. Kingdom
Revelation

Article 5

5. Daniel—Power Encounters

Frequently a ministry breakthrough involves power ministry in which God intervenes miraculously to authenticate His reality, power, and superiority. One such example of power ministry was coded by Tippett as a power encounter.[18]

Definition   A power encounter identifies a situation in which the power of God is tested over against some other god's power.

Several elements that should be present in classical power encounters: a) A crisis between people representing God and other people must be differentiated clearly. b) There must be recognition that the issue is one of power confrontation in the supernatural realm. c) There must be public recognition of the pre-encounter terms (If...Then...). d) There is an actual crisis/confrontation event (the more public usually the better will be the aftermath). e) There must be confirmation that God has done the delivering as the power encounter resolves. f) Celebration to bring closure and insure continuation of God's purpose in the power event.

Biblical examples of power encounters include the classic example of Elijah on Mt. Carmel, 1 Ki 18:17-40, Jephthah and the Ammonites in Judges 11:12-32 and the power encounters in Daniel 3 and 5. A N.T. example involves the spiritual warfare in Acts 19:10-20 where Paul demonstrates God's power in a mighty way. This power ministry display climaxed when Paul destroyed the demonic paraphernalia of many converts. Not all the elements of an ideal power encounter occur in all of the power encounters. But the essential element, God's breakthrough in power and demonstration of superiority is always seen.

Table Hab 5-1 details the two power encounters in Daniel showing which elements were present or absent. √ means absent or implied; √√ means clearly seen. Dan 3 involves the spectacular fiery furnace incident with Nebuchadnezzar and Dan 5 the awesome handwriting on the wall with Belshazzar.

Table Hab 5-1. Elements of Power Encounter Seen In Daniel

Power Encounter Element	Dan 3	Dan 5
a) A crisis between people representing god and other people must be differentiated clearly.	√√	√√
b) There must be recognition that the issue is one of power confrontation in the supernatural realm.	√	√

---

[18] Power encounter is a phrase that was first defined by a missiologist A. R. Tippett, Professor of Anthropology at the School of World Mission of Fuller Theological Seminary. It identifies a situation in which the power of God is tested over against some other god's power. Tippet first observed this in field studies in the southwest Pacific islands. Later he saw the same concept in the Scriptures. See his classic, **Solomon Island Christianity**.

5. Daniel—Power Encounters   page 51

c) There must be public recognition of the pre-encounter terms (If...Then...).	√	√
d) There is an actual crisis/confrontation event (the more public usually the better will be the aftermath).	√√	√√
e) There must be confirmation that God has done the delivering as the power encounter resolves.	√√	√√

Both power encounters in Da along with the other power ministry incidents in ch 2, Revelatory Breakthrough—Nebuchadnezzar's Image Dream, ch 4, Revelatory Breakthrough—Nebuchadnezzar's Tree Dream and ch 6, Daniel's deliverance from certain death in the lions' pit, give accumulative overwhelming evidence that God is powerful. All five power incidents endorse Daniel's theme,

> **The Most High (Sovereign God) Rules In The Affairs Of Individuals, Nations, And History.**

Application Today

Today it is the use of power gifts which will decisively authenticate a leader's backing by God. Table Hab 5-2 gives three major clusters of gifts. It is the power gifts that must be used to resolve power encounters and demonstrate that God is all powerful.

Table Hab 5-2. Giftedness and Overall Results

Giftedness	Gifts Involved	What is Demonstrated
Word	Exhortation, teaching, apostleship, ruling, prophecy, faith, pastoring, evangelism, word of wisdom, word of knowledge.	These word gifts all help us understand about God including His nature, His purposes and how we can relate to Him and be a part of His purposes.
Love	Governments, giving, mercy, helps, pastoring, evangelism, healing, word of wisdom, word of knowledge.	These love gifts all demonstrate the beauty of the unseen God's works in lives in such a way as to attract others to want this same kind of relationship.
Power	Faith, word of knowledge, discernings of spirits, miracles, tongues, interpretation of tongues, healing, word of wisdom, prophecy.	These power gifts help demonstrate the reality of the unseen God. They authenticate is power, presence, and superiority.

It is still true today.

> **The essential ingredient of leadership is the powerful presence of God in the life and ministry of the leader.**

Daniel demonstrated this. Power ministry, of which power encounters are one example, are desperately needed today.

See *giftedness, spiritual gifts, power ministry, power shift, power gifts,* **Glossary**. See **Articles**, *Spiritual Gift Clusters; Spiritual Gifts, Giftedness and Development; Apostolic Functions; Impartation of Gifts. All from the Titus Commentary.*

Article 6

6. Figures and Idioms In The Bible

Introduction to Figures

All language is governed by law—that is, it has normal patterns that are followed. But in order to increase the power of a word or the force of expression, these patterns are deliberately departed from, and words and sentences are thrown into and used in unusual forms or patterns which we call figures. A figure then is a use of language in a special way for the purpose of giving additional force, more life, intensified feeling and greater emphasis. A figure of speech is the author's way of underlining. He/She is saying, "Hey, take note! This is important enough for me to use a special form of language to emphasize it!" And when we remember the fact that the Holy Spirit has inspired this product we have—the Bible—we are not far wrong in saying figures are the Holy Spirit's own underlining in our Bibles. We certainly need to be sensitive to figurative language.

Definition   A *figure* is the unusual use of a word or words differing from the normal use in order to draw special attention to some point of interest.

For a figure, the unusual use itself follows a set pattern. The pattern can be identified and used to interpret the figure in normal language. Here are some examples from the Bible. I will make you fishers of people. Go tell that fox. Quench not the Holy Spirit. I came not to send peace but a sword. As students of the Bible we need to be sensitive to figures and know how to interpret and catch their emphatic meaning.

Definition   A figure or idiom is said to be *captured* when one can display the intended emphatic meaning in non-figurative simple words.

One of the most familiar figures in the Bible is Psalm 23:1. The Lord is my shepherd. I shall not lack. *Captured*: God personally provides for my every need.

E.W. Bullinger, an expert on figurative language, lists over 400 different kinds of figures. he lists over 8000 references in the Bible containing figures. In Romans alone, Bullinger lists 253 passages containing figurative language. However, we do not need to know all of those figures for the most commonly occurring figures number much less than 400. Figure Hab 4-1, below, lists the 11 most common figures occurring in the Bible. If we know them we are well on our way to becoming better interpreters of the Scripture. In fact, you can group these 11 figures under three main sub-categories, which simplifies learning about them.

6. Figures and Idioms In The Bible

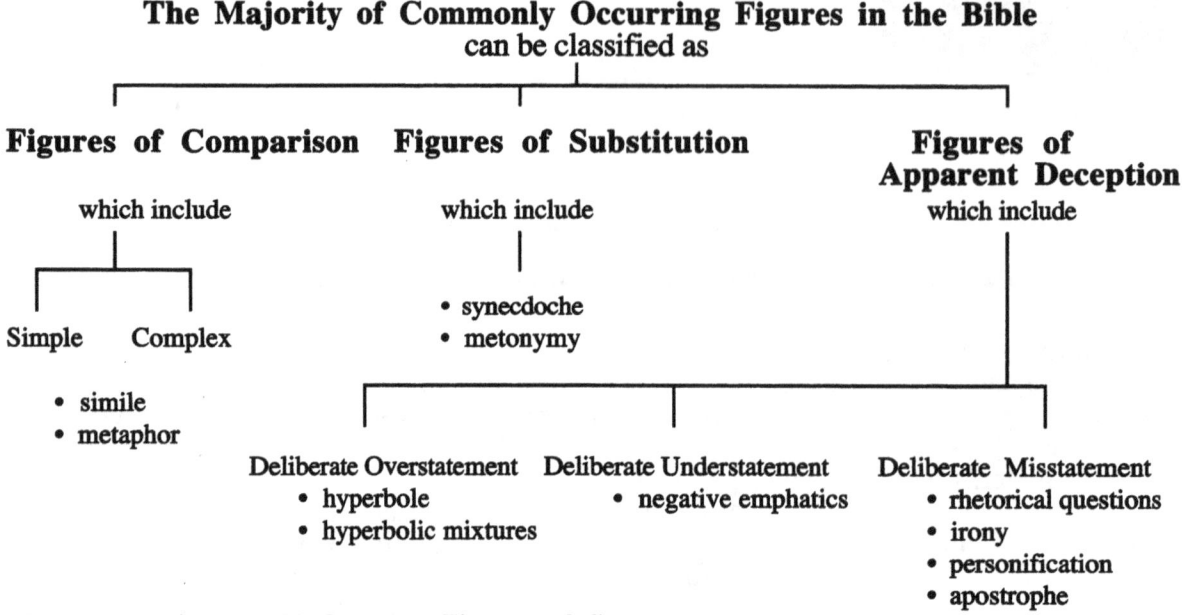

Figure Hab 6-1.   11 Common Figures of Speech

Table Hab 6-1 below gives these 11 figures of speech, a Scriptural reference containing the figure, and the basic definition of each of these figures.

Table Hab 6-1. 11 Figures in the Bible Defined

Category/ Figure	Scriptural Example	Definition
Figures of Comparison: 1. Simile 2. Metaphor	simile—Isa 53:6 metaphor—Ps 23:1	A <u>simile</u> is a stated comparison of two unlike items (one called the real item and the other the picture item) in order to display one graphic point of comparison. A <u>metaphor</u> is an implied comparison in which two unlike items (a real item and a picture item) are equated to point out one point of resemblance.
Figures of Substitution 3. Metonymy 4. Synecdoche	metonymy—Ac 15:21 Moses for what he wrote synecdoche— Mt 8:8 roof for the whole house.	A <u>metonymy</u> is a figure of speech in which (usually) one word is substituted for another word to which it is closely related in order to emphasize something indicated by the relationship. A <u>synecdoche</u> is a special case of metonymy in which (again usually) one word is substituted for another to which it is related as, a part to a whole or a whole to a part.
Figures of Apparent Deception— Deliberate Overstatement: 5. Hyperbole 6. Hyperbolic mixtures	hyperbole—1 Co 4:14-16 ten thousand instructors hyperbolic mixture—2 Sa 1:23 swifter	A <u>hyperbole</u> is the use of conscious exaggeration (an overstatement of truth) in order to emphasize or strikingly excite interest in the truth. Hyperbole is sometimes combined with other figures such as comparison and substitution. When such is the case it is called a <u>hyperbolic mixture</u> figure.

6. Figures and Idioms In The Bible

	than eagles, stronger than lions	
Figures of Apparent Deception—Deliberate understatement: 7. Negative emphatics	negative emphatics—Mk 12:34 not far = very near	A figure of <u>negative emphasis</u> represents the deliberate use of words to diminish a concept and thus call attention to it or the negating of a concept to call attention to the opposite positive concept (I have deliberately merged two figures, litotes and tapenosis into one because of the basic sameness of negative emphasis).
Figures of Apparent Deception—Deliberate Misstatement: 8. Rhetorical questions 9. Irony 10. Personification 11. Apostrophe	rhetorical question—1Ti 3:5 irony—2Co 12:13 personification—Heb 4:12 apostrophe—1 Co 15:55	A <u>rhetorical question</u> is a figure of speech in which a question is not used to obtain information but is used to indirectly communicate, (1) an affirmative or negative statement, or (2) the importance of some thought by focusing attention on it, or (3) one's own feeling or attitudes about something. <u>Irony</u> is the use of words by a speaker in which his/her intended meaning is the opposite of (or in disharmony with) the literal use of the words. <u>Personification</u> is the use of words to speak of animals, ideas, abstractions, and inanimate objects as if they had human form, character, or intelligence in order to vividly portray truth. <u>Apostrophe</u> is a special case of personification in which the speaker addresses the thing personified as if it were alive and listening.

I have developed in-depth explanations for all of the above figures. I have developed study sheets to aid one in analysis of them. Further I have actually identified many of these in the Scriptures and captured a number of them.[19]

Introduction to Idioms
Idioms are much more complicated that figures of speech.

Definition　　An <u>idiom</u> is a group of words, which have a corporate meaning that can not be deduced from a compilation of the meanings of the individual words making up the idiom.

What makes idioms difficult is that some of them follow patterns while others do not. For the patterned idioms, like figures, you basically reverse the pattern and capture the idiom. Table Hab 6-2 lists the patterned idioms I have identified in the Bible.

Table Hab 6-2.　　13 Patterned Idioms

Idiom	Example	Definitive principle/ Description
Three Certainty Idioms: 1. Double certainty (pos/neg) 2. Fulfilled (promised/proposed)	double certainty—1Ki 18:36 fulfilled—Ge 15:18 prophetic past—Jn	<u>double certainty</u>—a negative and positive statement (in either order) are often used to express or imply certainty. <u>fulfillment</u>—in the fulfillment idiom things are spoken of as given, done, or possessed, which are only promised or proposed. <u>prophetic past</u>—in the prophetic past idiom the

---

[19] See my self-study manual, **Interpreting the Scriptures: Figures and Idioms**.

6. Figures and Idioms In The Bible

3. Prophetic past	13:31	past tense is used to describe or express the certainty of future action.
4. Superlative (repetitive superlative)	Ge 9:25 servant of servants Isa 26:3 peace, peace = perfect peace 2Ti 4:7	The Hebrew superlative is often shown by the repetition of the word. Paul uses a variation of this by often using the noun form and a verb form of the same word either back to back or in close proximity. (the good struggle I have struggled).
5. Emphatic comparisons	1Pe 3:3,4	This takes three forms: absolute for relative: one thing (importance or focus item) is emphasized as being much more important in comparison with the other thing (the denial item). The form not A but B really means A is less important than B. relative for absolute: One thing is positively compared to another when in effect it is meant to be taken absolutely and the other denied altogether. abbreviated emphatic comparisons: Half of the comparison is not given (either the focus item or denial items). Half of the statement is given. The half missing is an example of ellipsis and is to be supplied by the reader.
6. Climactic arrangement	Pr 6:16-19 Ro 3:10-18	To emphasize a particular item it is sometimes placed at the bottom of a list of other items and is thus stressed in the given context as being the most important item being considered.
7. Broadened kinship	Ge 29:5	Sometimes the terms son of, daughter of, mother of, father of, brother of, sister of, or begat, which in English imply a close relationship have a much wider connotation in the Bible. Brother and sister could include various male and female relatives such as cousins; mother and father could include relatives such as grandparents or great-great-grandparents, in the direct family line; begat may simply mean was directly in the family line of ancestors.
8. Imitator	Ge 6:2, 11:5	to indicate that people or things are governed by or are characterized by some quality, they are called children of or a son of. or daughter of that quality.
9. Linked noun	Lk 21:15	Occasionally two nouns are linked together with a conjunction in which the second noun is really to be used like an adjective modifying the first noun.
Indicator Idioms: 10. City indicator 11. List indicator 12. Strength Indicator	city indicator La 1:16, daughter of Zion list indicator Pr 6:16, these 6 yea	city indicator—idiomatic words, daughter of or virgin of or mother of. list indicator—2 consecutive numbers—designates an incomplete list of items of which the ones on the list are representative; other like items could be included. strength indicator—a horn denotes aggressive strength or power or authority.

	7 Strength indicator 1Sa 2:1,10	
13. Anthropomorphism	Lk 11:20	In order to convey concepts of God, <u>human passions, or actions, or attributes are used to describe God.</u>

In addition, to the patterned idioms there are a number of miscellaneous idioms, which either occur infrequently or have no discernible pattern. I have labeled 32. Their meaning must be learned from context, from other original language sources, or from language experts' comments, etc.

Table Hab 6-3. 15 Body Language Idioms

Name	Word, Phrase, Usually Seen	Example	Meaning or Concept Involved
1. Foot gesture	shake off the dust	Mt 10:14, Lk 9:5 et al	have nothing more to do with them
2. Mouth gesture	gnash on them with teeth; gnashing of teeth	Ps 35:16; 37:12 Ac 7:54 et al	indicates angry and cursing words given with deep emotion and feeling
3. Invitation	I have stretched forth my hand(s)	Ro 10:21; Pr 1:24; Is 49:22	indicates to invite, or to receive or welcome or call for mercy
4. New desire	enlighten my eyes, lighten my eyes	Ps 13:3; 19:8; 1Sa 14:29; Ezr 9:8	to give renewed desire to live; sometimes physical problem, sometimes motivational inward attitude problem
5. Judgment	to stretch forth the hand; to put forth the hand	Ex 7:5; Ps 138:7; Job 1:11	to send judgment upon; to inflict with providential punishment
6. Fear	to shake the hand, to not find the hand, knees tremble	Is 19:16; Ps 76:8	to be afraid; to be paralyzed with fear and incapable of action.
7. Increase punishment	to make the hand heavy	Ps 32:4	to make the punishment more severe
8. Decreased punishment	to make the hands light	1Sa 6:5	to make punishment less severe
9. Remove punishment	to withdraw the hands	Eze 20:22	to stop punishment
10. Repeat punishment	to turn the hand upon	Is 1:25	to repeat again some punishment which was not previously heeded
11.	to open the	Ps 104:28;	to generously give or bestow

6. Figures and Idioms In The Bible

Generosity	hand	145:16	
12. Anger	to clap the hands together	Eze 21;17; 22:13	to show anger; to express derision
13. Oath	to lift up the hand	Ex 6:8; 17:16; De 32:40; Eze 20:5,6	to swear in a solemn way; take an oath; an indicator of one's integrity to consider worthy to be accepted; to accept someone or be accepted by someone
14. Promise	to strike with the hands (with someone else)	Pr 6:1; Job 17:3	become a co-signer on a loan; to conclude a bargain
15. Accept	to lift up the face	Nu 6:26; Ezr 9:6; Job 22:26	to consider worthy to be accepted; to accept someone or be accepted by someone

Table Hab 6-4.   14 Miscellaneous Idioms

Name	Word, Phrase, Usually Seen	Example	Meaning or Concept Involved
1. Success	tree of life	Pr 3:18; 11:30; 13:12; 15:4	idea of success, guarantee of success, source of motivation to successful life
2. Speech cue	answered and said	Mt 11:25; 13:2 and many others	indicates manner of speaking denoted by context; e.g. responded prayed, asked, addressed, etc.
3. Notice	verily, verily	Many times in Jn	I am revealing absolute and important truth; give close attention (this is a form of the superlative idiom)
4. Time	___ days and ___ nights	Jn 1:17; Mt 12:40; 1Sa 30:11; Est 4:16	any portion of time of a day is indicated by or represented by the entire day
5. Lifetime	forever and ever	Ps 48;14 and many others	does not mean eternal life as we commonly use it but means all through my life; as long as I live
6. Separation	what have I to do with you	Jn 2:4; Jdg 11;12; 2Sa 16:10; 1Ki 17;18; 2Ki 3;13; Mt 8:29; Mk 5:7; Lk 8:28	an expression of indignation or contempt between two parties having a difference or more specifically not having something in common; usually infers that some action about to take place should not take place
7. Reaction	heap coals of fire	Ro 12:20; Pr 25:21	to incur God's favor by reacting positively to a situation in which revenge would be normal
8. Orate	open the mouth	Job 3:1	to speak at great length with great liberty or freedom

6. Figures and Idioms In The Bible

9. Claim	you say	Mt 26:25,63,64	means it is your opinion
10. Excellency	living, lively	Jn 4:10,11 Ac 7:38; Heb 10:20; 1Pe 2:4,5; Rev 1:17	used to express the excellency of perfection of that to which it refers
11. Abundance	riches	Ro 2:4; Eph 1:7; 3:8; Col 1:27; 2:2	used to describe abundance of or a great supply
12. Preeminence	firstborn	Ps 89:27; Ro 8:29; Col 1;15, 18; Heb 12:23	special place of preeminence; first place among many others
13. Freedom	enlarge my feet; enlarge	2Sa 22:37; Ps 4:1; 18:36	freed me; brought me into a situation that has taken the pressure off, taken on to bigger and better things
14. Reverential respect for	fear and trembling	Ps 55:5; Mk 5:33; Lk 8:47; 1Co 2:3; 2 Co 7:15; Eph 6:5, Php 2:12	describes an attitude of appropriate respect for something. The something could be God, could a person, or could be a combination including some process. Sometimes indicates confronting a difficult situation or thing with a strong awareness of it and possible consequences

Again I would recommend you refer to my manual **Figures and Idioms** to see the approach for capturing the patterned idioms.

Figures and Idioms should be appreciated, understood, and should be interpreted with emphasis. Hardly any passage which is any one of the seven leadership genre will be without some figure or idiom.

Article 7

7. Future Perfect Paradigm

Stanley B. Davis caused quite a stir in when he introduced the notion of the future perfect paradigm[20] in 1982 as a major framework for strategic planning. Christian leaders studying change dynamics with me saw in this paradigm an underlying Bible framework.[21] They immediately embraced this paradigm as an enhancement for visionary leadership. What is this paradigm? Why is it important? What does a leader need to know about it to embrace it?

All leaders view leadership through mental perspectives that have accumulated due to their experience. We call these more formulated mental constructs by the term, paradigms.

Definition   A <u>paradigm</u> is a controlling perspective, which allows one to perceive (symbolized by r) and understand reality (symbolized by R).

So then when we talk about a future perfect paradigm we are talking about a mental framework for viewing something.

Definition: The <u>future perfect paradigm</u> refers to a way of viewing a future reality as if it were already present which in turn,

- inspires one's leadership,
- challenges followers to the vision,
- affects decision making, and
- causes one to persevere in faith,

and results in the future reality coming into being.

Perhaps some examples might help clarify the concept. World class athletes frequently envision the final act of their events in their minds before it actually happens. They actually go through the event twice, once in their mind—a future perfect way of thinking, and then when it actually happens. And they make decisions in the present based on that envisioned reality. They work hard to get ready for the event. Discipline in the present is in light of the future perfect reality they have seen. The Bible speaks of speaking a word of faith and bringing something into existence. God does this in Hebrews 11. He thinks something,

---

[20] See Stanley B. Davis, *Transforming Organizations: The Key To Strategy Is Context* in **Organizational Dynamics**, Winter, 1982. Later he refined and reproduced his article in a book length treatment. See **Future Perfect**. New York: Addison-Wesley, 1987.

[21] One of my ThM students (who also holds a PhD in ecology) did an analysis of this paradigm from a Biblical perspective, missiological perspective, and a theological perspective. His research affirmed this otherwise secular theory as a valid Biblical approach to inspirational leadership. See *inspirational leadership*, **Glossary**. See **Article**, 27. *Leadership Functions, Three High Level Generic Functions*.

7. Future Perfect Paradigm

our world, and then speaks it into existence. Hebrews 11 further details this kind of thinking as it highlights Old Testament saints who lived by faith. They moved toward something, a vision, which they kept always before them. Some did not reach these visions but they walked in light of them and toward them and with hope in them. Table Hab 7-1 lists some Biblical leaders who moved through their ministries with a future perfect paradigm.

Table Hab 7-1. Biblical Leaders And The Future Perfect Paradigm

Leader	The Future Perfect Seen
Abraham	A better land (pilgrim here).
Joseph	Destiny—Preserve People in the Land.
Moses	People in the land.
Joshua	People in the land.
Ezekiel	Final Judgment on nations.
Daniel	God, the Ancient of Days, sovereignly ruling over all; His purposes fulfilled.
Hosea	God's reconciling love bringing His people to Himself.
Jeremiah	God's Final Judgment on nations.
Nehemiah	Fortified City
Haggai	Centralized religion re-established—The Temple in place and people meeting God there.
Jesus	The Cross/ Uniting of all things.
Paul	Resurrection Life; The Gentiles fully worshipping God and accepted by God.
John	The New Heaven/ Bride in place.

Christian leaders are those who influence specific groups of God's people toward God's purposes for them. Getting external direction from God, that is, vision for the future for the group, involves an act of faith. Leaders with vision are able then to interpret present happenings of today in terms of this future state which they envision as already having taken place. They can live in the tension of the *what shall be as if it were* with the *anomalies of the present*. Such a time paradigm, as the future perfect paradigm, is very helpful to a leader. Figure Hab 7-1 gives a helpful perspective for viewing the future perfect paradigm in terms of two concepts, one known and one introduced in terms of that known one.

Future Perfect Time Perspective

|---|

Past Perfect　　　　　　　　　　　　　　　　　　　　　　　**Future Perfect**
*- - - - - - - - - -> Aftermath　　　　　　　　　　　　Beforemath <- - - - - - - - *

Examples:　　　　　　　　　　　　　　　　　Examples:
1. etymology: mown grass resprouting.　　　1. New word coined by
2. The San Francisco earthquake/ still　　　　　Davis.
   has after effects not repaired.　　　　　　　2. Diagnosis of terminal cancer.
3. The Cross—impacting our world　　　　　3. Announcement of
   today and the future too.　　　　　　　　　　　Pregnancy.

Figure Hab 7-1. The Future Perfect Paradigm on a Continuum

7. Future Perfect Paradigm

The new concept beforemath is more readily seen when thinking of its counterpart, aftermath.

Definition   <u>Aftermath</u> refers to the after effects and ramifications of some past act or event which has continuing influence of the present.

Definition   <u>Beforemath</u> refers to the effects and implications of some future event or state which has influence reaching back into the present, at least to the eye of the leader holding the future perfect vision by faith.

5 Stages Leading to the Future Perfect Paradigm

It is helpful to recognize that arriving at a future paradigm viewpoint does not happen all at once for all people. For some this will happen. For others there is a process that brings about the paradigm shift. This process is described in Table Hab 7-2.

Table Hab 7-2. 5 Stages Leading to the Future Perfect Paradigm

Stage	Explanation
1. Dream/ Vision	A leader begins to see something possible in his/her leadership—something that may happen in the future.
2. Destiny— Consciousness of God in it.	God begins to confirm this future possibility as something He is involved in. There is a growing sense of partnering with God in it. There is a growing sense that God is going to enable this.

3. The Inner Paradigm Shift	Something happens. The leader now sees this as a done deal, an accomplished thing—at least in his/her mind. So then the leader responds by acting on this faith venture by:
	   a. Working on the Beforemath
	   b. Recognizing the paradox, yet maintaining hope in the future reality.
	      (1) Decision making in light of the future/ not past.
	      (2) Affirmation of the future—always seeing progress.
	      (3) renewal--ministry and divine affirmation experiences.

4. Living in the Paradox, present but not yet present	Every item that confirms the future perfect vision is affirmed. There is the recognition that not everything is there yet, but it will be.
5. Realization— the Reality Present	The vision happens. Something that wasn't there now is. God is honored and praised. The leader's faith is built up. God now has something in place He will use.

Application

By definition a leader is a person with God-given capacity, a God-given burden who is influencing a specific group of God's people toward God's purposes. To do this it is imperative that a leader receive direction from God about the future for those people being led. The future perfect paradigm is one way God may well give a leader direction for the future.[22] For many leaders to accept the future perfect paradigm, they will need to go through a paradigm shift.

---

[22] Apostolic leaders, those gifted with the gift of apostleship, will naturally be drawn to this paradigm. Intercessors, especially those with the gift of faith will likewise be drawn to this paradigm. Leaders with the

7. Future Perfect Paradigm

Definition — A <u>paradigm shift</u> is the change of a controlling perspective and the perceptive result of that change (little r) so that one perceives (a new little r') and understands REALITY (Big R) in a different way.

Have you already embraced this kind of paradigm? Can you, if you have not? Characteristics of those working from a future perfect paradigm include:

a. They identify the beforemath issues that invade the present if the future perfect is to be realized. And then they begin working on the beforemath issues.
b. They recognize the paradox, yet maintain hope in the future reality.[23]
c. They make decisions always in light of the future, what will be, and not the past.
d. They affirm every indication of the future perfect—always seeing progress. They inspire others to see it too.
e. They will often see repeated renewals—both ministry and divine affirmation experiences—to stimulate their future perfect vision.

Here is an exercise for you that may help you bring closure to this explanation of the future perfect paradigm. Examine the stages of entering into a future perfect paradigm. If you are in process on some future perfect paradigm, then check where you are. Identify your *Future Perfect Paradigm* by giving it a descriptive label, then check the stage you are in. Examine the stages of the future perfect paradigm. If you are in process on some future perfect paradigm, then check where you are. Identify *the Future Perfect Paradigm* by some descriptive label, then check the stage you are in.

Label for Your Future Perfect Paradigm:
___ 1. Dream/ Vision
___ 2. Destiny--Consciousness of God in it
___ 3. The Inner Paradigm Shift
    ___ (a) Working on the Beforemath
    ___ (b) Recognizing the paradox, yet maintaining hope in the future reality.
    ___ (c) Decision making in light of the future/ not past.
    ___ (d) Affirmation of the future--always seeing progress.
    ___ (e) renewal--ministry and divine affirmation experiences.
___ 4. Living in the Paradox, present but not yet present
___ 5. Realization--the Reality Present

If you are not currently anywhere in these stages, then reflect again on the Bible leaders and their future perfect vision as seen in Table Hab 7-1. Join this group. Let them challenge you. You too can have a future perfect vision that can inspire you. Ask God to give you a future perfect vision for your leadership.

Conclusion

Daniel highlighted the need for perspective on the future. He had a hunger to know God's plans. Out of his leadership era, The Post-Kingdom Leadership Era emerged this important macro lesson. Daniel lived with it during all of his long and productive ministry. Embrace it for your own leadership.

---

gift of prophecy, especially those with a futuristic bent, will embrace this paradigm as well. But the paradigm is not limited to just those who have gifts relating to the future. All leaders must move their people toward God's future vision for them.

[23] This is analogous to the Kingdom of God paradigm. Many leaders recognize the Kingdom of God as God's ideal. They know of what it means for it to be realized. And they know it has not been realized. But that Kingdom has invaded our kingdom now and that Kingdom is present yet still future.

7. Future Perfect Paradigm

23.[24] Future Perfect — A primary function of all leadership is to walk by faith with a future perfect paradigm so as to inspire followers with certainty of God's accomplishment of ultimate purposes.

A leader who would inspire and bring hope to a generation of hopeless people will need a future perfect paradigm.

---

[24] This number refers to the identification of this macro lesson. There are 41 macro lessons, almost 7 each for the six leadership eras. See *macro lesson*, **Glossary**. See **30.** Macro Lessons: *List of 41 Macro Lessons Across Six Leadership Eras*.

Article 8

8. Getting God's Perspective, A Leader's Necessity

Introduction
The difference between leaders and followers is perspective. The difference between effective leaders and other leaders is better perspective. One issue highlighted in the book of Habakkuk stresses the importance of a leader getting perspective from God. One important major leadership lesson seen in the comparative study of leaders can be stated as:

Effective Leaders View Present Ministry in Terms Of A Life Time Perspective.[25]

In fact, in Habakkuk's case we can modify this lesson further.

> Effective Leaders View Present Ministry in Terms Of A Life Time Perspective and beyond.

Habakkuk, in the midst of crisis moment in his own ministry, got alone with God to get some answers concerning what he saw around him—things that seemed to deny God's existence and intervening influence. What can we see about perspective from studying God's meeting Habakkuk and giving an answer that startled Habakkuk? Let me suggest six macro lessons[26] that touch on perspective and are reflected in Habakkuk's case.

The Faith Perspective
Probably the most important perspective lesson reflected in the book of Habakkuk is the faith lesson. It is succinctly captured in the contrasting parallelisms of Habakkuk 2:4.

---

[25] This is one of seven major leadership lessons that have emerged in my studies of leadership over the past 21 years. They are: (1) Effective Leaders View Present Ministry in Terms Of A Life Time Perspective. (2) Effective Leaders Maintain A Learning Posture Throughout Life. (3) Effective Leaders Value Spiritual Authority As A Primary Power Base. (4) Effective Leaders Who Are Productive Over A Lifetime Have A Dynamic Ministry Philosophy. (5) Effective Leaders View Leadership Selection And Development As A Priority Function In Their Ministry. (6) Effective Leaders See Relational Empowerment As Both A Means And A Goal Of Ministry. (7) Effective Leaders Evince A Growing Awareness Of Their Sense Of Destiny. It is the first one I am referring to in this suggested idea. See **Article**, *Leadership Lessons—Seven Major Lessons Identified*.

[26] A macro-lesson is a high level generalization of a leadership observation (suggestion, guideline, requirement), stated as a lesson, which repeatedly occurs throughout different leadership eras, and thus has potential as a leadership absolute. See **Articles**, 29. *Macro Lessons—Defined;* 30. *Macro Lessons—List of 41 Across Six Leadership eras*.

8. Getting God's Perspective, A Leader's Necessity page 65

Habakkuk Chapter 2
4 Consider carefully the message:
   Those who are evil will not survive,
   But those who are righteous will live
   because they trust in God.[27]

The first two lines refer to the Babylonians who will be destroyed eventually. Pusey puts it so appropriately.

> The swelling pride and self-dependence of the Chaldee stands in contrast
> with the trustful submission of faith. Of the one God says it has no ground
> of uprightness, and consequently will not stand before God; of faith, he
> says, the righteous shall live by it. (Pusey 1907:4)[28]

The rest of chapter 2 describes God's judgment on them (see the 5 Woes). The last two lines refer to those, like Habakkuk, who are followers of God. They must learn to trust God. Or in the old King James words,

The Just Shall Live By His Faith.

This is probably the most important perspective in the book of Habakkuk. The Babylonians will not survive. But those, like Habakkuk himself, who learn to trust God shall live. This is quoted three times in the New Testament: Romans 1:17; Gal 3:11; and Heb 10:38. In each of those cases it is used in relationship to some aspect of being made right with God as opposed to some sort of earning one's righteousness before God. Here in Habakkuk, it is talking about those who belong to God trusting in God for their future. Leaders must trust God. The macro lesson describing this is the faith macro, first seen in the Patriarchal Leadership Era[29] and then in other leadership eras.

6. Faith
Biblical Leaders must learn to trust in the unseen God, sense His presence, sense His revelation, and follow Him by faith.

Habakkuk evinces this macro. He caught God's vision. Notice his faith response in the closing testimony of chapter 3. From *a doubting whether or not God is real* in the opening verses to *these final triumphant trusting words*, it is clear, Habakkuk has met the unseen God, sensed His presence, heard from Him, got revelation and is now trusting in that God. Trusting God peals loudly in Habakkuk's closing words.

16 I hear your message, and I am weak with fear,
    My lips quiver fearfully.
    My bones feel like they are giving way.
    I stumble as I walk.
    I will quietly wait for the day of judgment,
    When disaster will come upon the people who invade us.
17 Though the fig tree quits blossoming,

---

[27] See **Article, 15. *Habakkuk, The Crucial Faith Words.***
[28] See The Rev E. B. Pusey, D.D., **The Minor Prophets With a Commentary, Vol. VI, Habakkuk and Malachi**, London: James Nisbet and Co, 1907.
[29] I have identified six leadership eras in the Scriptures: 1. Patriarchal; 2. Pre-Kingdom; 3. Kingdom; 4. Post-Kingdom; 5. Pre-Church; 6. Church. See **Articles**, *36. Six Biblical Leadership Eras, Approaching the Bible with Leadership Eyes*; *26. Leadership Eras In The Bible, Six Identified*

8. Getting God's Perspective, A Leader's Necessity   page 66

> There is no fruit on the vines,
> The olive trees do not produce,
> The fields yield no food,
> The flock be cut off from the fold,
> And there be no herd in the stalls,
> 18 Yet I will rejoice in Jehovah,
> I will joy in the God of my salvation.
> 19 Jehovah, the Master, is my strength.
> He makes my feet like hinds' feet.
> He makes me tread upon my high places.

Responding to God's Word does not necessarily mean an easy path is ahead. Habakkuk recognizes that what lies ahead is going to be tough. He fears it deeply. But he has stilled his heart to respond to God in the things that will come.

These lines of verse 17 show that Habakkuk understands the ramifications of God's revelation. Prosperity as it has been known in Judah will be destroyed. Financial ruin lies ahead.

Yet I will rejoice translates one Hebrew word (SRN 05937).[30] That word carries with it the sense of rejoicing but also of exulting and doing so triumphantly. Note, Habakkuk's triumphant rejoicing is not in the circumstances but in God: Jehovah the eternal one (SRN 3068); Elohim—the God who delivers (SRN 0430; 03468); Jehovah Master (Adonai) (SRN 3068; SRN 0136). Habakkuk gives evidence that he is trusting God, the God who can deliver.

This faith perspective is a must for all leaders. It is never illustrated any more clearly in the Bible than in this book of Habakkuk.

Table Hab 8-1 lists the other 5 macro lessons touching on perspective seen in the intervening action of God in Habakkuk's life.

Table Hab 8-1. Other Perspective Macros Seen in Habakkuk

Macro Lesson	Label	First Seen	Statement/Comments
13	Challenge	Pre-Kingdom	Leaders receive vision from God, which sets before them challenges that inspire their leadership./ Habakkuk responded to God's faith challenge shaping. From a despairing ministry in the midst of rampant sinfulness and injustice Habakkuk moves to a trust in God to correct it. He sees that correction is a long term thing. He sees that God can be trusted to work out just solutions. He sees that God is moving forward in His plans for the world.
21	Recrudescence	Kingdom	God will attempt to bring renewal to His people until they no longer respond to Him./ Habakkuk has known of God's working in the past among His

---

[30] SRN stands for Strong's Reference Number. See Strong's **Exhaustive Concordance of the Bible** which gives a reference number to all Biblical words along with definitions and usages throughout the Bible.

8. Getting God's Perspective, A Leader's Necessity page 67

			people. Now he learns more about God. God can work through others. And further he learns God is going to destroy the southern Kingdom of Judah. Has God given up on Judah? No more recrudescence attempts. It sounds so. But I actually think God was giving Habakkuk a chance to intercede (like He did Moses in Exodus 33). And Habakkuk does remind God that He has worked with His people in the past. And Habakkuk asks for mercy. We do know that in Josiah's time there was a mini-renewal. Perhaps Habakkuk's prayers were answered. But in the long run, the southern Kingdom did not respond and recrudescence efforts ended.
22	By-pass	Kingdom	God will by-pass leadership and structures that do not respond to Him and will institute new leadership and structures./ Habakkuk could not see the new structures that might come. But he could foresee that the southern Kingdom was judged and being set aside.
24	Perspective	Post-Kingdom	Leaders must know the value of perspective and interpret present happenings in terms of God's broader purposes./ When God tells Habakkuk emphatically to carefully observe (1:5) what is going on up north with the Babylonian empire and to see it through God's eyes, Habakkuk is being introduced to the broader purposes of God. Babylon will be used of God but also will later be punished. God is working out justice in a complex world.
27	Persever-ance	Post-Kingdom	Once known, leaders must persevere with the vision God has given./ Habakkuk's closing testimony shows he will persevere through what is coming, because the vision has been grasped and Habakkuk knows it is from God.

Closure

One valuable lesson we should see from a study of Habakkuk is a simple one.

> Much perspective can be gained by leaders by the study of the Bible using leadership eyes.

I suggest for follow-up work on this the study of my handbook, **Having A Ministry That Lasts—By Becoming a Bible Centered Leader.** This book will give frameworks that will help you study the Bible for leadership insights. Study of all of the Biblical Leadership Commentary series will also greatly aid you in seeing leadership things in the Bible. But whatever you do don't forget, as a leader you need better and better perspectives that will inform your leadership. Habakkuk learned this lesson. You must too.

Article 9

9. God's Judgment on the Babylonians

Introduction

God promises[31] judgment on the nation of Babylon through at least three prophets.

1. Habakkuk notes the five woes

In chapter 2, each of the five woes promises God's judgmental activity against Babylon.

2. Isaiah also has strong judgmental prophecies about Babylon.

Isaiah 13, 14 give these judgmental prophecies. Several isolated statements about these judgmental prophecies being fulfilled also occur in Isaiah 47, 48.

3. Jeremiah Also Predicted Judgment on Babylon

Jeremiah prophesied strong judgment to come upon Babylon. Jeremiah 50,51 touches on this.

So then Habakkuk, Isaiah and Jeremiah, though all recognizing that Babylon was being used of God (*Left Hand of God*),[32] also saw that God would bring judgment on Babylon later.

Lets examine these judgments and see what happened.

Habakkuk's Five Woes

Table Hab 9-1 lists the five woes of Habakkuk chapter 2 and the description of judgment.

Table Hab 9-1. Habakkuk's Prophecy of Judgment on Babylon

Woe	Thrust of Woe	What Happened
1	The Babylonians will be paid pack for their plundering from many different peoples. The remnants of these peoples will pay back cruelty.	The Medo-Persians captured the Babylonians.
2	The defensive systems that the Babylonians trusted in will not save them. The pay back will be absolutely just.	The Medo-Persians broke through into the city by draining the water supply and going in under the wall.
3	While the Babylonians might	This lesson of God ruling behind the

---

[31] See **Article**, *10. God The Promise Keeper; 33. Promises of God.*

[32] See **Articles**, *21. Habakkuk, Left Hand of God; 28. Left Hand of God;*

9. God's Judgment on the Babylonians   page 69

	have thought they were above the law in doing what they did, God claims to be the one ultimately behind any justice. He will bring justice on the Babylonians and will be known everywhere.	scenes is given five times in Daniel (chapter 1, 2, 3, 4, and 5). Nebuchadnezzar finally learns it but other rulers do not. But God ultimately was ruling behind the scenes (Left Hand of God).
4	The Babylonian violence and destructive acts will be repaid.	Final judgment came through Darius the Mede's conquering of the city. We do not know of all that went on in the city. We do know the Babylon empire ended and was taken over by the alliance, Medes and Persians.
5.	The Babylonian idols will be shown to be powerless. God will be more powerful.	It was the power encounter in Chapter 5 of Daniel[33] in which the Babylonian gods were defeated. Daniel's brave interpretation of the handwriting on the wall preceded the immediate judgment—that very night Babylon fell.

Isaiah's Description of Judgment on the Babylonians

Isaiah who ministered during the reigns of Uzziah, Jotham, Ahaz, and Hezekiah also wrote of judgment on Babylon. What does Isaiah say about the judgment?

1. God will deal with the *arrogant* Babylonians

Isaiah 13
11 And I will punish the world for their evil, and the wicked for their iniquity; and I will cause the arrogancy of the proud to cease, and will lay low the haughtiness of the terrible.

2. Very few Males will be left Alive—They will be scattered and running for their lives.

Isaiah 13
12 I will make a man more precious than fine gold; even a man than the golden wedge of Ophir... 14 And it shall be as the chased roe, and as a sheep that no man takes up: they shall every man turn to his own people, and flee every one into his own land.

3. Cruelty Repaid—Just as Predicted Also in Habakkuk

Isaiah 13
15 Every one that is found shall be thrust through; and every one that is joined unto them shall fall by the sword. 16 Their children also shall be dashed to pieces before their eyes; their houses shall be spoiled, and their wives ravished.

4. The Medes Shall Be The Left Hand of God—They can't be bribed away from this task. And they will repay the cruelty the Babylonians have shown to others.

---

[33] See **Articles**, *5. Daniel—Power Encounters; 2. Babylonians—Power Encounter;*

9. God's Judgment on the Babylonians

Isaiah 13
17 Behold, I will stir up the Medes against them, which shall not regard silver; and as for gold, they shall not delight in it. 18 Their bows also shall dash the young men to pieces; and they shall have no pity on the fruit of the womb; their eye shall not spare children.

5. Desolation—Babylon Totally Wiped Out

Isaiah 13
19 And Babylon, the glory of kingdoms, the beauty of the Chaldees' excellency, shall be as when God overthrew Sodom and Gomorrah. 20 It shall never be inhabited, neither shall it be dwelt in from generation to generation: neither shall the Arabian pitch tent there; neither shall the shepherds make their fold there. 21 But wild beasts of the desert shall lie there; and their houses shall be full of doleful creatures; and owls shall dwell there, and satyrs shall dance there.22 And the wild beasts of the islands shall cry in their desolate houses, and dragons in [their] pleasant palaces: and her time is near to come, and her days shall not be prolonged.

6. Babylon's Splendor and Magnificence—All Destroyed

Isaiah 14
4 That thou shall take up this proverb against the king of Babylon, and say, How hath the oppressor ceased! the golden city ceased! 5 The LORD hath broken the staff of the wicked, and the scepter of the rulers. 6 He who smote the people in wrath with a continual stroke, he that ruled the nations in anger, is persecuted, and none hindered. ...11 Thy pomp is brought down to the grave, and the noise of thy viols: the worm is spread under thee, and the worms cover thee... 23 I will also make it a possession for the bittern, and pools of water: and I will sweep it with the besom of destruction, says the LORD of hosts. 24 The LORD of hosts hath sworn, saying, Surely as I have thought, so shall it come to pass; and as I have purposed, so shall it stand. 26 This is the purpose that is purposed upon the whole earth: and this [is] the hand that is stretched out upon all the nations. 27 For the LORD of hosts has purposed, and who shall disannul it? and his hand is stretched out, and who shall turn it back?

Jeremiah's Description of Judgment on the Babylonians
Jeremiah, who lived through the final stages of the Babylonian conquest of Judah and saw first hand the final end of Jerusalem also wrote concerning God's judgment on Babylon. What did he predict?

1. Power Encounter--God Would Be Supreme Against the Babylonian Deities

Jeremiah 50
2 Declare ye among the nations, and publish, and set up a standard; publish, and conceal not: say, Babylon is taken, Bel is confounded, Merodach is broken in pieces; her idols are confounded, her images are broken in pieces.

2. Prediction of Medes the Destroying Force—Left Hand of God

Jeremiah 50
3 For out of the north there cometh up a nation against her, which shall make her land desolate, and none shall dwell therein: they shall remove, they shall depart,

9. God's Judgment on the Babylonians   page 71

> both man and beast. For, lo, I will raise and cause to come up against Babylon an assembly of great nations from the north country: and they shall set themselves in array against her; from thence she shall be taken: their arrows shall be as of a mighty expert man; none shall return in vain.

More is said about this in 50:41-46. In chapter 51 the Medes are explicitly identified twice.

3. Babylon Made Desolate—Revenge Seen For Her Past Conduct

Jeremiah 50
> 13 Because of the wrath of the LORD it shall not be inhabited, but it shall be wholly desolate: every one that goes by Babylon shall be astonished, and hiss at all her plagues…15 Shout against her round about: she hath given her hand: her foundations are fallen, her walls are thrown down: for it is the vengeance of the LORD: take vengeance upon her; as she hath done, do unto her. 16 Cut off the sower from Babylon, and him that handles the sickle in the time of harvest: for fear of the oppressing sword they shall turn every one to his people, and they shall flee every one to his own land.

4. Chaldean Rulers Finally Set Aside

Jeremiah 50
> 17 Israel is a scattered sheep; the lions have driven him away: first the king of Assyria hath devoured him; and last this Nebuchadrezzar king of Babylon hath broken his bones. 18 Therefore thus says the LORD of hosts, the God of Israel; Behold, I will punish the king of Babylon and his land, as I have punished the king of Assyria.

5. Jeremiah Declares this Destruction and Desolation as being God's Work

Jeremiah 50
> 22 A sound of battle is in the land, and of great destruction.23 How is the hammer of the whole earth cut asunder and broken! how is Babylon become a desolation among the nations! 24 I have laid a snare for thee, and thou art also taken, O Babylon, and you were not aware: thou art found, and also caught, because thou hast striven against the LORD. 25 The LORD hath opened his armory, and hath brought forth the weapons of his indignation: for this is the work of the Lord GOD of hosts in the land of the Chaldeans. 26 Come against her from the utmost border, open her storehouses: cast her up as heaps, and destroy her utterly: let nothing of her be left. 27 Slay all her bullocks; let them go down to the slaughter: woe unto them! for their day is come, the time of their visitation. 28 The voice of them that flee and escape out of the land of Babylon, to declare in Zion the vengeance of the LORD our God, the vengeance of his temple. 29 Call together the archers against Babylon: all ye that bend the bow, camp against it round about; let none thereof escape: recompense her according to her work; according to all that she hath done, do unto her: for she hath been proud against the LORD, against the Holy One of Israel.30 Therefore shall her young men fall in the streets, and all her men of war shall be cut off in that day, says the LORD.31 Behold, I am against thee, O you most proud, says the Lord GOD of hosts: for thy day is come, the time that I will visit you. 32 And the most proud shall stumble and fall, and none shall raise him up: and I will kindle a fire in his cities, and it shall devour all round about him…35 A sword is upon the Chaldeans, says the LORD, and upon the inhabitants of Babylon, and upon her princes, and upon her wise men.36 A sword is upon the liars; and they shall

9. God's Judgment on the Babylonians

> dote: a sword is upon her mighty men; and they shall be dismayed. 37 A sword is upon their horses, and upon their chariots, and upon all the mingled people that are in the midst of her; and they shall become as women: a sword is upon her treasures; and they shall be robbed. 38 A drought is upon her waters; and they shall be dried up: for it is the land of graven images, and they are mad upon their idols. 39 Therefore the wild beasts of the desert with the wild beasts of the islands shall dwell there, and the owls shall dwell therein: and it shall be no more inhabited for ever; neither shall it be dwelt in from generation to generation. 40 As God overthrew Sodom and Gomorrah and the neighbor cities thereof, says the LORD; so shall no man abide there, neither shall any son of man dwell therein.

Much more detail is given in chapter 51 of Jeremiah but basically repeating the five major themes I have identified here.

Closure

God will bring ultimate justice to our world. We do not understand how all this will happen. God's *Left Hand Work* is often complex. Three different prophets, living at different times, all concur that God would bring judgment on Babylon. None of the three actually saw this judgment happen. Habakkuk understood this predictive action of God by faith and waited to see it happen. He did not see the actual judgment on Babylon but he knew by faith that God would do it. God's two encouraging words in Habakkuk steel us to face the complex injustices of our own day. He is working!

Encouraging Word 1—Habakkuk Chapter 2

> 13 Consider carefully, is it not from the all powerful Lord,
> That judgment comes upon evil people,
> And nations come to nothing?
> *14 For the earth will be filled,*
> *With the knowledge of the glory of Jehovah,*
> *As the waters cover the sea.*

The glory of Jehovah, that is, His manifest power and presence will someday be known all around our world. He will put an end to injustice.

Encouraging Word 2. Daniel 2

> 20 **BUT** Jehovah is in his holy temple;
> Let all the earth keep silence before him.

Nothing is left of Babylon today. God's judgment on Babylon is a token of His work in bringing all injustice to an end in our world. God is moving toward His purposes. God will be vindicated. No one will be able to say He was not just. Be encouraged, fellow leader.

Article 10

10. God The Promise Keeper

Introduction

Have you been to a *Promise Keepers'* event? That is an oft asked question these days. I smile and answer that question with another one. Do you know **The Promise Keeper**? Great as those promise keepers' events are they are nothing when compared to **The Promise Keeper** meeting with you.

Promises of God

When I was a little boy my friends and I would often say, "I promise." And the other person would say, "Cross your heart and hope to die?" The meaning was, "Do you really mean it?" Now little boys make and break promises about as fast as can be. But with God it is not so. One, He does not promise helter-skelter-like. And when He does promise He can be trusted. Our problem is learning to hear Him promise and being sure what we heard was a promise from Him, for us.

Definition   A *promise from God* is an assertion from God, specific or general or a truth in harmony with God's character, which is perceived in one's heart or mind concerning what He will do or not do for that one and which is sealed in our inner most being by a quickening action of the Holy Spirit and on which that one then counts.

There are three parts to the promise:

1. the cognitive part which refers to the assertion and its understanding, and
2. the affective part which is the inner most testimony to the promise, and
3. the volitional act of faith on our part which believes the assertion and feelings and thereafter counts upon it.

A leader can err in three ways, concerning promises. One, the leader may misread the assertion. That is, misinterpret what he/she thinks God will do or not do. Or two, the leader may wrongly apply some assertion to himself/herself which is does not apply. It may even be a true assertion but not for that leader or that time. Or the leader may misread the inner witness. It may not be God's Spirit quickening of the leader.

10. God The Promise Keeper

Sometimes the assertion comes from a command, or a principle, or even a direct statement of a promise God makes. The promise may be made generally to all who follow God or specifically to some. It may be for all time or for a limited time. Commands or principles are not in themselves promises. But it is when the Holy Spirit brings some truth out of them that He wants to apply to our lives that they may become promises. Such truths almost always bear on the character of God.

One thing we can know for certain, if indeed we do have a promise from God, then He will fulfill it. For Titus 1:2 asserts an important truth about God.

God can not lie.

He is **The Promise Keeper**. This is an image of God that all leaders need.

Examples of God As The Promise Keeper

God keeps his promises. He is the Promise Keeper. Table Hab 10-1 gives some examples to shore up our faith in **The Promise Keeper**. I could have chosen 100s of promises.[34]

Table Hab 10-1. God The Promise Keeper—Examples

To Whom	Vs	Basic Promise/ Results
Abraham	Gen 12:1,2	Bless the world through Abraham. Give descendants. Spawn nations. Give a land. / This has happened and continues to happen.
Nahum	Whole book	Judgment on Nineveh/ Assyria. Promises fulfilled.
Obadiah	Whole book	Judgment on Edom. Promises fulfilled.
Habakkuk	Ch 2	Judgment on Babylon. Promises fulfilled. See Da 5.
Zechariah	Lk 1:13	Birth of John the Baptist. Promise fulfilled.
Mary	Lk 1:35	Birth of Jesus. Promise fulfilled.
Hezekiah	Isa 39:1ff, especially vs 5-7	Babylonian captivity. Royal hostages taken (Daniel was one of these). Promise fulfilled.
Daniel	Ch 2	The broad outlines of history/ nations and God's purposes. Promise fulfilled in part with more to come.
Daniel	Ch 9	Messiah and work of cross. Promise fulfilled.
Daniel	Ch 10-11:35	Again the broad outline of history particularly with reference to Israel. Everything up to 11:35 has taken place in detail as promises. The rest is yet to come.

Conclusion

The dictionary defines a promise as giving a pledge, committing oneself to do something, to make a declaration assuring that something will or will not be done or to afford a basis for expectation. Synonyms for promise include: covenant, engage, pledge, plight, swear, vow. The central meaning shared by these verbs is *to declare solemnly that one will perform or refrain from a particular course of action*. God is **The Promise Keeper**. As children of His we should learn to hear His promises and to receive them for

---

[34] Over the years I have kept a listing of promises I felt God has made to me and my wife. Many of these have been fulfilled. In December of 1997 I reviewed all of these—an encouraging faith building exercise.

10. God The Promise Keeper

our lives. As a leader you most likely will not make it over the long haul if you do not know God **as The Promise Keeper.**

One of the six characteristics[35] of a leader who finishes well is described as,

> **Truth is lived out in their lives so that convictions and promises of God are seen to be real.**

A leader who has God's promises and lives by them will exemplify this characteristic.[36] Paul did. Paul, the model N.T. church leader knew God as **The Promise Keeper**. Do you?

---

[35] The six characteristics include: 1. They maintain a personal vibrant relationship with God right up to the end. 2. They maintain a learning posture and can learn from various kinds of sources—life especially. 3. They manifest Christ-likeness in character as evidenced by the fruit of the Spirit in their lives. 4. Truth is lived out in their lives so that convictions and promises of God are seen to be real. 5. They leave behind one or more ultimate contributions. 6. They walk with a growing awareness of a sense of destiny and see some or all of it fulfilled.

[36] One of the symptoms of a plateaued leader is failure to get new fresh truth from God—especially failure to get new promises from God. Such a leader will also lack faith to see old promises fulfilled.

Article 11

11. God's Shaping Processes with Leaders

Introduction

One major leadership lesson derived from comparative study of effective leaders states,

Effective leaders see present ministry in light of a life time perspective.[37]

This article deals with God's shaping processes with a leader.[38] It gives important aspects of perspective that all leaders need. Six observations of God's shaping processes with leaders include the following.

1. God first works in a leader and then through that leader.
2. God intends to develop a leader to reach the maximum potential and accomplish those things for which the leader has been gifted.
3. God shapes or develops a leader over an entire lifetime.
4. A time perspective provides many keys. When using a time perspective, the life can be seen in terms of several time periods, each yielding valuable informative lessons. Each leader has a unique time-line describing his/her development.[39]
5. Shaping processes can be identified, labeled, and analyzed to contribute long lasting lessons.[40]
6. An awareness of God's shaping processes can enhance a leader's response to these processes.

Figure Hab 11-1. Describes a generalized time line and some of the processes used by God over a lifetime.

---

[37] I have identified seven which repeatedly occur in effective leaders: 1. Life Time Perspective—Effective Leaders View Present Ministry In Terms Of A Life Time Perspective. 2. Learning Posture—Effective Leaders Maintain A Learning Posture Throughout Life. 3. Spiritual Authority—Effective Leaders Value Spiritual Authority As A Primary Power Base. 4. Dynamic Ministry Philosophy—Effective Leaders Who Are Productive Over A Lifetime Have A Dynamic Ministry Philosophy Which Is Made Up Of An Unchanging Core And A Changing Periphery Which Expands Due To A Growing Discovery Of Giftedness, Changing Leadership Situations, And Greater Understanding Of The Scriptures. 5. Leadership Selection And Development—Effective Leaders View Leadership Selection And Development As A Priority Function In Their Ministry. 6. Relational Empowerment—Effective Leaders See Relational Empowerment As Both A Means And A Goal Of Ministry. 7. Sense Of Destiny—Effective Leaders Evince A Growing Awareness Of Their Sense Of Destiny. See the **Article**, *Leadership Lessons—Seven Major Identified*.

[38] See also the **Article**, *Leadership Selection* which gives an overview across time of the major benchmarks of God's development of a leader.

[39] See **Article**, *Time-Lines: Defined for Biblical Leaders*.

[40] See **For Further Study Bibliography**, Clinton's **Leadership Emergence Theory**, a self-study manual which gives detailed findings from research on God's shaping processes with leaders. This manual describes 50 shaping processes in detail. This article touches on only a few of these shaping processes.

11. God's Shaping Processes With Leaders

I. Ministry Foundations	II. Early Ministry	III. Middle Ministry	IV. Latter Ministry	V. Finishing Well
• character shaping	• leadership committal • authority insights • giftedness discovery • guidance	• ministry insights • conflict • paradigm shifts • leadership backlash • challenges	• spiritual warfare • deep processing • power processes	• destiny fulfillment

Figure Hab 11-1. Some Major Shaping Processes Across The Time-Line

Shaping in Early Ministry —In and Then Through

Most younger emerging leaders in their initial exuberance for ministry feel they are accomplishing much. But in fact, God is doing much more in them than through them. The first years in ministry are tremendous learning years for a young leader who is sensitive to God's working in his/her life. God works on character first, even before a leader moves into full time leadership. Table Hab 11-1 lists four major shaping processes dealing with character and four major shaping processes dealing with early ministry.

Table Hab 11-1. Early Shaping Processes Identified and Defined

Type	Name	Explanation/ Biblical Example
Character	Integrity Check	A shaping process to test heart intent and consistency of inner beliefs and outward practice./ Daniel 1:3,4.
Character	Obedience Check	A shaping process to test a leader's will for obedience to God. /See Abraham, Ge 22.
Character	Word Check	A shaping process to test a leader's ability to hear from God./ See Samuel ch 3.
Character	Ministry Task	A shaping process to test a leader's faithfulness in performing ministry./ See Titus, Corinth trip (references in both 1,2Co).
Foundational Ministry	Leadership Committal	A shaping process, part of Guidance, to recruit a leader into ministry and to continue to engage that leader along the ministry path destined for him/her. /See Paul, Ac 9,22,26.
Foundational Ministry	Authority Insights	A shaping process to help leaders learn how to deal with leaders over them and folks under them./ See Ac 13 Barnabas and Paul.
Foundational Ministry	Giftedness Discovery	A shaping process in which a leader learns about natural abilities, acquired skills, and spiritual gifts that God wants to use through that leader./ See Phillip, Ac 8.
Long Term Ministry	Guidance	A shaping process in which God intervenes in the life of a leader at critical points to direct that leader along the ministry path destined for him/her./ See Paul, Ac 16.

11. God's Shaping Processes With Leaders

Shaping in Middle Ministry — Efficient Ministry

During middle ministry the leader now sees God working through as much as in the leader. Leaders identify giftedness. They learn how to influence; they are learning to lead. They gain many perspectives that channel their ministry toward effectiveness. Table Hab 11-2 lists some of the more important shaping processes that happen during this developmental phase.

Table Hab 11-2. Middle Ministry Shaping Processes—Identified, Defined

Type	Name	Explanation/ Biblical Example
Character/ Ministry	Conflict	A shaping process in which a leader learns perseverance, surfaces defects in character, gets new perspective on issues, and learns how to influence in less than ideal conditions./ See Paul, Ac 19 Ephesus.
Breakthroughs in Ministry	Paradigm Shifts	A shaping process in which God gives breakthrough insights that allow a broadening of perspective so as to propel the leader forward in ministry. /See Paul, Ac 9.
Character/ Ministry	Leadership Backlash	A shaping process in which a leader learns about follower reactions and about perseverance, hearing from God, and inspirational leadership./ See Moses, Ex 5.
Renewal/ Long Term	Challenges	A shaping process in which a leader is induced along the lines of new ministry; a part of the guidance process to take a leader along the life path. /See Paul and Barnabas, Ac 13.

Latter Ministry And Finishing Well — Effective Ministry

The essential difference between middle ministry and latter ministry has to do with focus.[41] In middle ministry the leader learns to be efficient in ministry—that is, to do things well. In latter ministry and the finishing well time the leader learns to be effective—that is, to do the right things well. There is a further deepening of character which enhances the leader's spiritual authority. There is a growing awareness of spiritual warfare. The leader learns to minister with power. Table Hab 11-3 lists some of the shaping processes that take place in the latter part of a leader's lifetime.

Table Hab 11-3. Latter Ministry Shaping Processes—Identified and Defined

Type	Name	Explanation/ Biblical Example
Deep Processing	Crises	A shaping process in which a leader's person or ministry is threatened with discontinuation; an overwhelming time in which the leader feels intense issues which could torpedo his/her whole ministry./ See Paul, 2Co.
Deep Processing	Isolation	A shaping process in which a leader is set aside from ministry and goes through a searching time about identity and a deepening trust of God./ See Paul, Php.
Long Term Guidance	Negative Preparation	A shaping process in which an accumulative effect of a number of negative things in the life and ministry of a leader is used by God to release that leader from some previous ministry and give freedom to enter another ministry./ See Paul, 2Co.
Long Term Guidance	Divine Contacts	A shaping process in which God uses some person in a timely fashion to intervene in a leader's life to give perspective—could be directed toward personhood, ministry, or long term guidance./ See Paul and Barnabas, Ac 9:27.

---

[41] See **Article**, *Focused Life*.

11. God's Shaping Processes With Leaders

Long Term Guidance	Double Confirmation	A shaping process in which God gives clear guidance by inward conviction and by external conviction (unsought)./ See Paul and Ananias, Ac 9.
Effective Ministry	Power Issues	A group of shaping processes including power encounters, gifted power, networking power and prayer power. The leader learns balance between own effort and God's enabling through him/her. The leader learns to minister effectively with God's power./ See Elijah, 1Ki 18 et al.

Conclusion

Awareness of these shaping processes allows a leader to combat the usually overwhelming attitude of *why me*? By seeing that these shaping processes occur in many leaders lives, leaders are affirmed that they are not way off base. It is part of God's way of developing a leader. A leader who understands what is happening in his/her life stands a better chance of responding to the processes and learning the lessons of God in them than one who is blindsided by these processes.

See *Integrity Check; Obedience Check; Word Check; Ministry Task; Leadership Committal; Authority Insights; Giftedness Discovery; Guidance; Conflict; Paradigm Shifts; Leadership Backlash; Faith Challenge; Leadership Challenge; Crises; Isolation; Negative Preparation; Divine Contacts; Double Confirmation; Power Encounters; Prayer Power; Gifted Power; Networking Power;* **Glossary**. See **Articles**, *Sovereign Mindset; Isolation Processing—Learning Deep Lessons from God; Spiritual Authority—Defined, Six Characteristics*. See **For Further Study Bibliography—The Making of A Leader; Leadership Emergence Theory;** *The Life Cycle of a Leader*.

Article 12

12. God's Timing and Leadership

Introduction
What do these verses have in common?

<u>Joseph's birth:</u>
22 And God remembered Rachel, and God hearkened to her, and opened her womb. 23 And she conceived, and bare a son; and said, God hath taken away my reproach: 24 And she called his name Joseph; and said, The LORD shall add to me another son. Gen 30

<u>Jesus Ministry:</u>
4 But when the fullness of the **time** was come, God sent forth his Son, made of a woman, made under the law, 5 To redeem them that were under the law, that we might receive the adoption of sons. Gal 4:4

<u>From John Quoting Jesus:</u>
John: Jesus said unto her, Woman, what have I to do with thee? my **hour** is not yet come. Jn 2:4

Then Jesus said unto them, **My time** is not yet come: but your time is always ready. Jn 7:6

I am not going to the feast, yet; for **my time** is not yet full come. Jn 7:8

Then they sought to take him: but no man laid hands on him, because his **hour** was not yet come. Jn 7:30

These words spoke Jesus in the treasury, as he taught in the temple: and no man laid hands on him; for his **hour** was not yet come. Jn 8:20

And Jesus answered them, saying, The **hour** is come, that the Son of man should be glorified. Jn 12:23

Now is my soul troubled; and what shall I say? Father, save me from this **hour**: but for this cause came I unto this **hour**. Jn 12:27

12. God's Timing and Leadership

> Now before the feast of the Passover, when Jesus knew that his **hour** was come that he should depart out of this world unto the Father, having loved his own which were in the world, he loved them unto the end. Jn 13:1

All have to do with God's timing. One of the major macro lessons first seen in *the Patriarchal Leadership Era* and then in every other leadership era thereafter states,

God's timing is crucial to the accomplishment of God's purposes.[42]

Effective leaders are increasingly aware of the timing of God's interventions in their lives and ministry. They move when he moves. They wait. They confidently expect. Leaders must learn to be sensitive to God's timing. God's direction includes *What, How, and When*. All are important.

This is a leadership lesson that all leaders must learn. Strong leaders, such as apostolic leaders desperately need to learn this. Such leaders usually have a strong sense of destiny. Such leaders usually have a strong vision they want to accomplish. Often these strong leaders tie their vision to some prophecy or other revelatory word. While they may know the *what* and even the *how* of the vision they may well be off in the *when*. They often move ahead of God's timing. God's timing is crucial. Less bold and forceful leaders also need to learn about God's timing. Frequently, they lag behind God's timing. What can we learn from some Bible characters about God's timing?

Thirteen Bible Characters and God's Timing

Table Hab 12-1 lists thirteen Bible characters and implications about God's timing.

Table Hab 12-1. 13 Bible Characters and God's Timing

Character	Leadership Era	Timing Issue	Observations/ Lessons
Abraham/ Sarah	Patriarchal	Birth of Isaac/ Israel's deliverance 400 years later	Isaac: *The promises of God include what, how, and when. Abraham and Sarah only knew what. The how they tried to manipulate. The when—they went ahead of God. God was true to his promise. The what, how, when all came together. God's timing was crucial.* Israel's Promised Deliverance from Egypt: *Sometimes God's timing is well beyond a leader's own lifetime. Such a promise can enable one to live with hope and faith though they may never see the fulfillment of that promise.*
Jacob/ Rachael	Patriarchal	Birth of Joseph	Joseph's birth, as to timing was important. The birth order was necessary to God's purposes for him—both favored status and his brothers jealousy. The time of birth was important; he was to deliver in 39 years. *Manipulation of God's timing can bring problems. Manipulation begets manipulation.*
Joseph	Patriarchal	Fulfillment of Certainty	Throughout the Joseph narrative timing is important (dreams at 17; caravan; in jail with

---

[42] See **Article**, 29. *Macro Lessons—Defined*; 30. *Macro Lessons—List of 41 Across Six Leadership eras.*

12. God's Timing and Leadership

		Guidance— 2 Dreams	two of Pharaoh's servants; God's dreams about drought, etc.) Most important lesson. *The way up is often down and may take a long time for God to accomplish.*
Moses	Pre-Kingdom	Deliverance of Israel from Egypt	Deliverance from Egypt: Moses was a strong leader who went ahead of God to deliver Israel from Egypt. He learned a major lesson that strong leaders often learn—The Death of a Vision. *A strong ego leader must surrender a vision and give it back to God. God will bring it about in his own way and timing. Don't move ahead of God. Make sure the how of guidance is God's how.* Crossing the Red Sea: *The when of God's guidance is crucial. It takes faith to believe in exact timing of God's intervention.* Failure to Enter the Land: *Failure to heed God's intervention time can bring long term ramifications—* *40 years in the desert, loss of a generation* Going in to the land: *God's progressive timing has underlying reasons behind it. Development of an armed force takes time.*
Joshua	Pre-Kingdom	Generational leadership/ Capture of Jericho/ Gibeon (flesh act)	Desert Wandering: *A leader often pays a price due to followership. A leader needs time to enculterate and be enculterated to a new generation of followers.* Crossing the Jordan: They could have crossed in non-flood season without God's help. They needed this God intervention for courage and to give Joshua spiritual authority. The three days they camped beside the flood waters built anticipation and fearfulness. Fall of Jericho: *The How and When must be obtained from God in a major achievement.* Gibeon: *Moving ahead of God, making a decision in the flesh with hearing from God and then asking God to approve your decision often results in major negative ramifications that you must live with.*
Caleb	Pre-Kingdom	Generational Leadership; Fulfillment of Promise	Desert Wandering: *Leaders who model whole hearted obedience to God can impact a new generation with the importance of believing God and obeying Him.* Land: *The promises of God will be fulfilled in His timing. Respond with courage.*
Samuel	Pre-Kingdom	Moving from decentralized	Sons: *The what of God's intervention is as important as the when and how. Samuel's sons were not God's answer to the leadership need.:*

12. God's Timing and Leadership

		leadership to a Kingdom	Saul: *Obedience to God's timing is necessary. Failure to obey God as to His timing may well imply lack of integrity and an eventual setting aside by God.*
David	Kingdom	Made King	Uniting the Kingdom: *Time is involved even when the what is known.*
Hezekiah	Kingdom	Sickness Unto Death/ Babylonian Envoy (flesh act)	Changing God's Timing: *Hezekiah's prolonged life brought ramifications he probably didn't foresee. The birth of Manasseh occurred in this time.* Babylonian envoy: *To move ahead of God, make a decision without consulting God, can bring ramifications (later Babylonian captivity). To be safe in one's own generation may well bode problems for future generations.*
Daniel	Post-Kingdom	70 Years Captivity Fulfilled	Learning Posture: *Daniel's maintaining a learning posture, studying the Scriptures, brought out the what and when and hints as to the how of God's plans. God's timing is exact. He will fulfill His promises on time.*
Jesus	Pre-Church	The Cross	World Scene: *The timing was perfect for Jesus birth.* Sensitivity: *Jesus was sensitive to God's timing for his life, throughout his ministry. He never went ahead; he never lagged behind. Jesus models perfectly the whole notion of what, when, and how in following God's plans.*
Peter	Church	Impulsive Actions; Coming of Holy Spirit	Impulsive: *Peter's tendencies to move too quickly throughout the disciples training serves as a negative model. See Jesus' reactions and training of Peter.* Pentecost: *God's promise of power was fulfilled exactly on time. Waiting was involved.* Lagging Behind: *The church failed to expand. God brought persecution to get them to expand.*
Paul	Church	Reaching of Gentiles/ Kings	Antioch Call: *A leader may be called upon to do something at a time (when is clear). But the what and how are hazy. The what and when may be revealed over time.* Macedonian call: *God's timing may involve pre-preparation about the what and how. The move to Europe involved a pre-prepared receptive group ready to hear and respond.*

Four Reasons For Delay In Timing

In a number of the Biblical examples given above God delayed what He was going to do. Some possible reasons for delay include:

12. God's Timing and Leadership   page 84

1. **Dealing With a Strong Ego Leader**—The *Death of a Vision* as seen in Moses' case involved dealing with the right vision but the wrong motivation, wrong power base, and wrong timing.
2. **God's Working out of other purposes**—In the promise to Abraham (400 years) God pointed out that He was dealing with the nations in the land and that their iniquity was not yet full. That is, He was giving them time to repent. That time wasn't up yet when Moses made his first attempt at deliverance.
3. **Foundational Character Shaping**—Moses' isolation period brought about a humility in character (Nu 12:3) which made him a pliable vessel in God's hands. He would need this humility because God would reveal power through his ministry which could be dangerous with a strong unfettered ego leader.
4. **Remedial Training**—God is doing remedial training. He is giving time for certain disciplines to be built in the life of the leader. Moses was a desert leader. He learned about desert disciplines as a shepherd wandering over desert land taking care of sheep.

Three Reasons To Move Fast in God's Timing

Just as some leaders have a tendency to move too fast and God has to delay their actions, some leaders move to slowly. Why should leaders move faster? Here are some reasons:

1. **Windows of Opportunity**—God knows that sometimes the needed action must take place within a certain time period or an opportunity to accomplish something may be lost.
2. **Networks/ onward guidance**—Sometimes the timing is such that obedience will connect to other things God has set up. The next piece of guidance will open up after obedience. To not move will be to miss it. Following an unusual apparently hurried intervention may lead to a series of people or events and give guidance that would not previously have been dreamed of.
3. **God's Doing**—Sometimes God moves a leader to action before things are apparently ready because He wants all to know that He alone is responsible and He alone will get credit for the results. That is, sometimes God has something happen fast because it would be impossible for it to happen unless God alone brought it about.

Four Implications of the Timing Lesson

Four observations can be drawn from a comparative study of God's timing with the leaders listed above:

1. **Ramifications.** Moving ahead of God's timing in guidance or in carrying out some aspect of ministry may accomplish the task; it will most certainly bring ramifications which will require remedial training and the repetition of incidents to teach us the dependence lesson.
2. **Guidance.** The *what*, *how*, and *when* are the major elements of guidance. We need clarity on all three. It is the *when* that is most in focus on the timing macro lesson.
3. **Sensitivity.** We must be sensitive to the Spirit in our lives. Timing can refer to daily interventions or long term guidance decisions. In either case we need to be sensitive to the Spirit. Seemingly small issues may turn out to be pivotal points. This implies that we as leaders especially need to develop the Spirit Sensitivity component of the Spirituality model.
4. **Negative Preparation and Flesh Act.** We need to be thoroughly familiar with these two process items including the various illustrations of them in Scripture so we will respond more quickly and carefully to incidents which God

12. God's Timing and Leadership

is using for this kind of processing. A *flesh act* means making a decision based on fleshly wisdom and moving ahead without getting God's guidance. *Negative preparation* refers to numerous negative happenings in the life. These may well be used by God to move a leader out of a situation.

Conclusion

Look again at the basic lesson.

God's Timing Is Crucial To Accomplishment Of God's Purposes.

Moses learned this lesson the hard way. But he learned it well. The latter stages of his desert leadership reflect his increased sensitivity to God's timing. The question is,

Are You Sensitive To God's Timing In The Little Things Of Daily Ministry As Well As The Big Things Of Major Guidance?

Some final advice should be noted, especially for major guidance decisions.

1. **Triple Confirmation.** Where possible never make a major decision unless you are clear on the *what*, the *how*, and the *when* of the issues. Should you be unclear on any, then it may be best to wait. Certainty guidance via double confirmation or divine contact should be sought on all three issues: what, when, how.
2. **Presumption.** Be careful of presuming to know God's intents on some aspects of ministry without clearing with Him first. Simply attempting to get His approval after the fact may prove fatal in the long run.
3. **Patterns.** Study the concept of timing in the Bible and identify patterns of sensitivity to God's timing. Note what to avoid as well as what to assert. Go back through the vignettes associated with the leaders given in Table Hab 12-1. Study them carefully and learn first hand what you need to know about God's timing and your leadership.

Let me repeat in closing. Effective Leaders Are Increasingly Aware Of The Timing Of God's Interventions In Their Lives And Ministry. They Move When He Moves. They Wait. They Confidently Expect. Leaders must learn to be sensitive to God's timing. God's direction includes *What*, *How*, and *When*. All are important.

See *flesh act; negative preparation; pivotal point; double confirmation; divine contact;* **Glossary**.

Article 13

13. Habakkuk, Celebration—A Leadership Function

Introduction
Note these words taken from the introduction to Habakkuk, chapter 3, verse 1 and the postscript to verse 19 of that same chapter.

1 A prayer of Habakkuk the prophet, set to Shigionoth.

19... To the choirmaster: with stringed instrument.

These portions are significant for several reasons.

One reason concerns the note of celebration. Habakkuk thought this experience with God worthy of celebrating it publicly with others. Celebration is a very important leadership function that falls under the notion of inspirational leadership.[43] There are three major overall high level leadership functions that a leader must make sure happen in his/her ministry: (1) Task Oriented Leadership Functions; (2) Relational Oriented Leadership Functions; (3) Inspirational Oriented Leadership Functions. Celebration falls under inspirational leadership. One thing that inspires people is public celebration, which rejoices in who God is and what He will do. Habakkuk does that. That is what chapter 3 is all about. When celebration includes personal testimony it carries an additional impact. Habakkuk does that. When a leader shares personally with his/her followers what God means to him/her, there will be impact. Followers will be inspired.

A second reason verse 1 and verse 19 are important is that they connect Habakkuk, a prophet, to the temple institution. Not much is known about Habakkuk, except that he was a prophet and ministered to the southern kingdom. Here we have indications that he may have served in the temple, perhaps as a priest or a worship leader. Certainly we get the idea that he was connected with the public ministry of the temple as well as being a prophet who spoke into situations. And we recognize his creative talent.

A third reason why these portions are significant concerns spiritual disciplines. Comparative study, of effective leaders who finished well, unearthed five factors,[44] which

---

[43] See **Article**, 27. *Leadership Functions, 3 High Level Generic Properties*
[44] The list of five enhancement factors includes the following. Enhancement 1—Perspective. Leaders need to have a lifetime perspective on ministry. Effective leaders view present ministry in terms of a lifetime perspective. Enhancement 2—Renewal. Special moments of intimacy with God, challenges from God, new vision from God and affirmation from God both for personhood and ministry will occur repeatedly to a growing leader. Enhancement 3—Disciplines. Leaders who have disciplines in their lives are more likely to persevere and finish well than those who do not. Enhancement 4—Learning Posture. The single most

13. Habakkuk, Celebration—A Leadership Function page 87

enhanced their perseverance and good finish. One of those was the presence of spiritual disciplines in the life of the leader.

> Leaders who have disciplines in their lives are more likely to persevere and finish well than those who do not.

For these three reasons, it is important to note Habakkuk's willingness to transparently celebrate his meeting with God with others, even though the news was hard to take.

Spiritual Disciplines

Leaders need discipline of all kinds. Especially is this true of spiritual disciplines.

Definition   Spiritual disciplines are activities of mind and body purposefully undertaken to bring personality and total being into effective cooperation with the Spirit of God so as to reflect Kingdom life.[45]

Figure Hab 13-1 categorizes spiritual disciplines. Note where celebration falls.

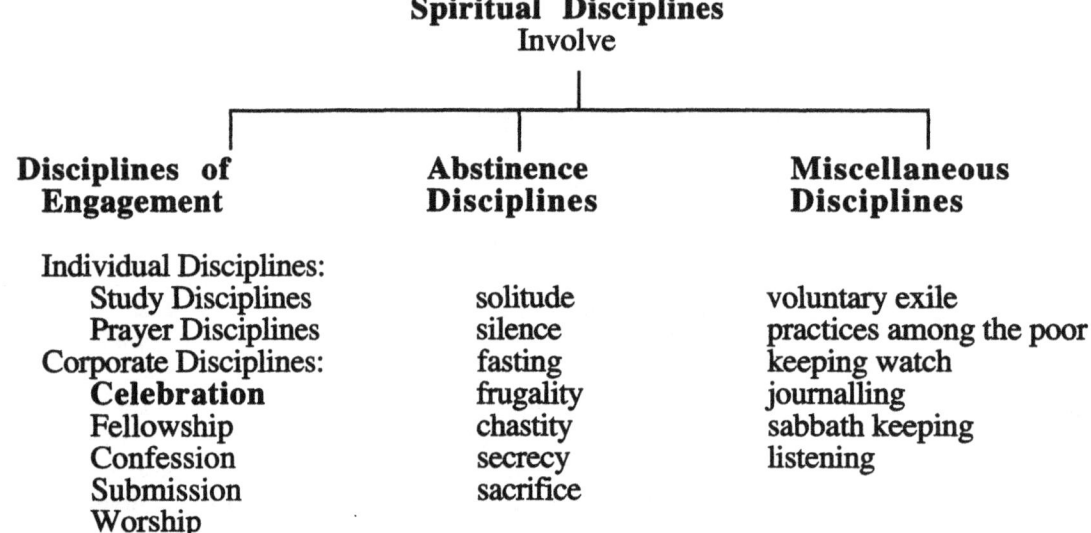

Figure Hab 13-1. Spiritual Disciplines Categorized

Note from Figure Hab 38-1 that celebration is a corporate function. It is done together with others who follow God.

Definition   Celebration refers to a corporate time, a gathering of a group of God's people, who recognize God for who He is and what He does, and worships Him, in such a way as to honor Him and to renew their committal to follow this God.

Numerous Biblical leaders saw celebration as an important leadership function.

---

important antidote to plateauing is a well developed learning posture Enhancement 5—Mentoring. Leaders who are effective and finish well will have from 10 to 15 significant people who came alongside at one time or another to help them.

[45] See **Article**, *37. Spiritual Disciplines—And On-going Leadership.*

13. Habakkuk, Celebration—A Leadership Function

Great Old Testament Biblical Leaders Who Celebrated

Table Hab 13-1 lists some instances of celebration by some of the great leaders in the Bible.

Table Hab 13-1. Biblical Leaders and Instances of Celebration

Leader	Form	Illustration of Public Celebration
Moses	Song	Ex 15:1-21
Miriam	Dance	Ex 15:20,21
Moses, Joshua	Song of Encouragement Tracing God's relationship, historically to Israel	De 31:19-22; 30; 32:1-44
Moses	Blessing; Public poetic passage of blessing for tribes of Israel	De 33:1-29
Joshua	Public Challenge to Follow God Leaders; then to followers	Jos 23, 24
Deborah	Song—Honoring God's Victory	Jdg 5:1-31
Samuel	Public Challenge to Follow God; Committal to pray for Israel	1 Sa 12
David	Many Psalms for use in public worship	See Psa 23 for just one example; many others written for public worship
David	Organizing the Temple Worship emphasizes importance of celebration; set up funding for worship leaders	1 Ch 15,16
Solomon	Public Prayer Dedicating The Temple; Blessing; one of the longest prayers in the Bible	1 Ki 8: 12-66
Hezekiah	Bringing Renewal; Public Sacrifices for sanctifying temple; Re-instituting the Feast of Unleavened Bread2	1 Ch 29:20 – Ch 30
Josiah	Brought Renewal and Re-instituted the Passover	2 Ki 23:21-23
Habakkuk	Public Testimony in song of trusting God for the Future	Habakkuk ch 3
Nehemiah/Ezra	Celebrate the completion of the wall; Re-instituting the Feast of Tabernacles; public worship using Word and Committal to Covenant following God's Law	Nehemiah Ch 8, 9, 10

Closure

Now note the closing stanzas of Habakkuk's testimony. In chapter 3:1-5 Habakkuk has just transparently shared how he is so fearful about what is to come. He has heard God's word of judgment on the southern kingdom, Judah. He has also heard God's word of judgment on Babylon. Now he concludes in verses 16-19 with this powerful testimony.

13. Habakkuk, Celebration—A Leadership Function

He wants it to be part of the public worship. He is transparent. He celebrates. He wants his people to celebrate.

These closing words from Habakkuk are the very essence of celebration.

Chapter 3
16 I hear your message, and I am weak with fear,
   My lips quiver fearfully.
   My bones feel like they are giving way.
   I stumble as I walk.
   I will quietly wait for the day of judgment,
   When disaster will come upon the people who invade us.
17 Though the fig tree quits blossoming,
   There is no fruit on the vines,
   The olive trees do not produce,
   The fields yield no food,
   The flock be cut off from the fold,
   And there be no herd in the stalls,
18 Yet I will rejoice in Jehovah,
   I will joy in the God of my salvation.
19 Jehovah, the Master, is my strength.
   He makes my feet like hinds' feet.
   He makes me tread upon my high places.

And, dear leader, learn to celebrate with your people, creatively and with impact.

Article 14

14. Habakkuk, Contextual Flow—Understanding the Argument

Introduction

It is helpful to recognize that the book of Habakkuk is not a monologue but a dialog. Habakkuk and God interweave a conversation. Recognition of this conversation illuminates the book.

Below is given the flow of the contextual statements through out the book. The larger three contextual units (chapters 1, 2, and 3) are printed in all capitals and use major ideas in topical form to summarize the larger unit.

For *smaller units of parallelism* (like a single verse), I give a simple reduction of the parallelism to its single meaningful statement. For *longer stanzas* (made up of several verses), I give the overall context statement. I also point out with the italicized statements the dialog between Habakkuk and God.

The book of Habakkuk is highly structured. Understanding its structure will make the difference in seeing its meaning—denotation and connotation.

Habakkuk: Contextual Flow of Book

I. (1:1-2:1) HABAKKUK'S HONEST STRUGGLE WITH FAITH

Habakkuk openly voices his complaint to God. (1:1-4)

1:1-4 **Context**: Habakkuk (because of the times and situations he is living in—that which he can see) is casting doubt on the character of God (particularly His faithfulness, His justice, and His Holiness).

    a. 1:2 **Reduction**: God is not answering Habakkuk's repeated prayers for deliverance from the violent sin going on in Israel (**The Faithfulness of God is at stake.**)

    b. 1:3 **Reduction**: Habakkuk is accusing God of allowing terrible sin to exist in Israel (**The Holiness of God is at stake.**)

    c. 1:4 **Reduction**: Habakkuk is accusing God of not being just in backing up His law (**The justice of God is at stake**).

God answers Habakkuk with an unusual and surprising answer.

14. Habakkuk, Contextual Flow—Understanding the Argument

1:5-11 **Context:** God is going to use the wicked warlike Chaldeans as his means for correcting Judah.

Habakkuk is appalled at this answer to his prayer. He makes a transition statement and then makes a counter criticism. Finally, he isolates himself to await God's reply.

1:12   **Reduction:** Habakkuk expresses hope that since God has made a covenant with Judah that this correction will not mean the end of Judah.
1:13-17 **Context:** How is it that you a Holy God will not only use but will permit the wicked Chaldeans to be so successful especially since their success causes them to trust further in their own might.
2:1   **Reduction:** Habakkuk puts himself in isolation to hear God's answer concerning this last accusation about the Chaldeans.

II. (2:2-2:20) HABAKKUK'S FAITH-WAIT RESPONSE REWARDED

God speaks with a general faith challenge, which He will clear up in the details which follow. **God** indicates prophetically what is going to happen to the Babylon nation. He points out 5 areas in which justice will be accomplished.

2:2-3   **Reduction:** God tells Habakkuk to very clearly write this answer and to recognize that the answer is sure to happen even though there seems like a long delay.
2:4-6   **Reduction:** God's follower can trust God to correct this Chaldean nation who pridefully and covetously wipes out nations.
2:6b-8   **Woe 1.** (Pusey's[46] 5 Great Sins: Ambition)
      The Remnant peoples of the conquered nations who have been victimized (murdered and robbed) are going to turn in revenge upon the Chaldeans.
2:9-11   **Woe 2.** (Pusey's 5 Great Sins: Covetousness)
      The Chaldeans think they are secure but their murderous action against other nations will prove their ultimate downfall because justice will be fulfilled.
2:12-14 **Woe 3.** (Pusey's 5 Great Sins: Violence)
      God does not appreciate the Chaldeans destroying what others have long labored to build and he will someday bring about his justice and ways so that all may see it.

---

[46] Pusey wrote a commentary series on the minor prophets. I found his exegetical work helpful. These 5 woes (I have translated the term "woe" by A miserable future is yours! You are doomed!) indicate areas of Babylonian actions needing God's justice. The topics suggested by Pusey sum it up well. See Pusey, E. B. **The Minor Prophets With a Commentary, Vol VI Habakkuk and Malachi**, James Nisbet & Co: London, 1907.

14. Habakkuk, Contextual Flow—Understanding the Argument

2:15-17 **Woe 4.** (Pusey's 5 Great Sins: Insolence)
The Chaldeans have caused many neighboring countries to openly suffer defeat but instead of earning glory for this they in turn will openly suffer defeat by God's direct action in history thus receiving justice for their evil actions.

2:18-20 **Woe 5.** (Pusey's 5 Great Sins: Idolatry)
God says, "The Chaldean foolishly trusts in his own hand made idols which can not reveal unknown trust as I have done for you. But I am alive and ruling. That should silence your questioning mind Habakkuk.

III. (3:1-19) HABAKKUK'S RESPONSE OF TRUE FAITH

Habakkuk makes a transition statement then a series of affirmations of God, who He is and what He has done (this could be prophetic past or a futuristic certainty like the past).

3:2 **Reduction:** Habakkuk fearfully believes God's answer and now asks God to show mercy in His correction by not giving up on His people.

3:3-6 **Context:** Habakkuk poetically describes God's dazzling glory and His mighty power.

3:7-15 **Context:** Habakkuk recognizes that God uses apparent natural disasters to protect His people and in His vision sees God's corrective hand being applied to Judah's enemies (apparently speaking in the prophetic past—or using something from the past as symbolic of future certainty—for sure he is emphasizing the certainty of what God will do.)

3:16-19 **Context:** Habakkuk concludes that though he is fearful he can in joy and with patience trust God to strengthen him in the difficulties which await him in the future.

The single thematic statement tying the larger contextual units (chapters) together is,

Subject of the Book: HABAKKUK'S STRUGGLE OF FAITH

Major Idea 1	• involved his honest questioning of God,
Major Idea 2	• was met by God's own explanation, and
Major Idea 3	• resulted in a joyous acceptance by faith of that which God was doing.

Article 15

15. Habakkuk, Crucial Faith Words

Introduction
God's basic answer to all of Habakkuk's questions is a simple one. In the KJV, the answer is,

2:4 The just shall live by faith.

This phrase occurs three times in the New Testament. How does Habbakuk's phrase differ from the other uses?

Basic Emphases of Phrase
The *just shall live by faith* is quoted three times in the New Testament: 1. Romans 1:17, 2. Galatians 3:11, 3. Hebrews 10:38.

Table Hab 15-1 gives the basic contextual emphases of the phrase and describes who it applies to, in a general sense.

Table Hab 15-1. The Just Shall Live By Faith—4 Occurrences

Where	Contextual Emphasis	Who For, Generally
1. Romans 1:17	Emphasis on *the just*	Christians who need to know what their righteousness is and that their righteousness is found in Christ.
2. Galatians 3:11	Emphasis on *shall live*	Christians who are legalistically trying to earn their salvation and need to learn of the finished work of Christ
3. Hebrews 10:38	Emphasis on *by faith*	Christians who need to be inspired by the faith warriors given in the Hall of Fame of Faith in Hebrews 11. Live lives by faith that will honor God—a full-orbed testimony of a lifetime for God.
4. Habakkuk 2:4	Emphasis on all three: *the just, shall live, and by faith*.	For **leaders** who want to know God, God's ways, and God's **timing** in their situations. **Trusting God to work out His plans in His timing is more important than knowing that timing.** Though knowing God's timing is important.

15. Habakkuk, Crucial Faith Words

The Macro Lesson Involved—A Needed Insight for All Leaders Anytime

What is a macro lesson?[47] A macro-lesson is a high level generalization of a leadership observation (suggestion, guideline, requirement), stated as a lesson, which repeatedly occurs throughout different leadership eras, and thus has potential as a leadership absolute. Macro lessons even at their weakest provide strong guidelines describing leadership insights. At their strongest they are requirements, or absolutes, that leaders should follow. Leaders ignore them to their detriment. The faith macro lesson given below and first seen in Abraham's leadership is an important insight that all leaders need to know.

> Biblical Leaders must learn to trust in the unseen God, sense His presence, sense His revelation, and follow Him by faith.

The basic answer that God gives, Habakkuk 2:4 reminds Habakkuk that a righteous person will have to learn to trust God whether or not he can see what God is doing or why God is doing it.

> **These crucial faith words from Habakkuk 2:4, underlying the faith macro lesson are needed in every leadership era.[48]**

Closure

I somehow suspect that leaders today sort of implicitly think it was easier in the days described in the Bible to hear from God and get God's will and sense His presence. But I don't think so. God is an unseen God. And the faith challenge of Habakkuk and its New Testament equivalent in Hebrews still remains.

> **Habakkuk 2:4 The just shall live by faith.**

> **Hebrews 11:6 But without faith it is impossible to please Him: for he that comes to God must believe that He is, and that He is a rewarder of them that diligently seek him.**

Be rewarded, dear leader, learn vicariously, Habakkuk's basic lesson. And go on your way rejoicing, as he did, knowing that God can be trusted to work out His purposes in your ministry, and beyond.

---

[47] 41 Macro Lessons have been identified. The numbers in the table which follow refer the to the list of macro lessons as given in the following articles. See **Articles**, 29. *Macro Lessons—Defined; 30. Macro Lessons: List of 41 Across Six Leadership Eras.*

[48] We have identified six leadership eras across the Bible. (1) The Patriarchal; (2) Pre-Kingdom; (3) Kingdom; (4) Post-Kingdom; (5) Pre-Church; (6) Church. See **Article**, 26. *Leadership Eras In The Bible, Six Identified.*

Article 16

16. Habakkuk, Four Shaping Activities

Introduction

One main reason the book of Habakkuk graces the canon of Scripture hinges around its lessons for leaders today. It shows us some of the important means God uses to mature a leader. It illustrates a leader who responded to God and grew in maturity. In leadership emergence theory, we have identified and labeled a number of shaping activities common to many leaders. God shapes them over a lifetime. We call these shaping activities[49] by the technical name of *process items*. That is, God uses these items to shape or process His leaders as He matures them. The book of Habakkuk includes four main process items:

- crisis,
- isolation,
- paradigm shift,
- faith challenge.

This article will define these four process items and then briefly illustrate them, as seen in the book of Habakkuk. The article will then list several macro lessons related to these kind of process items. From our comparative studies of leaders' lives we have noted that 90% or better of the leaders studied experience these four process items.[50] You should be familiar with them. The purpose of the article is then, to help you recognize God's shaping activities and some of the lessons He teaches through them.

The Four Shaping Activities[51]

Definition

A <u>process item</u> is the technical name in leadership emergence theory describing actual occurrences in a given leader's life including providential events, people, circumstances, special divine interventions, inner-life lessons and other like items which God uses to develop that leader by shaping leadership character, leadership skills, and leadership values.

---

[49] See **Article**, *11. God's Shaping Processes with Leaders*.
[50] We are in the neighborhood of 2500 leaders studied. This includes Biblical leaders, historical leaders and contemporary leaders. The largest majority of cases have been contemporary leaders.
[51] Actually there is a fifth process item but it is rather minor compared to the other four. God also brings a prayer challenge to Habakkuk. And Habakkuk does respond by interceding for his people. See *prayer challenge*, **Glossary**.

16. Habakkuk, Four Shaping Activities

These shaping things indicate leadership capacity and/or potential; they expand this potential; they confirm appointment to roles or responsibilities using that leadership capacity; they direct that leader along to God's appointed ministry level for realized potential. Some 51 process items (Synonym: shaping activities of God) have been identified in leadership emergence theory.[52]

Table Hab 16-1 contains the definitions of the four major process items seen in Habakkuk.

Table Hab 16-1. 4 Process Items Seen in the Book of Habakkuk

Name of Item	Description/ Definition
crisis	from leadership emergence theory. One of 51 process items that God uses to shape a leader./ Crisis process items refer to those special intense situations of pressure in human situations which are used by God to test and teach dependence.
isolation	from leadership emergence theory. One of 51 process items that God uses to shape a leader./ Isolation processing refers to the setting aside of a leader from normal ministry involvement in its natural context usually for an extended time in order to experience God in a new or deeper way.
paradigm shift	from leadership emergence theory. One of 51 process items that God uses to shape a leader./ A paradigm shift is a change of a controlling perspective so that one perceives and understands REALITY in a different way than previously.
faith challenge	from leadership emergence theory. One of 51 process items that God uses to shape a leader./ A faith challenge refers to those instances in ministry where a leader is challenged to take steps of faith in regards to ministry and sees God meet those steps of faith with divine affirmation and ministry affirmation and often with guidance into on going ministry leading to a focused life.

Habakkuk experienced these four shaping activities. The paradigm shift was the dominant shaping goal of the entire incident. That allowed for the positive response to the faith challenge. But it was the crisis processing which brought up the whole need for the paradigm shift and the positive response to the faith challenge.

Habakkuk goes through a *crisis* in his ministry (the first process item). He begins to doubt the reality of God. He questions God's lack of activity in dealing with sinfulness in Judah. Habakkuk does not see the justice of God. He sees this lack of justice as reflecting on God's holiness. He blames God for not dealing with the situation. He goes to prayer—a prayer of desperation—to hear what God may say to this. He is beginning to even doubt God's existence. Yet, he prays. It is sort of like, "if you are there, God, then hear my prayer and give me an answer." God does answer his prayer.

And his answer causes quite a stir. God is going to bring about justice and deal with Judah's sins by using the Babylonians to discipline them. This brings up a question in Habakkuk's thinking concerning God's sovereignty. Habakkuk needs to know how God

---

[52] *Leadership Emergence Theory* resulted from my doctoral work studying leadership cases of many leaders. It is a grounded theory. That is, the theory is grounded in data and studied comparatively among many cases, further validating the theoretical concepts arising from the analysis of the data.

16. Habakkuk, Four Shaping Activities

can be just and use a nation even more wicked than Judah to correct Judah. Habakkuk *isolates* himself (the second process item). That is, he gets alone, away from ministry and/or any other activity. He wants to hear from God himself.

God's basic answer is three fold:

1. Habakkuk 2:4 Live By Faith
He tells Habakkuk that the Babylonians will not live but that those who are righteous must learn to trust God. They will live by faith in God. Herein lies the *faith challenge* (the third process item). Habakkuk does not respond positively, yet, to this *faith challenge*.

2. Habakkuk Chapter 2, the Five Woes
He will also deal with Babylon bringing punishment to it for its wicked ways. The whole 2nd chapter of the book of Habakkuk tells how God will hold the Babylonians responsible for their wicked ways and will eventually destroy them.

3. Habakkuk 2: Earth will be filled, With the knowledge of the Glory of Jehovah,
In an almost aside-like comment, God assures Habakkuk that He will reveal Himself and His ways so all will know it (including his justice and working out of history toward His purposes). His glory shall be seen all around the world. Eventually God will bring history to a conclusion that will reveal His working all around the world. His glory will be seen by all.

Habakkuk reflects on what he has heard and then correlates it with what he knows of God's past working with Israel. After a deep time of reflecting, Habakkuk sees God's perspective and agrees with it (the fourth process item, the paradigm shift). Having gone through the paradigm shift and now viewing reality from God's perspective, Habakkuk accepts the *faith challenge*. The 3rd chapter reveals a joyful testimony of Habakkuk's acceptance of God's perspective.

Macro Lessons Associated With the Shaping Activities
What is a macro lesson?[53] A <u>macro-lesson</u> is a high level generalization of a leadership observation (suggestion, guideline, requirement), stated as a lesson, which repeatedly occurs throughout different leadership eras, and thus has potential as a leadership absolute. Macro lessons even at their weakest provide strong guidelines describing leadership insights. At their strongest they are requirements, or absolutes, that leaders should follow. Leaders ignore them to their detriment.

Table Hab 16-2 lists several macro lessons and suggest the process items that bring them about.

---

[53] 41 Macro Lessons have been identified. The numbers in the table which follow refer the to the list of macro lessons as given in the following articles. See **Articles**, 29. *Macro Lessons—Defined; 30. Macro Lessons: List of 41 Across Six Leadership Eras.*

16. Habakkuk, Four Shaping Activities

Lesson No. Label/ When First Seen[54]	Process Item(s)		Habakkuk
6. Faith/ Patriarchal	Faith check/ Faith Challenge	Biblical Leaders must learn to trust in the unseen God, sense His presence, sense His revelation, and follow Him by faith.	The basic answer that God gives, Habakkuk 2:4 reminds Habakkuk that a righteous person will have to learn to trust God whether or not he can see what God is doing or why God is doing it.
8. Intercession/ Pre-Kingdom	Prayer Challenge	Leaders called to a ministry are called to intercede for that ministry.	Habakkuk does intercede with God asking for His mercy as He works out his justice using the Babylonians. But this process item is minor compared to the four major ones.
10. Intimacy/ Pre-Kingdom	Crisis; faith challenge; isolation; prayer challenge	Leaders develop intimacy with God, which in turn overflows into all their ministry since ministry flows out of being.	All five of the process items were possible because Habakkuk had and developed further his intimacy with God.
13. Challenge/ Pre-Kingdom	Faith Challenge; Ministry Challenge	Leaders receive vision from God which sets before them challenges that inspire their leadership.	Habakkuk saw what God was going to do to Judah. He lived out his life with this perspective and joyfully accepted what came. He did not see the end result-Babylonians being destroyed but saw it to the eye of faith.
21. Recrudescence/ Kingdom	Ministry Challenge; Prayer Challenge	God will attempt to bring renewal to His people until they no longer respond to Him.	Habakkuk learns, disappointingly enough that God is going to bring an end to the southern kingdom. He has attempted renewal so many times and been thwarted. I actually think this was a prayer challenge to Habakkuk.
22. By-pass/ Kingdom	Ministry Challenge	God will by-pass leadership and structures that do not respond to Him and will institute new leadership and structures.	Habakkuk does not actually see this; Daniel did. But Habakkuk was warned of it.
24. Perspective/ Post-Kingdom	Paradigm shift	Leaders must know the value of perspective and interpret present happenings in terms of God's broader purposes.	The whole book of Habakkuk demonstrates this macro lesson.

Conclusion

God uses the book of Habakkuk to teach us, leaders today, of how He can shape us. The most important lessons have to do with trusting God by faith as we live out our lives and getting God's perspective on what is happening to us and our ministries. Sometimes it will take a paradigm shift for us to see God's perspective. We must be open for this.

---

[54] Study across the Bible has identified six leadership eras: (1) Patriarchal; (2) Pre-Kingdom; (3) Kingdom; (4) Post-Kingdom; (5) Pre-Church; (6) Church. Macro lessons have originated in each of the eras. At least they were first identified in an era and then checked backwards and forwards for occurrences in other eras.

16. Habakkuk, Four Shaping Activities

Paradigm shifts challenge us. All leaders will at one time or another face a faith crisis. Is God real. Is what I believe real? And God will meet them, if they go deep with God. Isolation, whether imposed from without or chosen, is one of the means God will use to take us deeper with Himself and reveal new perspectives to us. Forewarned is forearmed.

Article 17

17. Habakkuk, God's Timing

Introduction
Habakkuk cries out in his prayer to God in chapter 1 verse 2,

How long?

He is referring to a stop being brought to the wicked practices going on in the southern kingdom. He is wanting justice. God gives an answer. And it validates a macro lesson previously seen. One of the important leadership macro lessons[55] learned in the very first leadership era[56] was the timing macro lesson. Once identified it was seen repeated forcefully in the second leadership era. Then it was frequently observed throughout all the other leadership eras including the kingdom leadership era of which Habakkuk is a part.

Timing Macro-Lesson
God's Timing Is Crucial To Accomplishment Of God's Purposes.

Habakkuk is a leader who learned about the timing of God. It is a lesson all leaders need to learn.

Illustrations of the Timing of God in the Old Testament

Notice the following examples of this important macro lesson.

---

[55] A <u>macro-lesson</u> is a high level generalization of a leadership observation (suggestion, guideline, requirement), stated as a lesson, which repeatedly occurs throughout different leadership eras, and thus has potential as a leadership absolute. See **Articles**, 29. *Macro Lesson Defined and Macro Lessons;30. List of 41 Across Six Leadership Eras*.

[56] We have identified six leadership eras across the Bible. (1) The Patriarchal; (2) Pre-Kingdom; (3) Kingdom; (4) Post-Kingdom; (5) Pre-Church; (6) Church. See **Article**, *26. Leadership Eras In The Bible, Six Identified*.

17. Habakkuk, God's Timing

Table Hab 17-1. Some Examples of the Timing Macro Lesson

Era	Example(s)
I. Patriarchal Era	Abraham/ birth of child; Genesis 15, deliverance 400+ years later in Egypt
II. Pre-Kingdom Era: a. Desert Phase	Deliverance from Egypt, Exodus; Crossing the Red Sea; Failure to Enter the Land; 40 years in the desert; Going in to the land, Deuteronomy
b. Conquering the Land Phase	Crossing the Jordan, 3 days, flood season; Fall of Jericho
c. Conquered by the land	Deliverers, e.g. Gideon, Jephthah
III. Kingdom Era	**Samuel, transition to Kingdom leadership**
IV. Post-Kingdom Era	Daniel 9, Praying in the Return
V. Pre-Church Era	Galatians 4:4, Luke 1,2; Matthew 1,2
VI. Church Era	Pentecost; Macedonian call

God's will includes direction for what, how and <u>when</u>.

The Lesson Seen in Habakkuk

The book of Habakkuk illustrates this important timing macro lesson very explicitly. In this short little three chapter book, God emphasizes how crucial timing is—in three different ways.

1. **Judgment on the Southern Kingdom—Judah**
   Habakkuk questions God about dealing with the sinful, evil activity going on in the southern kingdom. God reveals that He is working on the problem but this involves a nation that He is raising up (the Babylonians) and it will take time. In fact, it probably did not occur in Habakkuk's lifetime or if it did it was in his very last years. The first of three sieges by Babylon occurred in 606 B.C. Daniel was carried away in this siege.

2. **Judgment on Babylon**
   Habakkuk does not like God's using the wicked Babylonians to bring judgment on the southern kingdom, which is less wicked than the Babylonians. God points out that He will also down-line bring judgment on the Babylonians. But much more time is involved. This final judgment occurred in 539 B.C. when the Medo-Persians captured Babylon and took over the empire. Chapter 2 of Habakkuk details the reasons why God is going to judge Babylon.

3. **The Challenge of Not Knowing When**
   In lieu of knowing when, God gives a basic alternative. This is a crucial lesson. God's basic answer to Habakkuk in 2:4 is that those who follow God (the just) shall live by faith (trust in God, who He is and what He is doing). The "just shall live by faith." The timing of God requires that a leader have a trusting relationship with God. The leader may not be able to see what God is doing (Habakkuk could

17. Habakkuk, God's Timing

not see God's left hand at work in the Babylonian nation). But that leader must learn to trust in God. However, note, Habakkuk seeks God's answer and God does reveal, at least somewhat the timing. Frequently, this is the case. A leader seeking to know God's timing on something will get an answer from God.

Some Observations
1. Note, God anticipates Habakkuk's queries at every stage and has an answer for them—timing is involved.
2. Habakkuk receives God's answer and finally agrees with it (goes through the paradigm shift necessary to understand God's judgment and justice).
3. *Left hand sensitivity* to current events is needed by leaders who must learn to see the left hand of God[57] at work.
4. Habakkuk was in a hurry. He wanted something done right away. God was already working on the situation. But it would take time to work it out. As leaders we are so frequently involved in our situations and their pressing need that we can not see them in terms of a bigger picture.
5. Habakkuk did respond to God's word about the timing. He accepted the basic admonition of living by faith. And he did so joyously though he knew much pain would be involved in the working out of God's purposes.

Conclusion
The book of Habakkuk is a good book to teach the timing macro lesson.

God's Timing Is Crucial To Accomplishment Of God's Purposes.[58]

The timing macro lesson is one of the top five macro lessons in the Bible. All leaders need to learn this valuable lesson. Seeing illustrations of the timing macro in the Bible helps sensitize one to discerning them in real life. And leaders must discern God's timing. Or in lieu of getting God's timing, leaders must learn the basic lesson,

The just shall live by faith.

---

[57] Left hand sensitivity refers to gaining a perspective on God's use of other nations and groups, apart from those dedicated to His service, to accomplish His purposes. See **Articles**, 28. *Left Hand of God*; 21. *Habakkuk, The Left Hand of God*; 31. *Needed—Sons of Issachar*.

[58] For further study, see **Article**, 12. *God's Timing and Leadership*.

Article 18

18. Habakkuk, Important Ideas to Communicate

Introduction
G. Campbell Morgan, in his book, **Living Messages of the Books of the Bible**, studied each book of the Bible for its contribution to the flow of truth in the Bible as a whole. He specifically identified truth from each book, which was applicable to present day situations. I have capitalized on that notion for Habakkuk. That book has some important ideas for leaders today.

Sometimes God, because God is who He is and He knows us and our problems, will take a particular problem common to us all and deal with it in Scripture. And He will deal with it in such a way as to give universal answers. Answers, that fit a leader who lived 100s of years ago, will still apply to leaders today. Such is the book of Habakkuk. Habakkuk is a book that primarily deals with God's shaping of a leader in a crisis moment in his life. What are some ideas from Habakkuk that apply today?

In order to identify those ideas, we need to know the background of the book. We need to know the situation of the leader, Habakkuk. We need to know the message of the book. We need to know the structure of the book that develops that message. We need to know the purposes of the book. From such an understanding, we can transfer the truth implied in that situation to similar situations today. From such an analysis, we can then pinpoint several ideas worth communicating today.

Understanding Habakkuk—The Story Line
Habakkuk is in a crisis in his life and ministry. He sees injustice and ungodliness all around him. He is beginning to doubt God, His character and His working. The book exposes his innermost feelings in this faith crisis situation. He voices his honest complaint to God and waits for God's answer. God's answer shocks Him and forces him to ask another question of God. God's next answer is so overwhelming that Habakkuk responds with awe, fear and joy in God's future work.

Understanding Habakkuk—The Structure of the Book
Tracing the interactive dialog between God and the leader Habakkuk leads to three major sections of the book. I have titled them from the response of Habakkuk to God's shaping activity.

 I. (1:1-2:1)   Habakkuk's Honest Struggle With Faith
II. (2:2-2:20) Habakkuk's Faith-Wait Response
III. (3:1-19)   Habakkuk's Response of True Faith

Understanding Habakkuk—The Theme of the Book
The overall message of the book easily flows from the three major sections.

18. Habakkuk, Important Ideas to Communicate

HABAKKUK'S STRUGGLE OF FAITH
- involved his honest questioning of God,
- was met by God's own explanation, and
- resulted in a joyous acceptance by faith of that which God was doing.

Understanding Habakkuk—Some Purposes of the Book
Some purposes of the book include the following. God wanted,

- to teach Habakkuk (and by implication, leaders of all time and God's people) to trust unconditionally in God's complex workings in history to bring about His just purposes,
- to mature Habakkuk's faith (and by implication to reveal to us today how God matures a leader in faith),
- to highlight the need always for a person of God to live by faith in God no matter what the situation he/she is facing,
- to indicate to Habakkuk (and by implication to us today) that when God uses nations in history for His purposes He is still true to His nature.
- to assure Habakkuk (and by implication us also) that God's justice will eventually permeate our world.

Implications for Us Today
All leaders must eventually learn to walk by faith, that is, trust in an unseen God's dealings with their own lives, ministry, events around them, and in the world. This is true, whether or not they can understand the complexity or see what God is doing. God's people must also learn this lesson. Habakkuk reveals several processes whereby God teaches this valuable Biblical lesson. Like Jonah and Job the book focuses not on ministry to others but on God's dealing with His leader. When there is increasing deterioration in the society, as was the case during Habakkuk's time, ungodliness will abound. And there will be unjust things going on with no apparent repercussions. It is in the midst of these things that we need to see a bigger perspective. We need to see the present happenings in terms of the larger picture, the history leading up to it and that, which is to come. God frequently does just that. He meets a leader in a crisis situation by broadening perspective. And we are thankful for just such processing, for otherwise we, like Habakkuk would be ready to give up.

Identifying Ideas From Habakkuk To Present Day Leadership Situations
When I teach the book of Habakkuk, I first give the information that I have just written above. When folks understand Habakkuk's situation and God's shaping of him, then they can see how the following 8 ideas are transferable to present day times. I usually choose 3 or 4 of these ideas to use in a short series. Table Hab 18-1 lists those ideas and gives a brief explanation about each one. I am applying these ideas directly to leaders since that is the thrust of this commentary. But these ideas could well apply to individual followers of God as well.

Table Hab 18-1. 8 Key Ideas From the Book of Habakkuk

Idea	Topic	STATEMENT/Discussion
1.	Doubting God	**ALL LEADERS HAVE TIMES IN THEIR MINISTRY WHEN THEY DOUBT GOD—HIS REALITY, HIS PRESENCE, HIS CHARACTER./** Such a leader was Habakkuk. God's answer to him still stands today. A leader must learn to walk by faith (Habakkuk 2:4). This is the essential principle that sustains a person over a lifetime with God. Application of this idea:

18. Habakkuk, Important Ideas to Communicate

		a. *Expect your faith to be tested.* Don't be blindsided when this happens to you. b. *One should be honest with God about his/her doubts.* Habakkuk was. And many of the Psalmist were also. c. *Expect God to meet your struggles of faith with a convincing solution.* Habakkuk questioned God. He then listened for God's answer. And he got God's answer. In fact, three of them. (1) Vs 1:5 I am working now; (2) Vs 2:1-4 I will tell you what I will do. You must trust me to do it. (3) Vs 2:20 I am holy. Trust me to reveal this. d. *Don't be satisfied with less that God's convincing answer to your personal problem of faith.* e. *Remember, the main thing about our faith is the object of your faith, God.* f. *Recognize, that truth faith always has in it an element of surrender to God.* **Summary** All leaders go through doubt. The issues will vary. But there is always something that will challenge a leader concerning God and God's actions. But God will meet such a leader. Habakkuk affirms the important sixth macro lesson seen first in the Patriarchal Leadership Era and then repeated in the Pre-Kingdom Leadership Era. **BIBLICAL LEADERS MUST LEARN TO TRUST IN THE UNSEEN GOD, SENSE HIS PRESENCE, SENSE HIS REVELATION, AND FOLLOW HIM BY FAITH.** See **Articles**, 29. *Macro Lessons Defined; Macro Lessons: 30. List of 41 Across Six Leadership Eras.*
2.	Broader Perspective	**EFFECTIVE LEADERS VIEW PRESENT MINISTRY IN LIGHT OF A LIFETIME (or even broader) PERSPECTIVE.**[59] God frequently meets a leader by giving that leader a broader perspective on his/her situation. We as leaders look at the given moment with its complexities including unfairness, crises, apparent injustice, etc. God helps us see the moment in light of the bigger picture. Such a broadening of perspective is seen in the book of Habakkuk. Sources of broadening of perspective include the Bible, history, life itself, other leaders or as in this case, revelation from God. Habakkuk got a broadened perspective on God's working and his justice, holiness, and faithfulness.

---

[59] This is one of seven major leadership lessons that have emerged in my studies of leadership over the past 21 years. They are: (1) Effective Leaders View Present Ministry In Terms Of A Life Time Perspective. (2) Effective Leaders Maintain A Learning Posture Throughout Life. (3) Effective Leaders Value Spiritual Authority As A Primary Power Base. (4) Effective Leaders Who Are Productive Over A Lifetime Have A Dynamic Ministry Philosophy. (5) Effective Leaders View Leadership Selection And Development As A Priority Function In Their Ministry. (6) Effective Leaders See Relational Empowerment As Both A Means And A Goal Of Ministry. (7) Effective Leaders Evince A Growing Awareness Of Their Sense Of Destiny. It is the first one I am referring to in this suggested idea. See **Article**, *Leadership Lessons—Seven Major Lessons Identified.*

3.	God's Shaping Activity	**GOD SHAPES A LEADER OVER A LIFETIME TO MOVE THAT LEADER TOWARD INHERENT POTENTIAL TO BE AND DO—THAT IS, TO FULFULL THAT LEADER'S DESTINY./** God patiently shapes a leader. He listens. He responds with answers, sometimes beyond that leader. The leader waits for a clarification or an overwhelming word from God. God gives it. The heart of it is simply that leaders who are righteous and follow God must walk in faithfulness, trusting God. Then God will sometimes tell that leader what He is doing. The leader can then respond in awe and with a joyful heart. Such a process is described in Habakkuk. Habakkuk was a leader who was patiently shaped by God and who is an exemplar of how we are to respond. In all of this, timing is crucial. God waits till the leader is ready for each stage in the process. Then at the right moment God gives His perspectives. God works in Habakkuk's case through four primary shaping activities (technical term, process items): crisis, isolation, faith challenge, paradigm shift. See **Article**, *16. Habakkuk, 4 Shaping Activities*.)
4.	Philosophy of History	**A LEADER NEEDS A FUNDAMENTAL APPROACH TO UNDERSTAND GOD'S WORKING IN HISTORY./** Two books in the Scripture especially show how God is working in history. Daniel is the most comprehensive. But Habakkuk shows the same thing on a smaller scale and in terms of one leader's understanding of what is going on in his ministry. God is working in history and the book of Habakkuk has as one of its major purposes to teach God's people to trust unconditionally in God's complex working in history to bring about His just purposes. At least four values are implied about God and history in this book: 1. God is controlling history to cause it to work to an absolutely just conclusion. 2. God can use any group of people as instruments to suit His purposes. 3. God is concerned about an individual (Habakkuk) in the course of history. 4. History cannot be rightly interpreted until all the data is in. We have but a partial picture from a limited perspective. Wait till the whole show is over. All the data is not in. Time is involved. God is working, indirectly behind the scenes (See **Article**, *The Left Hand of God*) and directly through His people.
5.	Faith Principles	**ANY LEADER CAN BE ENCOURAGED IN HIS/HER FAITH BY SEEING FAITH PRINCIPLES THAT HABAKKUK LEARNED./** The book of Habakkuk has some important principles about faith—the most important being Habakkuk 2:4. But there are some nine other principles: 1. Expect your faith to be tested in regards to your prayer life (1:1,2). 2. One should be absolutely honest with God about doubts (1:1-4). 3. In regards to your struggles of faith, expect God to meet with you with a convincing solution deep in your heart (3:2). 4. Do not be satisfied with anything less than God's convincing answer to your personal problem of faith (2:1). 5. Faith and righteousness are intertwined (2:4).

		6. A leader can trust God to work out the course of history to bring about absolute justice (Gen 18:25; Hab 2:14). 7. True faith is not incompatible with honest doubt or honest fears (1:1-4; 3:2,16). 8. Persevering faith ultimately results in a heart of joy in the midst of any circumstances (3:17-19; P.S. see Philippians). 9. The main thing about faith is the object of faith. Trust **GOD** not **TRUST** God.

6.	Essential Faith Principle	**THE JUST SHALL LIVE BY FAITH./**
		The essential spiritual principle is given in Habakkuk 2:4.
		
		2:4 Consider carefully the message:
		    Those who are evil will not survive,
		    But those who are righteous will live
		    because they trust in God.
		
		This statement is repeated 3 times in the New Testament:
		1. Romans 1:17 the **just** shall live by faith; (emphasis on just on who is righteous).
		3. Galatians 3:11 the just shall live **by faith** (emphasis on by faith and not works).
		4. Hebrews 10:38 the just shall **live** by faith (emphasis on live).
		
		In Habakkuk, the emphasis is on the *contrast* of those not living by faith and being punished (Babylonians) and those who must trust God (by faith) to work out His plans.

7.	Paradigm Shift	**GOD OFTEN MUST TAKE A LEADER THROUGH A MAJOR PARADIGM SHIFT IN ORDER FOR THAT LEADER TO UNDERSTAND GOD'S WORKING AND TO CONTINUE IN LEADERSHIP./** A most important paradigm shift occurred for Habakkuk. He was able to see beyond those things challenging his understanding of God and see God's working from a broader perspective. God used three major shaping activities to pull off this major paradigm shift (crisis, isolation, faith challenge). Habakkuk learned to walk by faith, trusting God to work His work, regardless of the local situation which seemed to deny God's character. How do we know Habakkuk went through this paradigm shift? We have the book. See **Article**, *Paradigms and Paradigm Shifts*.
8.	Hope	**A LEADER CAN ALWAYS COUNT ON GOD'S PAST WORKING AS A STABILIZING FACTOR THROUGH WHICH TO VIEW PRESENT HAPPENINGS AND HENCE RECEIVE HOPE./** Where does hope come from? For God's people, recollection of the past is one sure ground of hope for the future. See Habakkuk 3. See also Moses' farewell series in Deuteronomy.

Conclusion

There are great lessons in the book of Habakkuk; lessons, which apply today. I have not exhausted all the ideas that can be applied today from Habakkuk. But the ones listed above are certainly important ones. And they can make a difference in a leader who wants to finish well.

Article 19

19. Habakkuk, Important Words To Study

Introduction

The basic hermeneutical approach I use is the grammatical historical approach, modified by my studies in ethnotheology.[60] The approach takes into account:

- the importance of the author's situation,
- the place and purpose of the book in the Bible as a whole,
- the theme of the book,
- the structure of the book,
- the contextual flow, and
- the actual study of the **significant words** used in developing those contextual units.
- the communication models from ethnotheology dealing with interpretation,
- recognition of cross-cultural viewpoints in interpreting scripture.

This article is highlighting the study of words. The hermeneutical principle describing that study is,

> **In The Spirit, Prayerfully Study The Author's Words To Determine The Sense In Which He Uses Them In Developing A Given Context.**

I need to digress for a moment and introduce you to my pre-suppositions about interpreting the Bible. Then I will come back to this article proper.

The Bible is the Word of God written in the words of man. There are spiritual laws and language laws that apply to its study. I identify 7 General Language Laws and 7 Special Language forms that apply because the Bible is in the words of man and hence follows normal language principles. I identify 3 spiritual laws (there could be more), which apply because the Bible is the Word of God. I remind myself of the three spiritual laws by the phrase, *In the Spirit*, which prefaces each of the general language laws. Here are the three spiritual laws that the phrase, *In the Spirit*, reminds me of:

1. **To Understand God's Revealed Truth One Must Be A Child Of God And Thus Possess The Holy Spirit Who Is The Revealer.**
2. **To Understand God's Revealed Truth One Must Be Dependent Upon The Holy Spirit To Teach.**

---

[60] My doctorate in Missiology, done under Dr. Charles Kraft, focused on ethnotheology, which is Kraft's cross-cultural approach to interpreting the scriptures. It has a strong emphasis also on communication theory, which is very helpful when studying the Bible. My prior study in hermeneutics was under Buck Hatch at the graduate school of Columbia Bible College who taught me the systematized and integrated approach to the interpretation. I self-studied Milton S. Terry's classic, **Biblical Hermeneutics**.

19. Habakkuk, Important Words To Study   page 109

3. To Understand God's Revealed Truth One Must Be Yielded To Do The Will Of God (that is, respond obediently to the truth that is revealed).

Let me repeat. I begin the wording of each of the language laws which follow with a strange phrase, ***IN THE SPIRIT PRAYERFULLY***. I list this phrase <u>intentionally</u>. I do so to call to mind that the Bible is a unique, God-given book. It is more than just the words of men. It is revelation from God. It is God communicating His mind, His will, His intents, and Himself to people. I am trying, by using this phrase, to emphasize the divine side of the two-fold nature of the Bible. The Bible is the **WORD** of God in the words of men. That the Bible is written in the words of men demands that one be aware of and use the basic laws which language follows. That the Bible is also God's own revelation <u>demands that one be aware of and follow the spiritual principles which the Scriptures themselves indicate will affect one's understanding</u>. These last underlined words are what I mean by the phrase **IN THE SPIRIT PRAYERFULLY**, which you will soon see precedes each of the major language principles. I have not dealt exhaustively with all spiritual principles but have limited myself to those major ones affecting people who will minister in the Word and who study it to know and apply God's truth. I am seeking in wording these spiritual laws to describe the attitudes that should be embraced by those who seek to understand spiritual truth.

There are two implications flowing from these statements that I must emphasize.

- **These Spiritual Principles Are Indispensable For A Proper Understanding Of The Scriptures.**
- **An Interpreter Must Continuously Apply These Laws Before, During, And After Applying The Laws Of Language.**

This article also seeks to identify some of the **important words to study** from the book of Habakkuk. I will indicate some findings but leave the detailed work for you, the reader, to do. . The listing of the hermeneutical principles is given below in order that you may see where my study of words fits into the overall interpretative scheme. Figure Hab 19-1 gives an overview picture of the systematized and integrated scheme. Table Hab 19-1 then lists the actual principles. And Table Hab 19-2 shows how the principles are systematized to study a Bible book

19. Habakkuk, Important Words To Study

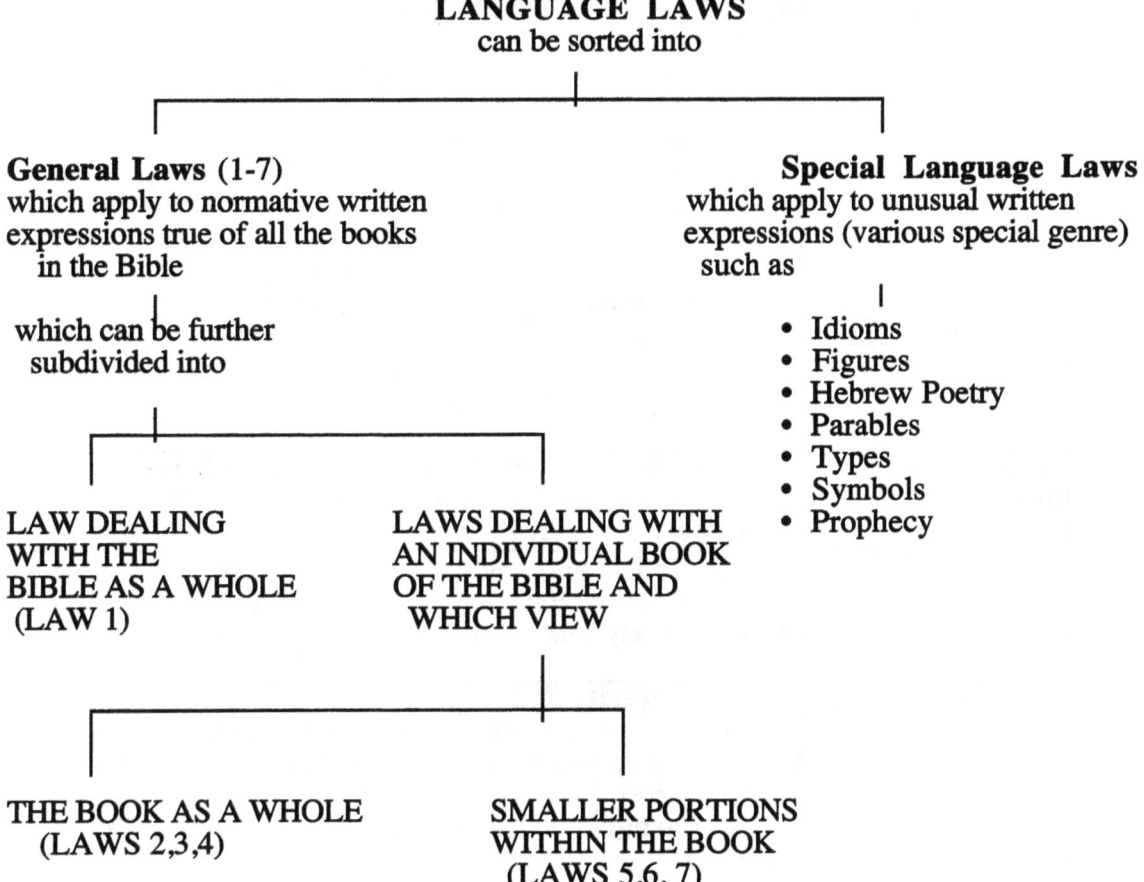

Figure Hab 19-1. Overall Scheme of Hermeneutical System

Table Hab 19-1. Statement Of The General Language Laws

Law	Dealing With	Statement

1	Book and Books, The Book in terms of the Whole Bible	**In The Spirit, Prayerfully Study The Book As A Whole In Terms Of Its Relationship To Other Books In The Bible** (i.e. the Bible as a whole) To Include:
		  a. its place in the progress of revelation,
		  b. its overall contribution to the whole of Bible literature (i.e. its *purposes—why is it in the Bible?*) and
		  c. its abiding contribution to present time.

19. Habakkuk, Important Words To Study

2	Historical Background	**In The Spirit, Prayerfully Study The Historical Background Of The Book Which Includes Such Information As:** a. the author of the book and the *historical perspective* from which he/she wrote, b. the *occasion* for the book, c. the *purpose* for the book including where pertinent the people for whom it was intended and their situation, and their need for it, d. any geographical or cultural factors bearing on the communication of the material.
3	Structure Of The Book	In The Spirit, Prayerfully Study The Book As A Whole Until You See The Author's Plan Or Structure Or The Way He Relates His Parts To The Whole Book To Accomplish His Purpose Or Develop His Theme.
4	Theme Of The Book	**In The Spirit, Prayerfully Study The Book As A Whole Until You Can Identify And State Concisely The Author's Theme Of The Book.**
5	Context	In The Spirit, Prayerfully Study The Author's Paragraphs And Sections In Relation To Each Other So That You Can Concisely State The Central Idea Of Each.
6	Grammar/ Syntax	**In The Spirit, Prayerfully Study The Author's Grammar** (i.e. the way he/she relates words, phrases, and sentences to develop paragraphs and larger sections) **In Order That You Can State Not Only The Context Of A Paragraph But The Flow Of Thought In Developing The Context In The Paragraph Or Larger Section.**
7	Words	In The Spirit, Prayerfully Study The Author's Words To Determine The Sense In Which He/She Uses Them In Developing A Given Context.

Table Hab 19-1. Hermeneutical Laws Explained

The general laws view a book as a unified written piece of literature. Each of these laws in its own way seeks to explain some factor of the book in terms of the book's unit. These laws integrally relate to each other. When applying a given law in studying the book one recognizes just how much each law interplays with the other laws. The following table gives the title of the law and its focus in study of a book. It also briefly describes the end result of applying the law to study of a book.

19. Habakkuk, Important Words To Study

Table Hab 19-2. The General Language Laws Related As To Focus

Law	Title Of Law	Focus	End Result When Used
1	Book And Books	Bible As A Whole	an understanding of how this book fits into the message of the Bible as a whole
2	Historical Background	Book As A Whole	uncovers historical factors which influence an understanding of the book as a whole
3	Theme	Book As A Whole	the unifying concept(s) developed by the book as a whole and to which all parts of the book relate
4	Structure	Book As A Whole	an understanding of how the author arranges the parts of his book to develop his theme or carry out his purpose
5	Context	Units Within Major Structure	an understanding of how the unit as a whole relates to the unifying concept of the major structural unit in which it is located
6	Grammar	Units Of Context	an understanding of how concepts within the unit develop the context
7	Words	Contextual Units	how the use of a word develops concepts within some given context

So then the hermeneutical law we are dealing with in this article is,

In The Spirit, Prayerfully Study The Author's Words To Determine The Sense In Which He/She Uses Them In Developing A Given Context.

Example: Habakkuk 1:5, Several Words Studied

I am going to use Habakkuk 1:5 as an example of what I mean by studying words. I am hoping you will catch the basic notion of seeing the usus loquendi (local uses of a word in various contexts which has a lot to do with connotation). I am hoping also to help you see connotation as well as denotation.[61] Then I will simply list other verses and words for study. I have studied each of the words I list. For each of the words given below in Tables I will give the Strong's Reference Number (SRN),[62] other references in the Old Testament where the word also occurs, the various uses in these Old Testament references, and a paraphrase which tries to indicate connotation as well as denotation.

Habakkuk 1:5 is a pivotal verse. God gets Habakkuk's attention very fast. Several words in that verse are worth noting.

5   Look (KJV Behold, SRN 7200) among the nations; look very carefully (KJV Regard, SRN 5027),
    There is something that will astonish (KJV wonder marvelously, SRN 8539) you,

---

[61] By denotation I am talking about the semantic meaning of the word. By connotation I am talking about the associated feelings or implications or the character of the word.

[62] **SRN** stands for Strong's Reference Number. See Strong's **Exhaustive Concordance of the Bible** which gives a reference number to all Biblical words along with definitions and usages throughout the Bible.

19. Habakkuk, Important Words To Study

For I am really doing something (KJV working a work; SRN 6466; SRN 6467) even as you speak,
Which, you won't believe (SRN 539), even when told.

Table Hab 19-3. Habakkuk 1:5 Look (KJV Behold);

Word/ SRN	Other References	How Used There	Comments Giving Denotation and Connotation
Look; (KJV Behold)/ 7200	1 Ch 21:12	*Advise* yourself; think very carefully so as to make an important decision;	Observing carefully enough to make a decision.
	Mal 3:18	*Discern*; Observe so that you can see the hand of God.	A discerning observation.
	Ecc 1:16	*Experience*; not seeing as an outsider but actually observing as one experiencing it firsthand	Observing as you experience what I am saying.
	Ecc 2:24	*Make...Enjoy*; literally make to enjoy; that is, observe with a realization that I am working, hence you will enjoy if because of that.	Joyful connotation because it comes from God.
	Isa 17:7	*Respect*; reverential fear	Understand who it is giving this and give the proper reverence deserved

Summary of Habakkuk 1:5 After *Look* Study (with connotative emphasis):

When I say behold or look I mean I want you to give a great deal of serious thought to what I am really already doing, discerning my hand in it, not as an onlooker, but actually participating in the experience with reverential fear, and yet looking forward to the fulfillment with a great deal of joy.

Table Hab 19-4. Habakkuk 1:5 Look Very Carefully (KJV Regard);

Look very carefully; (KJV	Ps 119:18	Behold with divine help	Trust God to reveal; know it is divine revelation.
	Pr 4:23-27	Look right at it; focused look not	Don't get side tracked by doubt or anything

19. Habakkuk, Important Words To Study

| regard) / SRN 5027 | 1 Ki 18:43 | distracted

Scan the sky looking for any indication | else.

Just as Elijah scanned the sky looking for the slightest indication of rain, you must by faith be looking to see what I am saying. |

Summary of Habakkuk 1:5 After *Look Very Carefully* Study (with connotative emphasis):

God says to Habakkuk. "I am working a great work in our day. I want you to look at it, to regard it, to give it a great deal of serious thought. Let nothing distract you from seeing it. Trust me to show you. I want you to discern my hand, looking for any indication of it. And I want you to do it with joy because I am in it."

Table Hab 19-5. Habakkuk 1:5 Astonish (KJV wonder marvelously);

Astonish; (KJV wonder marvelously)/ SRN 8539	Gen 43:33	Marveled—They were amazed at how Joseph could know their ages.	As I reveal this you will be astounded at what I am doing.
	Dan 4:1-3	Wonders; Twice used as Nebuchadnezzar reflects on God after fiery furnace. An element of the miraculous, the supernatural seen here.	You will catch the miraculous in it—seeing how I am controlling nations to accomplish my purpose.
	Dan 6:25-27	Wonders; Amazed at Daniel's experience in lions den; again an element of the miraculous.	An experiential understanding of divine intervention.
	Job 26:1-14 (vs 11)	Astonished; The very foundations of heaven are astonished at the amazing acts of God.	God's creative acts of the world astonish angelic beings. So this intervention by God using the Chaldeans should be sensed as an amazing thing.

Expanded Translation After Astonish Word Study (giving denotation/connotation):

God says to Habakkuk, "I am working a great work in your day, and I want you to look at it, to wonder marvelously at it. When I say I want you to look at it, I mean I want you to

19. Habakkuk, Important Words To Study

give this promise a great deal of serious thought, discerning My hand not as an outsider, but actually experiencing it, reverently, and yet looking forward to its fulfillment with a great deal of joy. Trust me to reveal things to you. When I say I want you look very carefully, I mean for you to consider this work asking God to open your eyes to see it. I want you to see My hand in it. Don't let anything divert your attention. But be on the lookout for the slightest indication of my involvement. Wonder marvelously knowing that there is a supernatural dimension. Be astonished at what I am doing.

Table Hab 19-6. Habakkuk 1:5 Emphatic Superlative (KJV working a work);

Really doing something;	Used many times; both words.	Work (SRN 6466); Work (SRN 6467)	The use of the repeated words is emphatic. I am really, really doing this.

Expanded Translation After Emphatic Superlative (giving denotation/connotation):

God says to Habakkuk, "I am really, really doing something, working a great work in your day, and I want you to look at it, to wonder marvelously at it. When I say I want you to look at it, I mean I want you to give this promise a great deal of serious thought, discerning My hand not as an outsider, but actually experiencing it, reverently, and yet looking forward to its fulfillment with a great deal of joy. Trust me to reveal things to you. When I say I want you look very carefully, I mean for you to consider this work asking God to open your eyes to see it. I want you to see My hand in it. Don't let anything divert your attention. But be on the lookout for the slightest indication of my involvement. Wonder marvelously knowing that there is a supernatural dimension. Be astonished at what I am doing.

Table Hab 19-7. Habakkuk 1:5 Believe (KJV believe);

Believe (SRN 539)	Dt 28:66	Believing lacking assurance; not total unbelief;	God is saying that there may come times when you will not believe it with assurance.
	Num 11:11,12	Nursing Father comforting a child;	God will be there for you, relationally, as you are tempted to doubt.

Finally Summary:

God says to Habakkuk, "I am really, really doing something, working a great work in your day, and I want you to look at it, to wonder marvelously at it. When I say I want you to look at it, I mean I want you to give this promise a great deal of serious thought, discerning My hand not as an outsider, but actually experiencing it, reverently, and yet looking forward to its fulfillment with a great deal of joy. Trust me to reveal things to you. When I say I want you look very carefully, I mean for you to consider this work asking God to open your eyes to see it. I want you to see My hand in it. Don't let anything divert your attention. But be on the lookout for the slightest indication of my involvement. Wonder marvelously knowing that there is a supernatural dimension. Be astonished at what I am doing. And know too, I recognize that you will have trouble believing this. I will be there for you to encourage you as you believe.

19. Habakkuk, Important Words To Study

Now note, there is a good bit of interpretive license taken when doing a connotative/denotative analysis of the important words. But you can know that when Habakkuk heard God say,

5 Look among the nations; look very carefully,
   There is something that will astonish you,
For I am really doing something even as you speak,
   Which, you won't believe even when told.

And as the revelation unfolded, he listened intently and was astonished (probably shocked). Notice he got alone with God, not wanting anything to detract his hearing from God. Notice he did see the divine intervention as the revelation clarified. The rest of the book of Habakkuk bears up my connotative/denotative interpretation.

Here are other significant words I have studied that are helpful in understanding some of the other important verses.

Table Hab 19-8. Some Other Words in Habakkuk For Word Study

Verse	Word in My Translation/ Word in KJV/ SRN
2:1	Doggedly set myself/ take my stand/ 05975 Watch tower/ tower/ 04692 **Watch carefully/ Look forth/ 06822** Answer, Answer/ 07725 Complaint/ complaint/ 08433
2:4[63]	**Because they trust/ faith/ 0530**
3:2	Heard, heard/ 08085
3:18	Jehovah/LORD/ 03068 God/ God/ 0430 Master/ God/ 0136

There are other words, especially in Habakkuk 3 which could be studied and might help clear up the allusions of Habakkuk. But at least these words given in this article are helpful

Closure
The study of an author's words in context can provide meaning that otherwise would not be grasped. But remember, one must trust God to reveal. And one must obediently respond to truth. But I hope you have sensed something of the importance of this hermeneutical principle:

In The Spirit, Prayerfully Study The Author's Words To Determine The Sense In Which He Uses Them In Developing A Given Context.

---

[63] See also the **15.**, *Habakkuk, Crucial Faith Words*, which treats this verse and the words in it.

Article 20

20. Habakkuk, Judgment and Revelation

Introduction

In a previous leadership article, I wrote about accountability[64] and a final judgment—beyond time and beginning of eternity. In this article, I want to suggest two principles about judgment by God in time—our history. They are brought out in Habakkuk, Nahum, and Obadiah. They are seen in various other portions of scripture as well. This will be a short article as it is suggestive at best and needs further research in the Scriptures. But I do want to mention it since it answers one of Habakkuk's questioning of God.

The Problem for Habakkuk

Note the following contextual statement, which sums up an objection from Habakkuk.

> **1:13-17 Context:**
> How is it that you a Holy God will not only use but will permit the wicked Chaldeans to be so successful especially since their success causes them to trust further in their own might.

Certainly God is aware of the wickedness of the Babylonians. He certainly demonstrates this in Chapters 1 and 2 when he describes the Babylonians. Note the following summary of characteristics of the Babylonians.

From chapter 1 we have these descriptors of the Chaldeans:

1. They were ruthless.
2. Their armies were massive and mobile.
3. They has specialized attack units, Cavalry Units which were very fast.
4. They captured cities and confiscated properties.
5. They were fierce. Surrounding nations feared them.
6. They were a law unto themselves.
7. They were adept at besieging fortified cities.
8. They operated on the principle that might is right.
9. Might was their god.
10. They were merciless in their destruction of nations.

From chapter 2 we have these descriptors of the Chaldeans:

---

[64] See **Article**, *Accountability—Standing Before God As A Leader*. That article is filled with Pauline principles which refer to leadership in the Church Leadership Era. This present article looks at God's ways with Israel, Judah, and other nations.

20. Judgment and Revelation

1. They are proud and will not survive.
2. They are arrogant.
3. The are restless. That is they are not satisfied with what they have.
5. They are greedy.
6. They make slaves of captured people.
7. They ransacked and looted the conquered nations.
8. They murdered many.
9. They were violent to peoples conquered.
10. They were self-reliant and felt secure in their defensive preparations in their homeland.
11. They brought dishonor to their country.
12. They destroyed cities.
13. They destroyed animals needlessly.
14. They were idolaters.

Yes, the Babylonians are more wicked than Judah. So how then, can we answer Habakkuk's question?

> **How is it that you a Holy God will not only use but will permit the wicked Chaldeans to be so successful especially since their success causes them to trust further in their own might.**

Two Principles of Judgment

I want to suggest two basic judgmental principles.

1. Revelation a Key
God judges those groups with more revelation of Himself and His ways with stricter accountability than those with less revelation.

2. God's Patience and Mercy, a Second Key
God mercifully gives groups of people as much time as possible to repent and turn to Him, before He finally brings final judgment on them.

God has given much light to the southern kingdom. They had the law and probably other writings. Many prophets had brought them God's word. And yet they refused to turn to God. The Babylonians had much less revelation. This seems to be in accord with Romans 2 which shows that God judges groups based on their living up to the revelation they have. This seems to be implied in Obadiah and Nahum where God brings strong final judgment on Edom and Assyria. God brought severe judgment on the Edomites, stressing their knowledge of and relationship, historically, to Israel.

The second principle, relating to God's Patience and Mercy, does not appear directly in Habakkuk. But it is seen in Genesis 15 in the prophetical words about God's people being in Egypt, until the judgment time had come on the nations in the land.

Genesis 15
12 And when the sun was going down, a deep sleep fell upon Abram; and, a horror of great darkness fell upon him. 13 And he said unto Abram, Know

20. Judgment and Revelation

for sure that your descendants shall be strangers in a land (Egypt) that is not theirs. They shall serve that nation; and that nation shall afflict them four hundred years; 14 And also that nation, whom they shall serve, will I judge: and afterward shall they come out with great substance. 15 But you will go to your ancestors in peace; you shall be buried after a long life. 16 But in the fourth generation your descendants shall come back to the land again: **for the iniquity of the Amorites is not yet full**.

17 And it came to pass, that, when the sun went down, and it was dark, behold a smoking furnace, and a burning lamp that passed between those pieces. 18 In the same day the LORD made a covenant with Abram, saying, Unto your descendants I have given this land, from the river of Egypt unto the great river, the river Euphrates: 19 The Kenites, and the Kenizzites, and the Kadmonites, 20 And the Hittites, and the Perizzites, and the Rephaims, 21 And the Amorites, and the Canaanites, and the Girgashites, and the Jebusites.

Perhaps the iniquity of the **Babylonians was not yet full**.

Closure

I speak with less certainty about these two observations, knowing I must do further research on them. I do know that Habakkuk was satisfied with God's answer. Habakkuk knew for certain that God would eventually bring judgment, fully deserved by the Babylonians. And this did happen in 539 B.C.

Article 21

21. Habakkuk, Left Hand of God

Introduction

In another leadership article, I attributed to Dr. Arthur Glasser the use of the phrase, the *Left Hand of God*, to call attention to God's use of non-believers to accomplish His purposes. This *Left Hand of God* is seen numerous times in the Old Testament. Table Hab 21-1 depicts just a few of them.

Table Hab 21-1. Some Occurrences of the Left Hand of God

Passage	Persons Involved	Explanation
Genesis 20, 21	Abraham, Sarah, Abimelech	Abraham lied to Abimelech about Sarah his wife. God protects her while she is with Abimelech and gives Abimelech a dream to let him know who Sarah is.
Genesis	Joseph, Pharaoh	God sends two dreams to Pharaoh, which need to be interpreted. Joseph comes to the forefront by interpreting these dreams and suggesting a wise course of action. Joseph is elevated to high position and is in place to deliver his people when the famine hits hardest.
Daniel	Nebuchadnezzar	Daniel ch 4 is one of the clearest examples of the king's heart being in the hand of Jehovah. God humbles Nebuchadnezzar, a very powerful ruler.
Isa 45	Cyrus; Daniel et al	God predicts He will use Cyrus and He does as noted in Table Hab 21.2 below.
Hag 1:1,2	Darius, Haggai	It is clear that Darius was used by God to help the remnant back in the land.
Ne ch 1 et al	Artaxerxes	Artaxerxes not only wrote decrees allowing the Jews to go back in the land, but he also helped fund their return.

With this article I want to add the book of Habakkuk to this list of those illustrating Left Hand workers for God. And I want to warn us. We need to become sensitive to this concept, the *Left Hand of God*. Otherwise, we will identify with Habakkuk the leader and be shocked to find out God has been working and we didn't even know it.

Habakkuk's Surprise

Habakkuk had a problem. As far as he could see God was not intervening in Judah to deal with sin and injustice. Imagine his initial shock and surprise when God gave him these words. I will quote from the commentary section in chapter 1.

God Speaks—I Am Doing Something About This

21. Habakkuk, Left Hand of God

5 Look among the nations; look very carefully,
   There is something that will astonish you,
 For I am doing something even as you speak,
   Which, you won't believe, even when told.
6 Consider: I am raising up the Babylonians,
   That ruthless and unruly nation,
   That marches all over the land,
   To possess homes and cities that are not theirs.
7 They are fierce and dreaded,
 They are a law unto themselves.
8 Their cavalry troops are swifter than leopards,
   And are more ferocious than the evening wolves.
 Their cavalry troops gallop rapidly on.
   Indeed, their horsemen cover ground rapidly.
 They move swiftly as an eagle that swoops to devour.
9 There whole army moves forward, eager to destroy.
 Like a desert wind their hordes break through.
   And they gather captives countless as the sand.
10 At kings they scoff;
 And of rulers they make sport.
 They are not dismayed by fortified cities.
 They raise siege-works and capture them.
11 Then they sweep by like the wind, and go on,
   guilty men, whose own might is their god.

Imagine Habakkuk's two-fold surprise as this revelation broke upon his consciousness:

1. That God was doing something;
2. That God was using the Babylonians to do it. Actually Habakkuk was shocked.

Left Hand of God—Sovereign Work of God

This is an illustration of the sovereign work of God in which He works through nations not having allegiance to Himself. They are not even aware that God is using them for His purposes. While the majority of the Babylonians would not even know that they were being used by God, some did.[65]

Habakkuk was rudely jolted into *left hand sensitivity*.

Definition

<u>Left hand sensitivity</u> refers to gaining a perspective on God's use of other nations and groups, apart from those dedicated to His service, to accomplish His purposes.

Habakkuk Has A New Problem—Understanding God's Work in History

Habakkuk's first problem had been addressed by God. God was doing something to deal with Judah's sins and ungodly situation. But it was complex and was taking time to be worked out. Now Habakkuk's immediate problem, sin permeating Judah with its criminal

---

[65] See the case of Nebuzaradan in Jeremiah 39: 1 The word that came to Jeremiah from the LORD, after that Nebuzaradan the captain of the guard had let him go from Ramah, when he had taken him being bound in chains among all that were carried away captive of Jerusalem and Judah, which were carried away captive unto Babylon.2 And the captain of the guard took Jeremiah, and said unto him, *The LORD thy God hath pronounced this evil upon this place.*

activity and injustice, becomes small in comparison with his new problem. How can God use a nation more undgodly than Judah to correct Judah's problems.

And so the rest of the book of Habakkuk deals with this problem. What Habakkuk needs to get is a view of God's working in history.

A LEADER NEEDS A FUNDAMENTAL APPROACH TO UNDERSTAND GOD'S WORKING IN HISTORY.

Three books in the Scripture especially show how God is working in history. Daniel is the most comprehensive in its sweep of history. And the Revelation deals with God's working in the end times. But Habakkuk does shows the same thing on a smaller scale and in terms of one leader's understanding of what is going on in his ministry. God is working in history and the book of Habakkuk has as one of its major purposes to teach God's people to trust unconditionally in God as He works in history to bring about His just purposes.

At least four values concerning a philosophy of God's working in history are implied about God and history in this book of Habakkuk:

1. God is controlling history to cause it to work to an absolutely just conclusion.[66]
2. God can use any group of people as instruments to suit His purposes.
3. God is concerned about an individual (Habakkuk) in the course of history.
4. History cannot be rightly interpreted until all the data is in.

We have but a partial picture from a limited perspective. We need to wait till the whole show is over. All the data is not in. Time is involved. God is working, indirectly behind the scenes and directly through His people.

Closure

We should see at least three things from this little book of Habakkuk.

1. It is difficult for God's people to acquire *Left Hand sensitivity*.

2. We must learn to embrace with joy, *God's Left Hand work*.

3. We must trust God and believe He is working His purposes, whether or not we understand what He is doing.

Habakkuk did all three of these things. It took a paradigm shift for him to see and finally agree with what God was doing. But his final response is what we as leaders need today. Habakkuk took joy in God's working. And we can be bolstered by God's basic answer (before His detailed explanation):

The Just Shall Live By Faith.

---

[66] One of Habakkuk's problems was the ungodly nation of Babylon. They abused their power. Habakkuk agreed with God's description of the Babylonian army. That was the problem. Just because a nation has power to do what it wants does not justify its doing what it wants. See also verse 11. Verses 8,9 point out that the Babylonians had military power. Though Babylon was being used by God, nevertheless they would be held accountable for their abuses. See the five woes of chapter 2 of Habakkuk. And the five woes of chapter 2 satisfied Habakkuk that God was indeed working to bring justice.

21. Habakkuk, Left Hand of God

These great faith words are foundational for us. We must live by trusting God whether or not we understand all that is going on. We live in ever increasingly complex leadership situations. We may not understand God's complex workings in history to accomplish His purposes. We may or may not have *Left Hand sensitivity*. God may or may not reveal what His *Left Hand Work* is. But we must always hang on to those important faith words.

Article 22

22. Habakkuk, Regaining Hope Via a God-Ordained Paradigm Shift

Introduction
Now listen to these words from Hebrews 11,

1 Now faith is the substance of things hoped for, the evidence of things not seen.

Relate these words to two important macro lessons.

What is a macro lesson?[67] A <u>macro-lesson</u> is a high level generalization of a leadership observation (suggestion, guideline, requirement), stated as a lesson, which repeatedly occurs throughout different leadership eras, and thus has potential as a leadership absolute. Macro lessons even at their weakest provide strong guidelines describing leadership insights. At their strongest they are requirements, or absolutes, that leaders should follow. Leaders ignore them to their detriment. The *faith macro lesson,* given below and first seen in Abraham's leadership in the Patricarchal Leadership Era, is an important insight that all leaders need to know. The *hope macro lesson,* first seen in Moses' leadership in the Pre-Kingdom Leadership Era, is what I am stressing in this article.

6. Faith Macro Lesson
Biblical Leaders must learn to trust in the unseen God, sense His presence, sense His revelation, and follow Him by faith.

12. Hope Macro Lesson
A primary function of all leadership is to inspire followers with hope in God and in what God is doing.

I contend that leaders today, in the Church Leadership Era, like Habbakkuk, years ago in the Kingdom Leadership Era, need both of these macro lessons in their lives. And not just head knowledge but experiential knowledge. Hope and Faith are linked. And frequently, it will take a paradigm shift directed by a God intervention to get these macro lessons.

Three Books Demonstrating the Importance of the Hope Macro Lesson
Three books in the Bible deal with God's working individually with leaders and not their ministry. Each of these prominently deal with a major paradigm shift needed in a

---

[67] 41 Macro Lessons have been identified. The numbers below, 6 and 12, refer the to the list of macro lessons as given in the following articles. See **Articles**, 29. *Macro Lessons—Defined;* 30. *Macro Lessons: List of 41 Across Six Leadership Eras.*

22. Habakkuk, Regaining Hope Via a God-Ordained Paradigm Shift

leader's life. These three are Job, Jonah, and Habakkuk. A fourth book containing both God's working individually with a leader and dealing with his ministry demonstrates the hope lesson powerfully. That is the book of Daniel. All four of these books show the importance of the hope macro lesson.

All four books also show that hope is most needed in desperate situations. Table Hab Hab 22-1 shows some commonalities across these 4 books.

Table Hab Hab 22-1. Hope Macro Lesson And Related Information

Leader	Need/Paradigm Shift	How Hope Seen
Job	Job is having tremendous physical problems and loss of finances. The prevailing paradigm at that time was that the righteous are rewarded and sinners punished. Job knew his situation did not fit that paradigm but did not know how to handle it. God gave a new paradigm.	Job comes out of a very difficult time with his faith in God vindicated. He goes deep with God during the deep processing. God gives hope to us all that we can trust Him even in difficult personal situations. One way a leader demonstrates hope is by a personal testimony of meeting with God and knowing God and God's ways. Job does this.
Jonah	Jonah does not want to preach God's prophetic message to the Ninevites because he actually wants God to bring judgment upon them. God providentially forces Jonah through a paradigm shift which allows him to see God's perspective on the Ninevites.	We have the book of Jonah, which shows that Jonah actually went through the paradigm shift, agreeing with God's desire to reach out to the nations, of which Assyria is typical. Jonah gives us hope. For we know God will use all of us to further His program for the world. One way a leader demonstrates hope is by a personal testimony of meeting with God and knowing God and God's ways. Jonah does this.
Habakkuk	Habakkuk needs to know that God is real and doing something about the evil he sees going on around him. God breaks through and reveals what He is doing. Time is involved.	One way a leader demonstrates hope is by a personal testimony of meeting with God and knowing God and God's ways. Habakkuk does this. He gets God's perspective on his situation. And he accepts it and gives a joyous testimony about it, though what he hears is potentially very painful news.
Daniel	Daniel lived in a most hopeless time. The program of God through the remnant nation of Judah had come to a screeching halt. Jerusalem was destroyed. Many had been taken away captive by Babylon. Daniel was one of those exiles. He needed to know God's perspective.	Daniel got God's perspective in varied ways. God's perspective was long term. Yet it encouraged Daniel. Daniel models how trusting God in a desperate time can be done. This kind of trust in a time when trusting God looks hopeless inspires hope for people today.

Habakkuk's Paradigm Shift[68]

Let me first define a paradigm and a paradigm shift.

---

[68] See **Article**, *32. Paradigms and Paradigm Shifts.*

22. Habakkuk, Regaining Hope Via a God-Ordained Paradigm Shift

Definition   A <u>paradigm</u> is a controlling perspective (symbolized by r) which allows one to perceive and understand **REALITY** ((symbolized by R).

Definition   A <u>paradigm shift</u> is the change of a controlling perspective and the perceptive result of that change (little **r**) so that one perceives (new little **r'**) and understands **REALITY** in a different way.

Essentially, then as we have described it a paradigm shift occurs by a changed little **r**, one's perception of reality, which in effect allows us to see more of **R** (absolute reality) or at least some different aspect of it.

Habakkuk goes through the following paradigm shift and his perception of reality is radically altered.

Before—God is unjust and unfaithful in His dealing with groups of people in history. He does not keep His promises.

Afterwards— God is just. He is complex in His dealings with nations. Ultimately His purposes and justice will be seen by all.

And notice the hope this gave Habakkuk. He begins in chapter 1 in despair, Habakkuk cries out in his prayer to God in chapter 1 verse 2,

How long?

He is referring to the need for God to stop the wicked practices going on in the southern kingdom. He is wanting justice. And he is beginning to doubt God's reality.

But notice how he ends up, after going through the paradigm shift. Here is Habakkuk's final fearful and joyful response to God's meeting him as seen in his closing passage in Chapter 3.

16 I hear your message, and I am **weak with fear**,
My lips **quiver fearfully**.
My bones **feel like they are giving way**.
I **stumble as I walk**.
I will quietly wait for the day of judgment,
When disaster will come upon the people who invade us.

17 Though the **fig tree quits blossoming**,
There is no **fruit on the vines**,
The **olive trees do not produce**,
The **fields yield no food**,
The **flock be cut off from the fold**,
And there be **no herd in the stalls**,
18 Yet I will rejoice[69] in Jehovah,
I will joy in the God of my salvation.

---

[69] *Yet I will rejoice* translates one Hebrew word (SRN 05937). That word carries with it the sense of rejoicing but also of exulting and doing so triumphantly. Note, Habakkuk's triumphant rejoicing is not in the circumstances but in God: Jehovah the eternal one (SRN 3068); Elohim—the God who delivers (SRN 0430; 03468); Jehovah Master (Adonai) (SRN 3068; SRN 0136). A leader's view of God is the most important thing about that leader. Habakkuk now has a good view of God.

22. Habakkuk, Regaining Hope Via a God-Ordained Paradigm Shift

19 <u>Jehovah, the Master, is my strength</u>.
   He makes my feet <u>like hinds' feet</u>.
   He makes me <u>tread upon my high places</u>.

To the choirmaster: with stringed instrument.

Does Habakkuk sound hopeful? I think so. He is a changed man. He has regained hope via a God-ordained paradigm shift.

Hope and Inspirational Leadership

Figure Hab 22-1 below, groups leadership functions into three generic categories: task oriented leadership, relational oriented leadership, and inspirational leadership.[70]

Three High Level Leadership Functions
include

Task-Oriented Leadership   Relational-Oriented Leadership   Inspirational Leadership

Figure Hab 22-1. Three High Level Leadership Functions

All need to happen. And the third function, inspirational leadership, is crucial. The hope macro is at the very heart of inspirational leadership.

> **12. Hope Macro Lesson**
> **A primary function of all leadership is to inspire followers with hope in God and in what God is doing.**

Habakkuk did that for all the followers who had access to his testimony. And Habakkuk does that for us today as we read his story in the Old Testament.

Generational Need

I have ministered mainly to a generation of leaders, called the boomers. Only in very recent years has my ministry faced the generation, called busters or Xers. These are very different generations in terms of how they view the world around them. Boomers see the world as offering opportunity and success. Xers see it as hopeless. I contend that as leaders, we must present the messages of Job, Jonah, Habakkuk and Daniel to the emerging leaders from this Xer generation. All of these leaders ministered in rather hopeless situations. But God brought paradigm shifts for each of them and perspectives which brought hope.

Closure

Habakkuk has demonstrated that hope can come through a God-ordained paradigm shift. It can be true for any leader today as well. Our responsibility, is to grasp these words,

> **1 Now faith is the substance of things hoped for, the evidence of things not seen.**

---

[70] See **Article**, 27. *Leadership Functions, 3 High Level Generic Properties.*

And then to learn affectively, cognitively, conatively, and experientially these two important macro lessons.

6. Faith Macro Lesson
Biblical Leaders must learn to trust in the unseen God, sense His presence, sense His revelation, and follow Him by faith.

12. Hope Macro Lesson
A primary function of all leadership is to inspire followers with hope in God and in what God is doing.

May it be so!

Article 23

23. Hebrew Poetry

Introduction

Perhaps your feeling concerning *Hebrew Poetry* can be expressed in these words, "Why bother?" or "Is it really necessary to study *Hebrew Poetry?*" You might think that there is little need for such knowledge. It might help you to pick up a **New English Bible** and to flip through the pages of the Old Testament. As you do, notice how much of the Old Testament is in the format of **Hebrew Poetry**. It is printed in a form so that it can be easily recognized at a glance. Unless I missed my count some 528 pages out of 1499 contain *Hebrew Poetry*. In many cases the entire page is *Hebrew Poetry*. Yes, *Hebrew Poetry* is important. And for Habakkuk it certainly is important. For the whole book is in *Hebrew Poetry*.

Understanding *Hebrew Poetry* requires some appreciation of its structure. *Hebrew Poetry* is not like *English Poetry*. To our ears there is a special beauty in *English Poetry* associated with the rhyme and rhythm of the words. The beauty in the words and rhythm help us feel emotionally the beauty described. Although *Hebrew Poetry* does have some emphasis on rhyming and rhythm, its essential beauty lies in a *balance of thought* rather than a balance of rhyme or rhythm. *Hebrew Poetry* contains a logical rhythm, which overshadows its metrical rhythm. PARALLELISM is the name usually given to describe the balance of thought seen in Hebrew Poetry.

Hebrew Poetry expresses one thought and then follows it with another parallel thought. The two thoughts are intimately related. Discovering the relationships between the thoughts is the key to grasping the meaning of *Hebrew Poetry*. When one begins to get used to this form of expression—parallel thought relationships—he/she soon sees a deeper beauty even than that felt in the rhyme and rhythm of *English Poetry*.

Hebrew Poetry like all poetry is the language of the heart. One must learn to become sensitive to it. Recognize that it deeply moved its author. It should move your heart as well as your mind. And remember, the author took special pains to communicate what he was feeling. Such is the case with Habakkuk. This was a crucial time in his life. His meeting with God, hearing God's answer, and responding to it were deeply moving to him. That is why he took the time to put it in *Hebrew Poetry*. He also wanted to use some of it in public worship—to be sung.

Some Values in Hebrew Poetry

1. Clarification of meaning.

One of the parallel phrases may explain the other phrase using other words so that the meaning is seen more clearly. I have identified several Hebrew Idioms because the parallel phrase explained them.

23. Hebrew Poetry

2. Recognition of the Deep Heart Intent Being Communicated
It is not just cognitive information that is being transmitted. The author wants you to know that he is shooting for *affect impact* as well. He has taken the time to clothe his message in a passionate form meant to move the heart.

3. Overall Thematic Intent of Extended Parallelism
By using the analysis method of reduction one can rather easily identify the overall intent of a stanza or several stanzas.

4. Most Public Worship Songs Were Hebrew Poetry Put To Music
Leaders need to inspire celebration. It is amazing to me to see just how many leaders in the Bible wrote music for public celebration. *Hebrew Poetry* was the medium.

Three Kinds of Parallelism
When analyzing couplets, that is, two lines of parallelism, I use a simplified classification of three types.

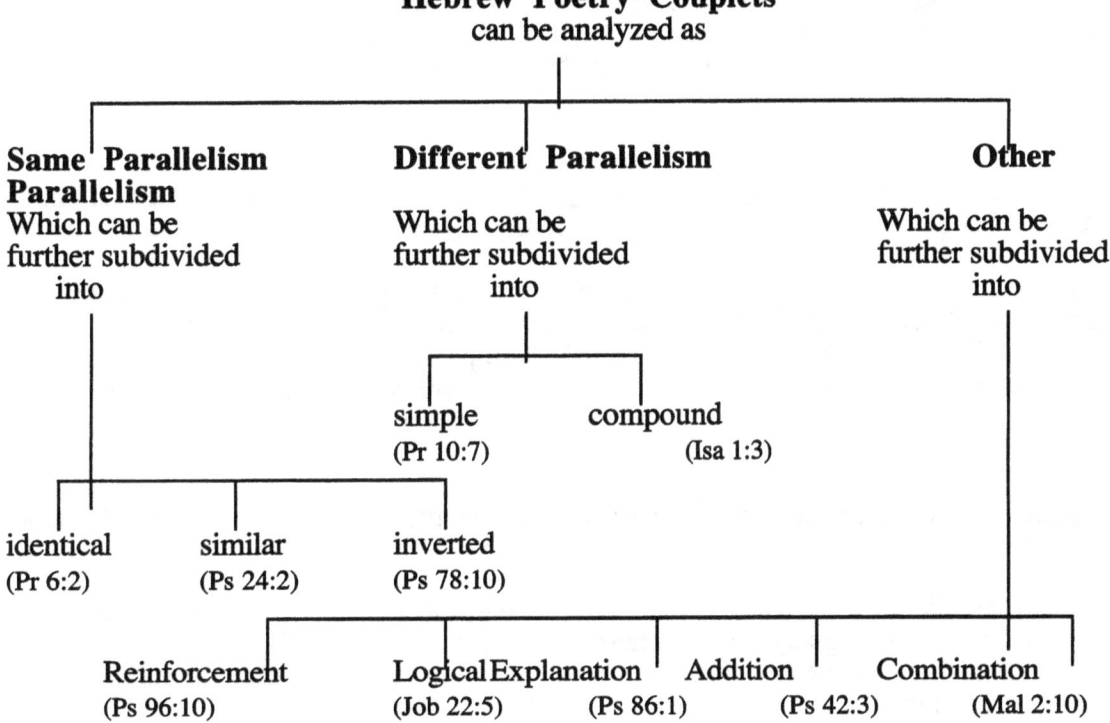

Figure Hab 23-1 Tree Diagram Giving Overview of 3 Types of Parallelisms

23. Hebrew Poetry

Some Basic Definitions of Hebrew Poetry

The basic pattern of *Hebrew Poetry* is the placing of thoughts one right after the other in which basic relationships are expressed between the thoughts or portions of the thoughts.

Definition

<u>Hebrew Poetry</u> is a way of expressing relationships between parallel thoughts in an emotional language. Usually it is the repetition of phrases in which member of one phrase relate to the members of the other phrase.

Definition

<u>Same parallelism</u> refers to the type of *Hebrew Poetry* in which members of one phrase relate to members of the parallel phrase in basically the same way.

The technical word describing same parallelism is *synonymous parallelism*. Terry[71] identifies 3 kinds of synonymous parallelism: (1) identical (when the different members are composed of the same or nearly the same words); (2) similar (when the language and figures differ slightly but the sentiment or intent of members is the same; (3) inverted (where the members are the same in intent or thought though the order of occurrence is not the same in the parallel phrases).

Definition

Hebrew Poetry is said to be <u>different parallelism</u> when one or more members of one phrase is in different correspondence with its related member of the parallel.

Different is here meant to broadly include contrast, or opposite, or unlike manner. The technical name describing different parallelism is *antithetic parallelism*. Terry[72] distinguishes 2 kinds of antithetic parallelism: (1) simple, where contrast occurs in one or more members of a simple couplet); (2) compound, where two or more phrases are contrasted.

Definition

<u>Other parallelism</u> relates to the broad classification of *Hebrew Poetry* not specifically same or different.

The two parallel phrases relate to each other in a number of ways. This is my catch-all category. In technical language each of these is given its own name. I prefer to simply recognize all of these as one category and try to explain in my own words the relationship I see between the phrases.

Here are some of the ways that *Other Parallelism* phrases relate to one anther:

- **Reinforcement**—one phrase reinforces the other through:
  -example;
  -figurative illustration;
  -non-figurative pictorial illustration.

- **Logical**—one phrase relates to the other by:
  -answering a question;
  -posing a question;
  -giving a reason why;

---

[71] See p. 96 Milton S. Terry, **Biblical Hermeneutics**.
[72] See p. 97 Milton S. Terry, **Biblical Hermeneutics**.

23. Hebrew Poetry

-drawing an implication;
-stating a conclusion;
-demanding an application.

- **Explanation**—one phrases clarifies the other by:
  -explaining something in particular about the entire phrase;
  -explaining what is meant in detail about one member of the phrase.

- **Addition**—one phrase introduces new thoughts:
  -adds an entire new thought—perhaps part of a buildup or progressive series of thoughts;
  -adds a new member which has no corresponding member in the other phrase.

- **Combination**—some combination of reinforcement, logical, explanation, or addition often occurs, that is, a given phrase may function in more than one way.

Habakkuk and Extended Parallelism—Some Basic Definitions

In Proverbs, from chapter 15 onwards, the *Hebrew Poetry* is frequently given in simple couplets. But in most of the *Hebrew Poetry* in the Old Testament, the couplets are combined into larger units. That is, couplets are grouped into stanzas. Not only is there parallelism between phrases in a couplet but there are also relationships between couplets. I call these stanza-like instances of *Hebrew Poetry*, extended parallelism. Habakkuk is entirely made up of extended parallelism.

Definition
Extended parallelism describes any unit of *Hebrew Poetry* larger than a couplet in which three or more phrases are placed in parallel. There exits the possibility of thought relationships between any of the phrases in parallel.

A helpful practice in analyzing extended parallelism is to reduce couplets to one line of emphatic meaning. Then extended relationships between lines often become more evident.

Definition
A reduction statement (sometimes shortened to reduction) is a one line summary statement representing the emphatic meaning of the couplet.

To be able to state concisely yet comprehensively what a whole stanza is saying is the object of a summary. One carefully observes analysis of reductions, lines, and connectors and then condenses what is seen into a comprehensive statement.

Definition
A summary statement is a condensed statement of the entire poetic unit. It consists of the subject of the unit and each major idea developed about the subject.

Definition
A connector word(s) is a word(s) such as *but, and, nevertheless*, which connects two phrases or two couplets or a line with a couplet and serves to help interpret the relationships between the things connected.

Definition
A connector phrase is a phrase placed between reduction statements or lines (inserted by the interpreter) to indicate the flow of thought in the extended parallelism.

23. Hebrew Poetry

Analysis Procedure

Table Hab 23-1 gives the basic procedure for analyzing extended *Hebrew Poetry*.

Table Hab 23-1. Basic Procedure—Analyzing Extended Hebrew Poetry

Step	Procedure	Details
1	**REDUCTION ANALYSIS** Recognize and analyze extended parallelism.	1. Identify the stanza to be analyzed. 2. Identify and label lines. 3. Identify and label the couplets. 4. Note all correspondences. 5. Form reductions for all couplets. 6. Analyze extended relationship between reductions, lines, and sub-units. 7. Insert connector words and phrases to bring out interpretive meaning.
2	**FLOW OF THOUGHT ANALYSIS** Interpret your reduction analysis.	1. From each extended sub-unit within a stanza conclude a major idea. 2. Determine a general subject to which all major ideas relate. 3. Condense subject and major ideas into a summary statement.

Some Examples From Habakkuk—Opening Stanza Chapter 1

Habakkuk Speaks—Are You There, O God

Line 1	2	O Jehovah, how long shall I beg for your help, When will you listen?
Line 2		I cry out unto you about violence, And you will not deliver.
Line 3	3	Why do you tolerate the iniquity I see,
Line 4		And cause me to experience such injustice?
Line 5		For destruction and violence are before me,
Line 6		And there is strife,
Line 7		And criminal activity all about.
Line 8	4	Therefore, the law is not enforced,
Line 9		And justice does not happen.
Line 10		For evil people outnumber the righteous.
Line 11		Therefore justice is distorted.

Lines 1 and 2 illustrate a *Same* relationship.

Reduction statement 1: I repeatedly ask for your intervention but you do not answer my prayers.

Lines 3 and 4 illustrate an *Other* relationship

The second phrase pinpoints the iniquity mentioned in the first phrase—it is sin that relates to injustice.

Reduction statement 2: I question your character since this sin results in injustice.

Lines 5, 6, and 7 go together to illustrate an *Other* relationship. Lines 6 and 7 build on or reinforce in a build-up manner line 5.

Reduction statement 3: Destruction, violence, strife and criminal activity abound.

23. Hebrew Poetry

Lines 8 and 9 illustrate a *Same* relationship.

Reduction statement 4: Not enforcing the law results in injustice.

Lines 10 and 11 illustrate an *Other* relationship. Line 10 explains why Line 11 happens.

Reduction statement 5: Justice does not exist since non-righteous people outnumber and influence what is happening.

Relating the reduction statements and supplying connector words looks like the following.

Reduction statement 1 WHICH CAUSES ME Reduction statement 2.
AND HERE IS WHY I SAY THAT
Reduction statement 3 RESULTING IN Reduction statement 4.
WITH THE FINAL RESULT OF Reduction statement 5.

I repeatedly ask for your intervention but you do not answer my prayers.
WHICH CAUSES ME
To question your character since this sin results in injustice.
AND HERE IS WHY I SAY THAT
Destruction, violence, strife and criminal activity abound.
RESULTING IN
Not enforcing the law and hence in injustice.
WITH THE FINAL RESULT OF
Justice does not exist since non-righteous people outnumber and influence what is happening.

Summary Statement for Stanza: God's failure to intervene in Habakkuk's situation allows sinful activities to abound and injustice prevail and non-righteous people to unduly influence the times.

Frequently, there is difficulty in getting exact identification of lines. Analysis is not an exact science. A lot of artistic license in taken by poets. But the basic procedure described above does usually work. And the most important thing is to derive the meaning, whether or not you can identify and label all the relationships exactly.

Illustration From Habakkuk—Value 2. Recognition of the Deep Heart Intent Being Communicated

Habakkuk faces a most crucial moment in his life. Is God real? If so, why doesn't He intervene in our situation. Criminal activity is all around. It is condoned by the system. If God is holy and just, why doesn't He do something. And so Habakkuk honestly questions God. God's character is at stake. And God answers this honest sincere intent by Habakkuk to understand God and God's actions. The final joyous surrender that Habakkuk gives and commits to music to be celebrated in public worship is one of the highlight testimonies in all of scripture. I close with it and then give a few comments on it. But it is not the understanding of the cognitive concepts that is in view here. In fact, I will not interpret it. I will just let you read and feel it. It is feeling with Habakkuk what this revelation from God means that is in view. It is seeing the response of Habakkuk. It is the Old Testament equivalent of Paul's testimony in Philippians. Joy does not have to be determined by our circumstances. Knowing God and trusting God can bring joy, no matter what the circumstances.

23. Hebrew Poetry

Habakkuk's final fearful and joyful response to God's meeting him.

16 I hear your message, and I am weak with fear,
    My lips quiver fearfully.
    My bones feel like they are giving way.
    I stumble as I walk.
    I will quietly wait for the day of judgment,
    When disaster will come upon the people who invade us.

17 Though the fig tree quits blossoming,
    There is no fruit on the vines,
    The olive trees do not produce,
    The fields yield no food,
    The flock be cut off from the fold,
    And there be no herd in the stalls,
18 Yet I will rejoice[73] in Jehovah,
    I will joy in the God of my salvation.
19 Jehovah, the Master, is my strength.
    He makes my feet like hinds' feet.
    He makes me tread upon my high places.

To the choirmaster: with stringed instrument.

Closure

    This whole critical incident in Habakkuk's life exemplifies how God shapes a leader. God did not do this in Habakkuk's life just for Habakkuk alone. And what is true of Habakkuk is true of leader's today. God's work in our lives does shape us and is crucial. But it is not only for us but for others also. Habakkuk was transparent. He shared what happened in his life knowing that it would encourage others. He exemplifies what a response should be to God's solution—the just shall live by faith. And Habakkuk joyfully accepted that solution. He did trust God. He believed God would deliver (God of my salvation). He did believe God would bring justice and reveal Himself someday to the whole earth. He did believe that God's character would be vindicated. And note the meaning of the beautiful simile he closes with—God will guide me step-by-step as I face each of the difficult moments, which will come.

    That should be the cry of leaders today. We must trust the unseen God. We can joyfully trust Him. And we can know that He will guide us step-by-step in the complexities of each difficult moment.

---

[73] *Yet I will rejoice* translates one Hebrew word (SRN 05937). That word carries with it the sense of rejoicing but also of exulting and doing so triumphantly. Note, Habakkuk's triumphant rejoicing is not in the circumstances but in God: Jehovah the eternal one (SRN 3068); Elohim—the God who delivers (SRN 0430; 03468); Jehovah Master (Adonai) (SRN 3068; SRN 0136). A leader's view of God is the most important thing about that leader. Habakkuk now has a good view of God.

Article 24

24. Isolation Processing —Learning Deep Lessons from God

Introduction

Leaders get set aside from ministry. Isolation is the term used to describe this process. Sometimes the leader is directly set aside by God, sometimes by others, sometimes by self. Whatever the case, isolation results in deep processing in the life of a leader. More than 90% of leaders will face one or more important isolation times in their lives. Most do not negotiate these times very well. Knowing about them and what God can accomplish in them can be a great help to a leader who then faces isolation.

Defining and Describing Isolation

What is isolation?

Definition   Isolation processing refers to the setting aside of a leader from normal ministry or leadership involvement due to involuntary causes, partially self-caused or voluntary causes for a period of time sufficient enough to cause and/or allow serious evaluation of life and ministry.

Some notable Biblical examples include Job, Joseph, Moses, Jonah, Elijah, Habakkuk, Jesus, Paul.

Usually this means the leader is away from his/her natural context usually for an extended time in order to experience God in a new or deeper way. Sometimes isolation can occur in the ministry context itself.

Isolation experiences can be short—like intensive time spent away in solitude to meet God. Or it can last up to several months and occasionally more than a year. Figure Hab 24-1 describes isolation in terms of three major categories.

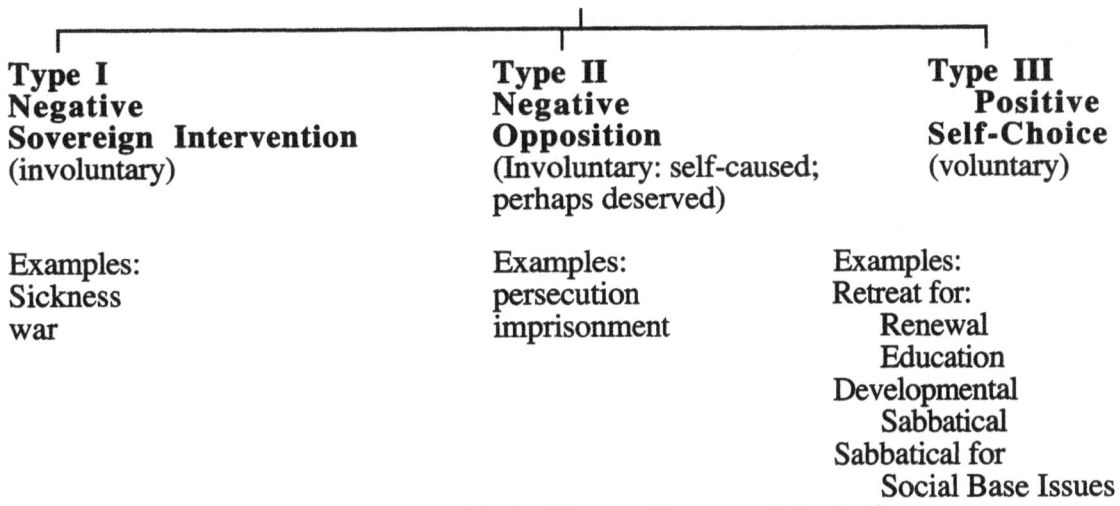

Figure Hab 24-1. Three Types of Isolations

24. Isolation Processing—Learning Deep Lessons from God

These isolation experiences can be viewed in terms of perceived intervention of God in them. Figure Hab 24-2 gives a continuum correlating the isolation experiences to a leader's understanding of God's place in them.

Clear—Divine Intervention		Less clear—Providential
TYPE I	**TYPE II**	**TYPE III**
• sickness	• personality conflicts	• self-choice renewal
	• prison	• organizational issues
	• persecution	• self-choice development
		• ministry issues
		• artificial, short intensive
		• self-choice for social base

Figure Hab 24-2. Isolation Sovereignty Continuum

Table Hab 24-1 gives results observed in comparative studies of leaders in isolation.

Table Hab 24-1. Isolation Results

Isolation Type	Results or Uses of Isolation
I. Negative/ Sovereign Intervention	lessons of brokenness; learning about supernatural healing; lessons about prayer; deepening of inner life; an intensified sense of urgency to accomplish; developing of mental facilities; submission to God; dependence upon God.
II. Negative/ Opposition	lessons of brokenness; submission to spiritual authority; value of other perspectives; dependence upon God
III. Positive/ Self-choice	new perspective on self and ministry; rekindling of sense of destiny; guidance; oneself to change; upon wider body of Christ

Overlapping Features in Many Isolation Experiences

Table Hab 24-2 lists some common things that happen to leaders in isolation.

Table Hab 24-2. Common Happenings in Isolation

Isolation	Some Happenings
I or II	1. Sense of Rejection
I or II	2. Sense of stripping away--getting down to core issues
I, II or III	3. Eventually a deep need for God
I, II or III	4. Searching for God
I, II, or III	5. Submission to God
I, II, or III	6. Dependence upon God
I, II, or III	7. Rekindling of desire to serve God in a deeper way

24. Isolation Processing—Learning Deep Lessons from God

Bible Characters and Isolation Lessons From Their Lives

Job, Moses, Elijah, and Paul provide some important isolation lessons. See the Tables, which follow listing each of these Bible Characters and observations about isolation.

Job

Job faced sickness, loss of life, loss of wealth, loss of friends, and loss of status as an important person. Table Hab 24-3 suggests some things that can be learned from Job's Type I isolation experience.

Table Hab 24-3. Job and Type I Isolation

Step	Explanation
1.	**Begin With The End In Mind** (need a framework/ perspective). In isolation, deep-seated ideas are challenged in such a way as to capture our attention and force us to come to essential values. Maybe it is only in isolation that they could be challenged. But know that isolation will end and God will teach lessons even about deep-seated ideas.
2.	**Analyze From The Known To The Unknown.** Apart from unusual revelation, we can only search out answers in terms of what we know. That is, the first step in the isolation process— search out what is happening in terms of what you do know (e.g. paradigms).
3.	**Recognize That The Unknown Can Serve Two Functions.** When anomalies arise we must recognize that they may not really be anomalies and will be cleared up in the end (in which case it is a matter of faith and waiting), or they are real and will force us into new paradigms.
4.	Expect God's Intervention. **God may give insight if a new paradigm is needed or may require a faith response.**
5.	**Believe In God's On-Going Answer.** The book of Job shows us that God is in charge of our individual processing—no matter how or through whom it may come, even including Satanic origin. We do not have all the answers. He does. We must trust Him in them.

Moses

In Ex 2:11-15, there is an incident in which Moses kills an Egyptian and then flees (He 11:23-28 and Ac 7:23 give an interpretation of this). Then in Ex 3:7 and following, God calls Moses to a major task, the very one he had tried on his own and given up. There is a major difference in the Moses of Ex 2 and the Moses of Ex 3. Nu 12:3 describes it. Something happened. I want to suggest that it was a brokenness[74] experience. And that brokenness experience was part of isolation processing for Moses.

Moses experienced this Type II isolation processing. It included aspects of geographical and cultural isolation. Three characteristics of geographic and cultural isolation include: 1. It is more powerful in its early effects; wears off with time and as assimilation occurs. (This is seen also in the life of Daniel.) 2. In Geographic/ cultural isolation there is a loss of self-esteem. The things you were and value in the old culture are usually not so respected and valued in the new. 3. There is often a loss of momentum and vision.

Table Hab 24-4. Moses and Type II Isolation

Lesson	Explanation/ Generalized
1	**Look for leadership committal processing as a means toward ending isolation.** Often isolation involves and may terminate with God's

---

[74] See *brokenness*, **Glossary**.

24. Isolation Processing—Learning Deep Lessons from God

	renewal of call. See *progressive calling;* **Glossary**.
2	**God has to sometimes take a vision away in order to later accomplish that vision in his way.** Keep an open hand to plans, visions, future work.
3	**Humility is often the fruit of isolation processing--an unhealthy egotism is broken.** God can unleash great power through a broken/ humble leader without fear of that leader abusing the power.

Elijah

Elijah had two impactful isolation experiences. The first was a Type I, clearly God directed. The second was a Type II. I do not think Elijah ever fully recovered from the second experience. Table Hab 24-5 gives some observations about the Type I experience. Table Hab 24-6 gives the Type II isolation experience which arose due to persecution.

Table Hab 24-5. Elijah's Type I Isolation Experience, 1Ki 17:1-6—Some Observations

Observation	Explained
1	Isolation was God-directed (vs 2,3)
2	Success brings problems (vs 7 brook dries up--he prayed for no rain)
3	God will provide in isolation (vs 4, 9, 14)
4	God protects in isolation (I Kings 18:10).

Elijah's Type II isolation experience was the fallout from one of the most successful ministry events recorded in the O. T. He has just seen God move mightily in a power encounter[75] with the prophets of Baal on top of Mount Carmel—a true mountain top experience. When he flees from persecution he moves into an isolation experience—again a mountain top experience—this time, Mount Sinai. Note that again as with the first experience, success brings with it problems.

Table Hab 24-6. Elijah's Type II Isolation Experience, 1Ki 19 —Persecution— Running For His Life

Observation	Explained
1. The Situation	Vs4 Desert Isolation— 1. Hope gone; despair; take my life, (vs 4,5) 2. Angel touches him--provision (vs 5,7) 3. Horeb--Mountain of God--40 days/ 40 nights); cave What are you doing? God shows up.
2. Notice the Steps	Step 1. The feelings: I alone/ stood up for God/ persecution Step 2. Presence of God—the antidote to the feelings. Step 3. God answers--not you alone (vs11), 7000 who have not bowed the
3. The Price To Pay	Power encounters can be costly--they drain away energy—After mountain- experiences expect attacks from Satan, evil forces; you may well crash hard in the valley. Elijah never again has a major ministry success?
4. Rejection/	In isolation there is a sense of personal rejection and a need for divine affirmation. Notice how God does this. **Small Still Voice**. Not the

---

[75] This is the classic power encounter which defines others. The steps of a *Power Encounter* include:
1. There is a confrontation between God and Evil. 2. The forces are recognized for that--the issues are who is more powerful and thus deserving of allegiance. 3. There is a public demonstration so that both forces can be seen by all as to who is more powerful. 4. God demonstrates publicly His power and defeats the evil forces so that there can be no doubt about to whom allegiance should be given. 5. Aftermath--God is glorified, evil forces are punished; there may be a response toward God. See *power encounter*, **Glossary**.

24. Isolation Processing—Learning Deep Lessons from God

God's Affirmation	spectacular like you might expect or hope for.
5. Leadership Selection	Elijah imparted power and authority to Elisha--one who was faithful, tenacious, wanted what Elijah had. He carried on Elijah's ministry with more power than Elijah. Elijah's isolation experiences brought spiritual authority. Emerging leaders are drawn to leaders with spiritual authority.

One of the most important things to see from Elijah's isolation experiences is that isolation is frequently accompanied by a sense of personal rejection. It is divine affirmation that we need. God will meet us--maybe not in the way we expect.

Paul

Paul had numerous isolation experiences. It is from his life that the concept of repeated isolation experiences occurring in a leader's life emerged. Five are worth noting—1) his short days in Damascus with Ananias, Ac 9; 2; 2) His 2 to 3 years in Arabia mentioned in Gal; 3) His short prison experience in Philippi seen in Ac 16:23; 4) His four years in Rome (during which Eph, Col, Phm, Php were written); 5) His short few months in Rome just before his death. Table Hab 24-7 suggests nine observations drawn from a comparative study of Paul's isolation experiences.

Table Hab 24-7. Nine Observations from Paul's Isolation Experiences

Isolation Experience	Description and Observations
Galatian Isolation 1. **Reflection**	Paul's Galatian/Arabia--Pre-Ministry isolation was a Type III self-choice isolation. It was a time of Reflection in which he worked out his Christology. Basic Principle: **Reflection is a major goal and means of processing during isolation.** Reflection will happen in isolation. Depending on the kind of isolation there will be questions. A seeking after something—time for thinking. (2Ti is especially filled with reflection; a looking back on a lifetime given to the Gospel.)
2. **Prison Isolation; Response Attitude**	A. In general, the following principle makes the difference in whether the isolation is profitable or not. **A sovereign mindset in processing makes the difference in immediate response and in long lasting results.** Attitude is everything. Notice Paul's attitude as reflected in: Eph 3:1; 4:1; Col 4:3,9,10; Phm 1; Php 1:12; 4:22. Paul saw a God-ordained purpose behind isolation. What does it mean to have a *sovereign mindset* in processing? It means to recognize that however the isolation may have come about—unjust determination, terrible circumstances, or whatever—you must recognize that God has an ultimate purposes in it: 1) to demonstrate the sufficiency of the supply of the Spirit of Christ, 2) to do specific things fitting the immediate situation, 3) to open up new thinking that could not have been possible, 4) to bring long-range productivity out of it (spiritual authority).
3. **Intense Focus**	**Critical issues come into focus during isolation processing.** Isolation forces one to focus usually first on why, causes of it, and then later on the purposes of it. And finally with a powerful concentration that allows for problem solving, new revelation to meet situations, and insights that could only come because of the situation.

24. Isolation Processing—Learning Deep Lessons from God

4. Evaluation— Divine Perspective	**Divine evaluation of character, leadership commitment, and perspective is in focus in isolation processing.** Frequently, what happens is a recognition that God is allowing you to search your life and ministry and evaluate it in light of the situation and often with resulting paradigm shifts that will affect your ministry philosophy and the rest of your life.
5. Deepened Relationship	**A deepened relationship with god is always a major goal of isolation processing.** Philippians, the last of the first set of prison epistles and the most positive upbeat of all of Paul's letter culminates four years of isolation which have been filled with crises. It is filled with the importance of union with Christ. Its message points out what can happen in isolation processing—a grasping of the sufficiency of Christ for life.
6. Basis for Long Range Productivity	**Long lasting productivity is often rooted in isolation processing.** The prison epistles may never have been written had Paul been on the go. But set aside, reflection time produced thinking in regard to his own personal sanctification intimacy with Christians (Php), church problems (Col), the nature of the church (Eph), the solving of a problematic social institution (Phm). But not just products, attitudes and ideas are born in isolation which may come to fruition down road. 1. Specific things—people touched, saved, advise given, etc. 2. Modeling—an intangible product 3. written achievements—one product of isolation.
7. The importance of praise	**Praise is a major weapon in isolation processing.** In external isolation you probably feel less like praising than almost anything else, yet it is at that juncture that praise is probably the most important faith challenge. See Php jail experience, Ac 16, and the tone of praise in all the prison epistles--most of the opening prayers carry that note of praise. Praise will release power, new perspective in isolation.
8. Short Isolation	**Life changing and ministry changing revelation may come even in a short isolation experience.** Moses, 40 days of isolation by self-choice (divine drawing); Paul in two different times (Ac 9, Ananias, Ac 16 Philippian jail experience)
9. Intensified Prayer	**Isolation processing often presses a person into intensified prayer burdens and efforts.**

   Let me summarize what we can see in Paul's isolation experiences. Such experiences will tell a leader whether or not that leader has a sovereign mindset. They will also force reflection and evaluation of one's self in relation to: God, truth, a ministry, the past, the future. Critical issues come into focus. Peripheral issues are seen for what they are. In normal times we worry about a lot of things--many peripheral and non-essential. But in isolation times we get down to basic issues: who we are, what we really know, where we are going, who God really is, what He wants from us, etc. A leader will deepen his/her relationship with God—because that is what really matters--more than our ministry, more than the problems around us. A leader may discover the importance of praise or see an intensified outpouring of prayer, or the roots for long range productivity in our lives.
   Knowing these things, so what? How can observing these principles in the life of Paul help us as we life schedule or as we work through a present isolation experience? How can we be proactive? Here are some suggestions:

24. Isolation Processing—Learning Deep Lessons from God

1. **Reflection**—If you are not a thinker or if you are a thinker but are confused in isolation, because you know that reflection is important, you should get with someone in the body of Christ who has either natural abilities of analytical skills, discernment, or spiritual gifts of exhortation, teaching, word of wisdom, word of knowledge and ask for help on getting an overall perspective on what the intent of God is in the isolation. In terms of mentor types, you need to get with a spiritual guide or mentor counselor.

2. **Response Attitude**—Acknowledge that God is in this isolation. By faith accept this and then move with a learning posture through it. I am going to learn great things from God. Others may be to blame but God is in it.

3. **Intense Focus**—Recognize that critical issues will be pointed out in the isolation processing.

4. **Divine Perspective Evaluation**—Do self-evaluation of your life and ministry. Some suggestions as to how to do this: Be alert to values. Expect new revelation. Know that paradigm shifts often occur in isolation.

5. **Deepened Relationship**—Spend time in intimacy disciplines with God; extended times of silence, solitude, prayer, Bible study, fasting.

Conclusion
Here are some final warnings and assurances about isolation.

1. **Expect it.** About 90% of leaders go through an isolation experience of Type I or II.
2. **Recognize that there will be a sense of rejection in it.** Because of this it is helpful to keep a log of your divine affirmation and ministry affirmation items. Review them alone with God and feel anew His acceptance.
3. **Determine beforehand to go deep with God.** He will take you into a place of more dependence, perhaps a place of intimacy that you could not have without this kind of processing.
4. **Know that God will indeed meet you in isolation** though at first He may appear remote. Do not try to move out of isolation on your own until God has met you. Otherwise, you may go through a repeated isolation experience.
5. **Know the uses of isolation** and seek to see and sense which of these God is working into your life.
6. For a Type III isolation experience **set goals** for personal growth that include dependence, intimacy, and a deeper walk with God.
7. **Talk to other Christians who have gone through deep processing.** They will give you perspective with a proper empathy.

As a leader you will face isolation. Will you meet God in it and see His purposes in it fulfilled? Remember, isolation processing comes to almost all leaders. Expect repeated isolation processing. It is needed throughout a lifetime. Don't forget, attitude is crucial. Perspective can make the difference—knowing what isolation does, that it does end, that it will accomplish many important things. If you sense you are plateauing then self-initiate an extended time of isolation—get help from mentor counselors and mentor spiritual guides.

Article 25

25. Leaders—Intercession Hints from Habakkuk

Introduction

In the small three chapter book of Habakkuk, the prophet Habakkuk is facing the crisis of his life. This crisis can make or break Habakkuk. How does he respond in this crisis—by praying? The entire book records Habakkuk's talking and listening to God about his crisis issues. The prayer goes back and forth. Here are the highlights of the dialog in my terse paraphrase.

<u>Habakkuk Speaks</u>.
Chapter 1:1-4
Are you there, O God? You don't seem to be taking care of the injustices I see.

<u>God Speaks.</u>
Chapter 1:5-11
I am doing something about this? I am raising up the Chaldeans to solve your problem.

<u>Habakkuk Speaks</u>
Chapter 1:12-2:1
I am waiting to hear what you will say to my accusation that your character won't let you do this.

<u>God speaks.</u>
Chapter 2:2b-20
What I am doing will happen. You need to trust me to work it out. But know I will also take care of punishing the Chaldeans. And I will be vindicated throughout the whole earth.

Habakkuk Sing His Response To God (A corporate celebration and prayer)
I am going to trust you and joyfully respond to the things that happen. You will enable me to do this.

Some Prayer Observations Seen in this Book of Prayer

I want to briefly comment on five observations about prayer that I see in this prayer book. Table Hab 25-1 below gives the brief statements.

Table Hab 25-1. 5 Prayer Observations Seen in Habakkuk

Observation	Topic	Statement
1.	Holiness	**A proper understanding of God's holiness causes one to have a burden to pray about social injustice.**

143

2.	Discerning Answers	God's answer to our prayers may be difficult to discern in our surrounding circumstances.
3.	Honesty in Prayer	A leader can be absolutely honest with God in prayer concerning how he/she feels or thinks.
4.	Dialogue	Prayer can be a dialogue in which the prayer talks and listens and God listens and speaks.
5.	Solitude	Listening for God's speaking in prayer may best be done in a time and place of solitude.

Brief Comments on Each Observation

Observation 1
A proper understanding of God's holiness causes one to have a burden to pray about social injustice.

Notice Habakkuk's words in chapter 1, verses 1-4.

2 O Jehovah, how long shall I beg for your help,
  When will you listen?
I cry out unto you about violence,
  And you will not deliver.

3 **Why do you tolerate the iniquity I see,**
     And cause me to experience such injustice?
  For destruction and violence are before me,
     And there is strife,
     And criminal activity all about.
4 Therefore, the law is not enforced,
     And justice does not happen.
     For evil people outnumber the righteous.
  Therefore justice is distorted.

Essentially what Habakkuk is seeing around him in his situation seems to contradict what he knows of God and God's ways. How can a holy God tolerate iniquity. Why doesn't God do something to bring about justice?

What Habakkuk does is to go to God in prayer about the situation. He honestly confronts God. He demonstrates a burden for seeing God (a holy God) deal with the sin and injustice around him.[76]

Observation 2
God's answer to our prayers may be difficult to discern in our surrounding circumstances.

---

[76] God did answer. I feel in this case, that if God had not answered, Habakkuk would have probably quit his ministry. However, sometimes God does not answer. How do we handle that?

25. Leaders, Intercession Hints from Habakkuk   page 145

When God answers Habakkuk, it is clear that He wants Habakkuk to listen and discern carefully.

5   Look among the nations; look very carefully,
    There is something that will astonish you,
  For I am doing something even as you speak,
    Which, you won't believe, even when told.
6   Consider: I am raising up the Babylonians,
    That ruthless and unruly nation,
    That marches all over the land,
    To possess homes and cities that are not theirs.

Three times in this short response, God tells Habakkuk to really listen and discern: look, look very carefully; consider. Apart from this revelatory information—Habakkuk would probably never have known that God was working in the emerging of the Babylonian empire. God tells Habakkuk that He is already working. It is clear from this astounding revelation that discerning answers to our prayers about complex situations can be hard to discern. We, like Habakkuk, will be forced to get God's revelatory word on current situations.

Observation 3
A leader can be absolutely honest with God in prayer concerning how he/she feels or thinks.

Notice again Habakkuk's words in chapter 1, verses 1-4.

2   O Jehovah, how long shall I beg for your help,
    When will you listen?
  I cry out unto you about violence,
    And you will not deliver.

3   **Why do you tolerate the iniquity I see,**
    And cause me to experience such injustice?
  For destruction and violence are before me,
    And there is strife,
    And criminal activity all about.
4   Therefore, the law is not enforced,
    And justice does not happen.
    For evil people outnumber the righteous.
  Therefore justice is distorted.

These are honest words. Habakkuk is accusing God of laxity in holiness; lack of intervention in a situation needing God's touch.

Look also at the following from Habakkuk 2. It sums up Habakkuk's accusative words towards God's use of the Babylonians (Hab 2:12-17).

2:1 I will doggedly set myself to wait for God's answer,
    And station myself on the watch tower,
    And watch carefully to perceive, what He will communicate to me.
    And then I will have an answer to my **complaint**.[77]

---

[77] Lines 3,4 seem to indicate that Habakkuk will persistently wait till he can **perceive what God is saying**. Habakkuk is hoping for some **restorative word** (answer SRN 07725) to his **complaint** (SRN

25. Leaders, Intercession Hints from Habakkuk

Habakkuk certainly demonstrates this prayer observation.

A leader can be absolutely honest with God in prayer concerning how he/she feels or thinks.

This prayer observation is seen repeatedly through a number of the Psalms. Being honest with God in our prayers is a major step forward to transparency and vulnerability—needed traits by leaders.

Observation 4
Prayer can be a dialogue in which the prayer talks and listens and God listens and speaks.

Habakkuk prays honestly to God. God answers Habakkuk with what He is doing. Habakkuk challenges this solution. God defends His plans and shows how he will bring justice, both in the situation Habakkuk is in presently and to the Babylonians as well. Habakkuk then talks to God about his awe inspiring interventions in the past. He also intercedes for mercy. And finally he tells God that he has heard and accepted God's revelation. This is a back and forth dialog in prayer. What it stresses to leaders today is the necessity to develop listening skills in one's prayer time. Disciplines of silence and listening must be cultivated in order to hear God's prayerful dialog.

Observation 5
Listening for God's speaking in prayer may best be done in a time and place of solitude.

Look again at the opening verses of chapter 2.

2:1 I will doggedly set myself to wait for God's answer,
And station myself on the watch tower,[78]
And watch carefully to perceive, what He will communicate to me.
And then I will have an answer to my **complaint**.

Habakkuk is seeking a place of solitude—a place where he can be alone and not distracted. He wants to hear God. Solitude is needed if a leader is to focus on God.

Closure

Now these observations are simple enough. But the real question is, do we have the outworking of these 5 observations in our life. Take a look at the five observations given below. Check on the continuum for each where you actually are with regard to using the observation in your own life.

0843) to God (the word complaint connotes rebuke—very honest expression toward God). How much time is involved in this is uncertain. But that Habakkuk is getting away from his normal way of life in order to especially hear from God is indicated.

[78] The sense of this stanza (the four lines of verse 1) seems to be that Habakkuk will isolate himself until he perceives God's reply to his complaint that God is unfair using the wicked Babylonians to bring about judgment on Judah. Lines 1 and 2 seem to indicate that Habakkuk will go into the outlying fields where observation towers were set up with sentries to watch for enemies attacking. Habakkuk is getting away from his normal way of life in order to especially hear from God is indicated.

25. Leaders, Intercession Hints from Habakkuk   page 147

Observation 1
My understanding of God's holiness causes me to have a burden to pray about social injustice.

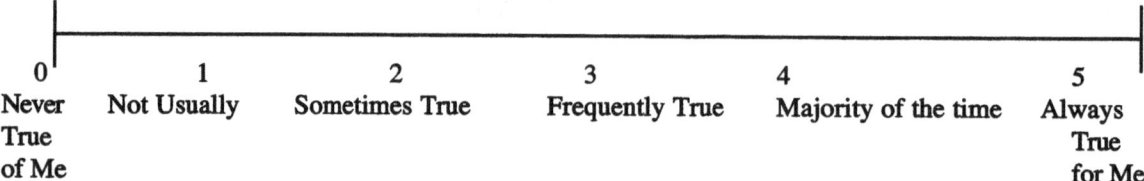

0	1	2	3	4	5
Never True of Me	Not Usually	Sometimes True	Frequently True	Majority of the time	Always True for Me

Observation 2
God's answer to my prayers is really difficult to discern in my complex situation.

0	1	2	3	4	5
Never True of Me	Not Usually	Sometimes True	Frequently True	Majority of the time	Always True for Me

Observation 3
I am absolutely honest with God in prayer concerning how I feel or think or otherwise see things.

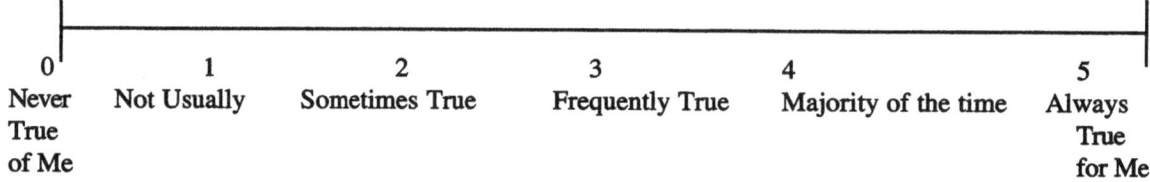

0	1	2	3	4	5
Never True of Me	Not Usually	Sometimes True	Frequently True	Majority of the time	Always True for Me

Observation 4
For me prayer is a dialogue in which God and I both talk and listen. I have developed my prayer listening skills to a high degree.

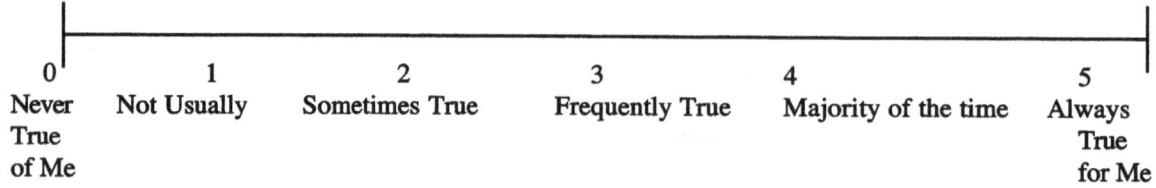

0	1	2	3	4	5
Never True of Me	Not Usually	Sometimes True	Frequently True	Majority of the time	Always True for Me

Observation 5
I have a regular time and a special place in which I practice solitude and my prayer listening skills.

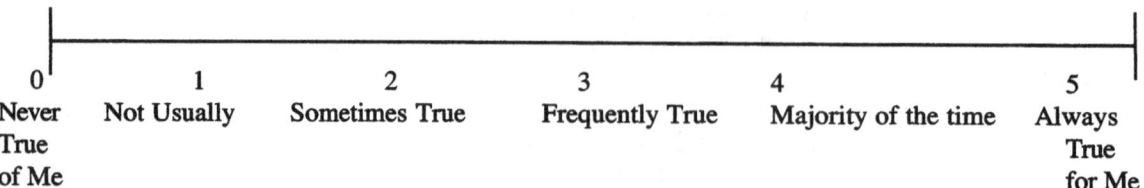

0	1	2	3	4	5
Never True of Me	Not Usually	Sometimes True	Frequently True	Majority of the time	Always True for Me

25. Leaders, Intercession Hints from Habakkuk

I am also modeling something in this article. When you study a Bible leader be sensitive to how that leader's prayer life is seen. Learn to draw out observations about a leader's prayer attitudes and habits. These leaders in the Bible can speak into our own lives, if we but have the eyes to see.

Article 26

26. Leadership Eras In The Bible, Six Identified

Introduction

A <u>Bible Centered leader</u> refers to a leader whose leadership is informed by the Bible, who has been personally shaped by Biblical values, has grasped the intent of Scriptural books and their content in such a way as to apply them to current situations and who uses the Bible in ministry so as to impact followers. Notice that first concept again—

whose leadership is informed by the Bible.

Two of the most helpful perspectives for becoming a Bible centered leader **whose leadership is informed by the Bible** include:

(1) recognizing the differences in leadership demands on leaders throughout the Bible, i.e. seeing the different leadership eras, and
(2) Recognizing and knowing how to draw out insights from the seven genre of leadership sources in the Bible.

This article overviews the first of these helpful perspective—seeing the leadership eras in the Bible.

The Six Leadership Eras

Let me start by giving you one of the most helpful perspectives, a first step toward getting leadership eyes, for recognizing leadership findings in the Bible. That first helpful perspective involves breaking down the leadership that takes place in the Bible into leadership eras which on the whole share common leadership assumptions and expectations for the time period. These assumptions and expectations differ from one leadership era to the next, though there are commonalties that bridge across the eras.

Definition   A <u>leadership era</u> is a period of time, usually several hundred years long, in which the major focus of leadership, the influence means, basic leadership functions, and followership have much in common and which basically change with time periods before or after it.

An outline of the six eras I have identified follows.

I. Patriarchal Era (Leadership Roots)—Family Base
II. Pre-Kingdom Leadership Era—Tribal Base
    A. The Desert Years
    B. The War Years--Conquering the Land,
    C. The Tribal Years/ Chaotic Years/ Decentralized Years--Conquered by the Land

26. Leadership Eras In The Bible, Six Identified   page 150

III. Kingdom Leadership Era—Nation Based
  A. The United Kingdom
  B. The Divided Kingdom
  C. The Single Kingdom--Southern Kingdom Only
IV. Post-Kingdom Leadership Era—Individual/ Remnant Based
  A. Exile--Individual Leadership Out of the Land
  B. Post Exilic--Leadership Back in the Land
  C. Interim--Between Testaments
V. New Testament Pre-Church Leadership—Spiritually Based in the Land
  A. Pre-Messianic
  B. Messianic
VI. New Testament Church Leadership—Decentralized Spiritually Based
  A. Jewish Era
  B. Gentile Era

I have used the following tree diagram[79] to provide an overview of leadership. The three overarching components of leadership include: the leadership basal elements (leader, follower, situation which make up the What of leadership); leadership influence means (individual and corporate leadership styles which make up the How of leadership); and leadership Value bases (Biblical and cultural values which make up the Why of leadership).

The Study Of Leadership
involves

Leadership Basal Elements	Leadership Influence Means	Leadership Value Bases
including	such as	including
• Leader	• Individual Means	• Cultural
• Followers	• Corporate Means	• Theological
• Situation	• Spiritual Means	

Figure Hab 26-1. Tree Diagram Categorizing the Basics of Leadership

It was this taxonomy which suggested questions that helped me see for the first time the six leadership eras of the Bible. Table 26-1 below gives the basic questions/subjects/categories that helped me identify the different leadership eras. It is these categories that allows comparison of different leadership periods in the Bible.

Table Hab 26-1. Basic Questions To Ask About Leadership Eras

1. **Major Focus**—Here we are looking at the overall purposes of leadership for the period in question. What was God doing or attempting to do through the leader? Sense of destiny? Leadership mandate?
2. **Influence means**—Here we are describing any of the power means available and used by the leaders in their leadership. We can use any of Wrong's categories or any of the leadership style categories I define. Note particularly in the Old Testament the use of force and manipulation as power means.

---

[79] This was derived in a research project, the historical study of leadership in the United States from the mid 18th century to the present—for further study see **A Short History of Leadership Theory**, 1986, by Dr. J. Robert Clinton. Altadena, CA: Barnabas Publishers. See **Further Study Bibliography**.

26. Leadership Eras In The Bible, Six Identified

3. **Basic leadership functions**—We list here the various achievement/responsibilities expected of the leaders: from God's standpoint, from the leader's own perception of leadership, from the followers. Usually they can all be categorized under the three major leadership functions of task, relational, and inspirational functions. But here we are after the specific functions.
4. **Followers**—Here we are after sphere of influence. Who are the followers? What are their relationship to leaders? Which of the 10 Commandments of followership are valid for these followers? What other things are helpful in describing followers?
5. **Local Leadership**—in the surrounding culture: Biblical leaders will be very much like the leaders in the cultures around them. Leadership styles will flow out of this cultural press. Here we are trying to identify leadership roles in the cultures in contact with our Biblical leaders.
6. **Other**—Miscellaneous catch all: such things as centralization or decentralization or hierarchical systems of leadership; joint (civil, political, military, religious) or separate roles.

   Thought Questions—Here try to synthesize the questions you would like answered about leaders and leadership if you could get those answers. We are dealing here with such things as the essence of a leader (being or doing), leadership itself, leadership selection and training, authority (centralized or decentralized), etc.

Using these leadership characteristics I studied leadership across the Bible and inductively generated the Six Leadership Eras as given above.[80] Table Hab 26-2 adds some descriptive elements of the eras.

Table Hab 26-2. Six Leadership Eras in the Bible—Brief Characterizations

Leadership Era	Example(s) of Leader	Definitive Characteristics
1. Foundational (also called patriarchal)	Abraham, Joseph	Family Leadership/ formally male dominated/ expanding into tribes and clans as families grew/ moves along kin ship lines
2. Pre-Kingdom	Moses, Joshua, Judges	Tribal Leadership/ Moving to National/ Military/ Spiritual Authority/ outside the land moving toward a centralized national leadership
3. Kingdom	David, Hezekiah	National Leadership/ Kingdom Structure/ Civil, Military/ Spiritual/ a national leadership—Prophetic call for renewal/ inside the land/ breakup of nation
4. Post-Kingdom	Ezekiel, Daniel, Ezra	Individual leadership/ Modeling/ Spiritual Authority
5. Pre-Church	Jesus/ Disciples	Selection/ Training/ spiritual leadership/ preparation for decentralization of Spiritual Authority/ initiation of a movement/

---

[80] I have a short form of answers to each of these questions for each of the six leadership eras. See **Article 36. Six Biblical Leadership Eras, Approaching the Bible With Leadership Eyes**, where I answer these questions for each era.

26. Leadership Eras In The Bible, Six Identified

6. Church	Peter/ Paul/ John	decentralized leadership/ cross-cultural structures led by leaders with spiritual authority which institutionalize the movement and spread it around the world

When we study a leader or a particular leadership issue in the Scriptures we must always do so in light of the leadership context in which it was taking place. We cannot judge past leadership by our present leadership standards. Conversely, we will find that major leadership lessons learned by these leaders will usually have broad implications for our leadership.

See **Articles**: *Leadership Genre—Seven Types; 29. Macro Lessons Defined; 30. Macro Lessons —List of 41 Across Six Leadership Eras; 36. Six Biblical Leadership Eras, Approaching the Bible With Leadership Eyes.*

Article 27

27. Leadership Functions, 3 High Level Generic Properties

Introduction
High level Christian leaders[81] perform many leadership functions. In addition to direct ministry functions based on giftedness there are those additional functions that characterize leaders simply because they are people responsible for others.

description   Leadership functions describe general activities that leaders must do and/or be responsible for in their influence responsibilities with followers.

Leadership studies in the mid-50s[82] analyzed the kinds of things leaders did in secular organizations. From a list of over a thousand they reduced them by factor analysis to two major categories. These two categories are roughly equivalent to what we would call today task-oriented leadership and relational-oriented leadership. In the early 80s and 90s leadership research began to identify another high level function, which I call inspirational leadership.[83]

Figure Hab 27-1 below groups leadership functions into three generic categories: task oriented leadership, relational oriented leadership, and inspirational leadership.

Three High Level Leadership Functions
include

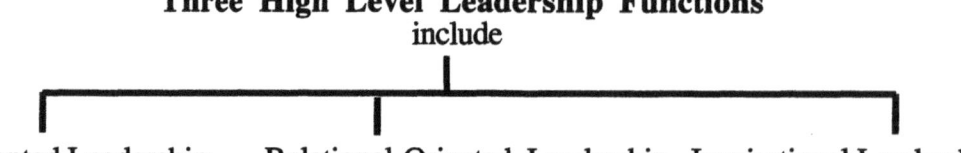

Task-Oriented Leadership   Relational-Oriented Leadership   Inspirational Leadership

Figure Hab 27-1. Three High Level Leadership Functions

Task Oriented Leadership
Task oriented leadership (technically called *Initiation of structure* in the Ohio State Research) groups all of those activities which a leader does to accomplish the task or vision

---

[81] I use a five-fold leadership typology adapted from McGavran: Type A—local internal influence in the church or Christian organization; Type B—local external influence in the church or Christian organization; Type C—local/regional influence; Type D—national influence; Type E—international influence. I am speaking mostly about Type C, D, and E leaders when I talk about generic leadership functions for high level leaders. See **Article, Leadership Levels—Looking At A Leadership Continuum**.
[82] The Ohio State Leadership Research (1948-1967) reduced the many observed functions of secular leadership by factor analysis to two major generic categories: consideration and initiation of structure.
[83] McGregor and others were doing research on motivation. There was also a growing interest in values underlying why leaders did things.

27. Leadership Functions, 3 High Level Generic Properties

for which the structure exists. Task behaviors involve clarifying goals, setting up structures to help reach them, holding people accountable, disciplining where necessary and in short, to act responsibly to accomplish goals. Table Hab 27-1 displays a list of typical task oriented leadership functions.

Table Hab 27-1. Typical Task-Oriented Leadership Functions
Christian leaders:
1. must provide structures which facilitate accomplishment of vision;
2. will be involved in crisis resolution related to structural issues;
3. must make decisions involving structures;
4. will do routine problem solving concerning structural issues;
5. will adjust structures where necessary to facilitate leadership transitions;
6. must do direct ministry relating to maintaining and changing structures (extent depends on giftedness).

Relational-Oriented Leadership

Relational-oriented leadership (technically called *Consideration* in the Ohio State research) groups all of those activities which a leader does to affirm followers, to provide an atmosphere congenial to accomplishing work, to give emotional and spiritual support for followers so that they can mature. In short, it is to act relationally with followers in order to enable them to develop and be effective in their contribution to the organization. Table Hab 27-2 lists some typical relational oriented leadership functions.

Table Hab 27-2. Typical Relational-Oriented Leadership Functions
Christian leaders:
1. must be involved in selection, development and release of emerging leaders;
2. are called upon to solve crises involving relationships between people;
3. will be called upon for decision-making focusing on people;
4. must do routine problem solving related to people issues;
5. will coordinate with subordinates, peers, and superiors;
6. must facilitate leadership transition—their own and others;
7. must do direct ministry relating to people (extent depends on giftedness).

Inspirational Leadership

Christian leadership is *externally directed*. That is, goals result from vision from God. Such leadership must move followers toward recognition of, acceptance of and participation in bringing about that God-given vision. Leaders will answer to God for their leadership.[84] Inspirational leadership is needed for this. Some typical inspirational functions are shown in Table Hab 27-3.

Table Hab 27-3. Typical Inspirational Leadership Functions
Christian leaders:
1. must motivate followers toward vision.
2. must encourage perseverance and faith of followers.
3. are responsible for the corporate integrity of the structures and organizations of which they are a part.
4. are responsible for developing and maintaining the welfare of the corporate culture of the organization.
5. are responsible for promoting the public image of the organization.
6. are responsible for the financial welfare of the organization.
7. are responsible for direct ministry along lines of giftedness which relate to inspirational functions.

---

[84] See **Article**, *Accountability—Standing Before God as a Leader*.

27. Leadership Functions, 3 High Level Generic Properties

8. must model (knowing, being, and doing) so as to inspire followers toward the reality of God's intervention in lives.
9. have corporate accountability to God for the organizations or structures in which they operate.

Summarizing Leadership Functions

There are common activities and unique activities for the three categories of leadership functions. A single list helps pinpoint the essential activities of Christian leaders.

1. Utilize giftedness for direct ministry to those in their sphere of influence.
2. Solve crises.
3. Make decisions.
4. Do routine problem solving.
5. Coordinate people, goals, and structures.
6. Select and develop leaders.
7. Facilitate leadership transition at all levels.
8. Facilitate structures to accomplish vision.
9. Motivate followers toward vision. This usually involves changing what is, and providing/ promoting a sense of progress.
10. Must encourage perseverance and faith of followers. This usually involves maintaining what is and creating a sense of stability. This is usually in dynamic tension with activity 9.
11. Accept responsibility for corporate functions of integrity, culture, finances, and accountability.
12. Must model so as to inspire followers toward the reality of God's intervention in lives and history.

Conclusion

These three functions must be carefully tended to if an organization is to go on.[85] Yet, a given leader usually has a predilection toward either task-oriented leadership or relational-oriented leadership. It is a rare leader who can do both well. But either a task-oriented leader or a relational-oriented leader can do inspirational leadership. That is, motivational functions can be done by either a task-oriented leader or relational-oriented leader. What ever the case, it is up to a high-level leader to make sure the functions are done despite his/her own particular bent. To do this a high-level leader must be willing to delegate, to depend on and release to others functions that are not his/her own strength.

See **Article**, *Leadership Levels*.

---

[85] Most task oriented Christian organizations simply assume that these are happening.

Article 28

28. Left Hand of God

Introduction

Vertical verses in a horizontal book like Proverbs demand our attention.[86] Note Proverbs 21:1 in the several translations given below.

21:1 The king's heart [is] in the hand of the LORD, [as] the rivers of water: he turneth it whithersoever he will. KJV

21:1 The king's heart is in the hand of Jehovah as the watercourses: He turneth it whithersoever he will. ASV

2:1 The king's heart is [like] channels of water in the hand of the LORD; He turns it wherever He wishes. NASB

21:1 The king's heart is in the hand of the LORD; he directs it like a watercourse wherever he pleases. NIV

21:1 The king's heart [is] in the hand of the LORD, [Like] the rivers of water; He turns it wherever He wishes. NKJV

21:1 The king's heart is a stream of water in the hand of the LORD; he turns it wherever he will. RSV

21:1 The Lord controls rulers, just as he determines the course of rivers. CEV

21:1 The Lord controls the mind of a king as easily as he directs the course of a stream. TEV

21:1 The king's heart is like a stream of water directed by the Lord; he turns it wherever he pleases. NLT

The terms used—rivers, watercourses, channels, stream, course could refer to a canal or channel of water such as an irrigation ditch. Just as the farmer directs the irrigation ditch so as to bring water where he wants it, so God directs kings and other rulers to do what He wants done.

---

[86] Psalms is a vertical book. That is, most of the Psalms are dealing with humans talking and/or hearing from God (vertical communication). Proverbs is dealing for the most part with humans relating to each other (horizontal relationships or activity). So then in a book dealing with horizontal relationships or activity it behooves us to note those few vertical passages. They demand our attention.

28. Left Hand of God, The

Every missionary better learn this verse and its view of God very quickly. For missionaries operate in countries controlled by others. They must abide by decisions made by political rulers—usually not in favor of their being in the country. Missionaries learn to trust God to move in the affairs of these pagan rulers.

Glasser Phrase

Dr. Arthur Glasser uses the phrase, the *Left Hand of God*, to call attention to God's use of non-believers to accomplish His purposes. This *Left Hand of God* is seen numerous times in the Old Testament. Table Hab 28-1 depicts just a few of them.

Table Hab 28-1. Some Occurrences of the Left Hand of God

Passage	Persons Involved	Explanation
Genesis 20, 21	Abraham, Sarah, Abimelech	Abraham lied to Abimelech about Sarah his wife. God protects her while she is with Abimelech and gives Abimelech a dream to let him know who Sarah is.
Genesis	Joseph, Pharaoh	God sends two dreams to Pharaoh, which need to be interpreted. Joseph comes to the forefront by interpreting these dreams and suggesting a wise course of action. Joseph is elevated to high position and is in place to deliver his people when the famine hits hardest.
Daniel	Nebuchadnezzar	Daniel ch 4 is one of the clearest examples of the king's heart being in the hand of Jehovah. God humbles Nebuchadnezzar, a very powerful ruler.
Isa 45	Cyrus; Daniel et al	God predicts He will use Cyrus and He does as noted in Table Hab 28-2 below.
Hag 1:1,2	Darius, Haggai	It is clear that Darius was used by God to help the remnant back in the land.
Ne ch 1 et al	Artaxerxes	Artaxerxes not only wrote decrees allowing the Jews to go back in the land, but he also helped fund their return.

Restoration Leaders

All the restoration leaders were very much aware of the Left Hand of God. They were rebuilding the work of God back in the land. They were there because God had moved in the hearts of pagan rulers, very powerful ones. Those rulers—particularly Cyrus, Darius, Xerxes, Artxerxes—were moved to aid God's people. Esther, Mordecai, Ezra, Nehemiah, Haggai, Zechariah, and Malachi were all aware of the Left Hand of God.

One of the astounding things is God's prediction that He will use these rulers to accomplish His purposes. A beautiful illustration of this is Isaiah's famous passage, Isa 45. Table Hab 28-2 below illustrates just a few of the passages referring to Cyrus.

28. Left Hand of God, The

Table Hab 28-2. God's Left Hand Working Through Cyrus

Passages Predicting	Passages Fulfilling
Isa 44:28 That saith of **Cyrus**, [He is] my shepherd, and shall perform all my pleasure: even saying to Jerusalem, Thou shalt be built; and to the temple, Thy foundation shall be laid.	
Isa 45:1 Thus saith the LORD to his anointed, to **Cyrus**, whose right hand I have holden, to subdue nations before him; and I will loose the loins of kings, to open before him the two leaved gates; and the gates shall not be shut;	
Isa 45:13 I have raised him (**Cyrus**) up in righteousness, and I will direct all his ways: he shall build my city, and he shall let go my captives, not for price nor reward, saith the LORD of hosts.	
	2Ch 36:22,23 Now in the first year of **Cyrus** king of Persia, that the word of the LORD [spoken] by the mouth of Jeremiah might be accomplished, the LORD stirred up the spirit of **Cyrus** king of Persia, that he made a proclamation throughout all his kingdom, and [put it] also in writing, saying, Thus saith **Cyrus** king of Persia, All the kingdoms of the earth hath the LORD God of heaven given me; and he hath charged me to build him an house in Jerusalem, which [is] in Judah. Who [is there] among you of all his people? The LORD his God [be] with him, and let him go up.
	Ezr 1:2, 7, 8 Thus saith **Cyrus** king of Persia, The LORD God of heaven hath given me all the kingdoms of the earth; and he hath charged me to build him an house at Jerusalem, which [is] in Judah. 7 Also **Cyrus** the king brought forth the vessels of the house of the LORD, which Nebuchadnezzar had brought forth out of Jerusalem, and had put them in the house of his gods; 8 Even those did **Cyrus** king of Persia bring forth by the hand of Mithredath the treasurer, and numbered them unto Sheshbazzar, the prince of Judah.

Closure

Most of us as leaders know something of the *Right Hand of God*. We have experienced God's intervention in our lives and ministries in such a way as to be awed by

28. Left Hand of God, The page 159

His power. But can we see His *Left Hand* working today. We need to be aware of this facet of God's power. And we need discernment, maybe even prophetic voices, to point out to us the *Left Hand of God*. It is especially comforting to believe we have a sovereign God in our world controlled by the most part by non-godly political leaders. May we see God turn the heart of the kings to accomplish His purposes.

See *Sovereign Mindset*; **Glossary**.

Article 29

29. Macro Lessons—Defined

Introduction to Macro lessons

Macro Lessons inform our leadership with potential leadership values that move toward the absolute. We live in a time when most do not believe there are absolutes. In my study of leadership in the Bible, I have defined a leadership truth continuum which recognizes the difficulty in deriving absolutes but does allow for them.[87] Figure Hab 29-1 depicts this.

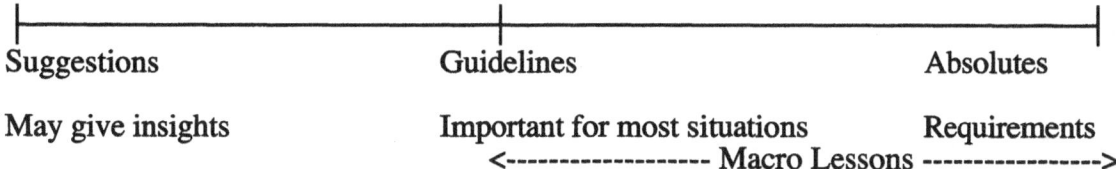

Suggestions   Guidelines   Absolutes

May give insights   Important for most situations   Requirements
                         <-------------------- Macro Lessons ----------------->

Figure Hab 29-1. Leadership Truth Continuum/Where Macro Lessons Occur

In the *Complexity Era* in which we now live,[88] the thrust of leadership theory has moved, toward the importance of leadership values. The questions being asked today are not as much what is leadership (the leadership basal elements—leader, followers, and situations) and how does it operate (leadership influence means—corporate and individual) as it is why do we do what we do (leadership value bases). The first three eras (Great Man, Trait, and Ohio State) answered the question, "What is leadership?" The Contingency and early part of the Complexity Era answered the question, "How do we do it?" Now we are grappling with, "Why do we lead? or What ought we to do?" We are looking for leadership values. A leadership value is an underlying assumption which affects how a leader behaves in or perceives leadership situations. They are usually statements that have *ought* or *must* or *should* in them. Macro-Lessons are statements of truth about leadership which have the potential for becoming leadership values. These macro-lessons are observations seen in the various leadership eras in the Bible. Many of these became values for numerous Bible leaders. These macro-lessons move toward the right (requirement, value) of the leadership truth continuum.

What is a macro lesson?

Definition   A <u>macro-lesson</u> is a high level generalization
- of a leadership observation (suggestion, guideline, requirement), stated as a lesson,
- which repeatedly occurs throughout different leadership eras,
- and thus has potential as a leadership absolute.

---

[87] See Clinton, **Leadership Perspectives** for a more detailed explanation of the continuum and for my approach to deriving principles from the scriptures. See **Article**, *Principles of Truth*.

[88] A study of leadership history in the United States from 1850 to the present uncovered 6 Eras (an era being a period of time in which some major leadership theory held sway): 1. Great Man Era (1840s to 1904); 2. Trait Theory (1904-1948); 3. Ohio State Era (1948-1967); Contingency Era (1967-1980); Complexity Era (1980-present). See Clinton, **A Short History of Leadership Theory**. Altadena, Ca.: Barnabas Publishers.

29. Macro Lessons—Defined

Macro lessons even at their weakest provide strong guidelines describing leadership insights. At their strongest they are requirements, or absolutes, that leaders should follow. Leaders ignore them to their detriment.

examples **Prayer Lesson**: If God has called you to a ministry then He has called you to pray for that ministry.
Accountability: Christian leaders minister ought always with a conscious view to ultimate accountability to God for their ministry.
Bible Centered: An effective leader who finishes well must have a Bible centered ministry.

Macro Lessons are derived from a comparative study of leadership in the Six Leadership Eras. These Six Leadership Eras and number of macro lessons identified are shown in Table Hab 29-1.

Table Hab 29-1. Leadership Eras and Number of Macro Lessons

Leadership Era	Number of Macro Lessons
1. Patriarchal Era	7
2. Pre-Kingdom Era	10
3. Kingdom Era	5
4. Post-Kingdom Era	5
5. Pre-Church Era	9
6. Church Era	5

I have identified 41 macro lessons, roughly 5 to 10 per leadership era. When a macro-lesson is seen to occur in varied situations and times and cultural settings and in several leadership eras it becomes a candidate for an absolute leadership lesson. When that same generalization becomes personal and is embraced by a leader as a driving force for how that leader sees or operates in ministry, it becomes a leadership value.

The top three Macro Lessons for the four O.T. Leadership Eras are listed in Table Hab 29-2.

Table Hab 29-2. Top Three Macro Lessons in O.T. Leadership Eras

Priority	Leadership Era	Label	Statement
1	Pre-Kingdom	Presence	The essential ingredient of leadership is the powerful presence of God in the leader's life and ministry. (*Therefore a leader must not minister without the powerful presence of God in his/her life.*)
2	Patriarchal	Character	Integrity is the essential character trait of a spiritual leader. (*Therefore, a leader must maintain integrity and respond to God's shaping of it.*)
3	Pre-Kingdom	Intimacy	Leaders develop intimacy with God which in turn overflows into all their ministry since ministry flows out of being. (*Therefore a leader must seek to develop intimacy with God.*)

The top three Macro Lessons for the two N.T. Leadership Eras are listed in Table Hab 29-3.

29. Macro Lessons—Defined

Table Hab 29-3. Top Three Macro Lessons in N.T. Leadership Eras

Priority	Leadership Era	Label	Statement
1	Church	Word Centered	*God's Word must be the primary source for equipping leaders and must be a vital part of any leader's ministry.*
2	Pre-Church	Harvest	*Leaders must seek to bring people into relationship with God.*
3	Pre-Church	Shepherd	*Leaders must preserve, protect, and develop those who belong to God's people.*

You will notice that some of these macro lessons are already described in value language (should, must, ought) while others are simply statements of observations. I have put in italics my attempt to give the value associated with the observation.

Comparative study across the six leadership eras for macro lessons makes up one of the seven leadership genres, i.e. sources for leadership findings from the Bible.

See **Articles**, *30. List of Macro Lessons; Leadership Genre—Seven Types (Macro Lessons, Biographical Material, Books as A Whole, Direct Context, Indirect Context, Leadership Acts, Parabolic).* See Clinton, **A Short History of Leadership Theory**. Altadena, Ca.: Barnabas Publishers. See also Clinton, **Leadership Perspectives**. Altadena, Ca.: Barnabas Publishers.

Article 30

30. Macro Lessons: List of 41 Across Six Leadership Eras

Introduction

Macro Lessons inform our leadership with potential leadership values that move toward the absolute. The following are the 41 lessons I have identified as I comparatively studied the six different leadership eras for leadership observations.

No.	Label	Leadership Era	Statement of Macro Lesson
1.	Blessing	Patriarchal	God mediates His blessing to His followers through leaders.
2.	Shaping	Patriarchal	God shapes leader's lives and ministry through critical incidents.
3.	Timing	Patriarchal	God's timing is crucial to accomplishment of God's purposes.
4.	Destiny	Patriarchal	Leaders must have a sense of destiny.
5.	Character	Patriarchal	Integrity is the essential character trait of a spiritual leader.
6.	Faith	Patriarchal	Biblical Leaders must learn to trust in the unseen God, sense His presence, sense His revelation, and follow Him by faith.
7.	Purity	Patriarchal	Leaders must personally learn of and respond to the holiness of God in order to have effective ministry.
8.	Intercession	Pre-Kingdom	Leaders called to a ministry are called to intercede for that ministry.
9.	Presence	Pre-Kingdom	The essential ingredient of leadership is the powerful presence of God in the leader's life and ministry.
10.	Intimacy	Pre-Kingdom	Leaders develop intimacy with God which in turn overflows into all their ministry since ministry flows out of being.
11.	Burden	Pre-Kingdom	Leaders feel a responsibility to God for their ministry.
12.	Hope	Pre-Kingdom	A primary function of all leadership is to inspire followers with hope in God and in what God is doing.
13.	Challenge	Pre-Kingdom	Leaders receive vision from God which sets before them challenges that inspire their leadership.
14.	Spiritual Authority	Pre-Kingdom	Spiritual authority is the dominant power base of a spiritual leader and comes through experiences with God, knowledge of God, godly character and gifted power.
15.	Transition	Pre-Kingdom	Leaders must transition other leaders into their work in order to maintain continuity and effectiveness.
16.	Weakness	Pre-Kingdom	God can work through weak spiritual leaders if they are available to Him.

30. Macro Lessons: List of 41 Across Six Leadership Eras

17.	Continuity	Pre-Kingdom	Leaders must provide for continuity to new leadership in order to preserve their leadership legacy.
18.	Unity	Kingdom	Unity of the people of God is a value that leaders must preserve.
19.	Stability	Kingdom	Preserving a ministry of God with life and vigor over time is as much if not more of a challenge to leadership than creating one.
20.	Spiritual Leadership	Kingdom	Spiritual leadership can make a difference even in the midst of difficult times.
21.	Recrudescence	Kingdom	God will attempt to bring renewal to His people until they no longer respond to Him.
22.	By-pass	Kingdom	God will by-pass leadership and structures that do not respond to Him and will institute new leadership and structures.
23.	Future Perfect	Post-Kingdom	A primary function of all leadership is to walk by faith with a future perfect paradigm so as to inspire followers with certainty of God's accomplishment of ultimate purposes.
24.	Perspective	Post-Kingdom	Leaders must know the value of perspective and interpret present happenings in terms of God's broader purposes.
25.	Modeling	Post-Kingdom	Leaders can most powerfully influence by modeling godly lives, the sufficiency and sovereignty of God at all times, and gifted power.
26.	Ultimate	Post-Kingdom	Leaders must remember that the ultimate goal of their lives and ministry is to manifest the glory of God.
27.	Perseverance	Post-Kingdom	Once known, leaders must persevere with the vision God has given.
28.	Selection	Pre-Church	The key to good leadership is the selection of good potential leaders which should be a priority of all leaders.
29.	Training	Pre-Church	Leaders should deliberately train potential leaders in their ministry by available and appropriate means.
30.	Focus	Pre-Church	Leaders should increasingly move toward a focus in their ministry which moves toward fulfillment of their calling and their ultimate contribution to God's purposes for them.
31.	Spirituality	Pre-Church	Leaders must develop interiority, spirit sensitivity, and fruitfulness in accord with their uniqueness since ministry flows out of being.
32.	Servant	Pre-Church	Leaders must maintain a dynamic tension as they lead by serving and serve by leading.
33.	Steward	Pre-Church	Leaders are endowed by God with natural abilities, acquired skills, spiritual gifts, opportunities, experiences, and privileges which must be developed and used for God.
34.	Harvest	Pre-Church	Leaders must seek to bring people into relationship with God.
35.	Shepherd	Pre-Church	Leaders must preserve, protect, and develop God's people.
36.	Movement	Pre-Church	Leaders recognize that movements are the way to penetrate society though they must be preserved via appropriate ongoing institutions.

30. Macro Lessons: List of 41 Across Six Leadership Eras

37.	Structure	Church	Leaders must vary structures to fit the needs of the times if they are to conserve gains and continue with renewed effort.
38.	Universal	Church	The church structure is inherently universal and can be made to fit various cultural situations if functions and not forms are in view.
39.	Giftedness	Church	Leaders are responsible to help God's people identify, develop, and use their resources for God.
40.	Word Centered	Church	God's Word is the primary source for equipping leaders and must be a vital part of any leaders ministry.
41.	Complexity	All eras	Leadership is complex, problematic, difficult and fraught with risk—which is why leadership is needed.

See Also **Article** 29. *Macro Lessons—Defined.*

Article 31

31. Needed, Sons of Issachar

Introduction

The difference between leaders and followers is perspective. Leaders have perspective that followers do not. The difference between leaders and more effective leaders is better perspective. The Old Testament has reference to a small group of folks who somehow had the ability to get needed perspective on what was happening and what could be done about it. Note the following:

> **1 Chronicles 12:32**
> 32 And of the children of Issachar, which were **men that had understanding of the times, to know what Israel ought to do**; the heads of them were two hundred; and all their brethren were at their commandment.

This verse occurs in a listing of men who were drawn to David while he was at Hebron and preparing to take over Saul's kingdom. This is a beautiful expression of what is needed for leadership today—in our multi-complex situations. Needed:

1. Leaders that have an understanding of the times;
2. Leaders who know what leadership ought to do.

Needed—Strategic Leadership Perspective

Leaders need to understand their times, that is the situations they face and what led up to them, and what is going on in them, and possible future scenarios involving them. And leaders need to know what to do as they motivate their followers toward God's purposes for them

Habakkuk was just such a leader. He was facing a situation that involved injustice and disregard for God and God's ways. He needed the Issachar Factor.

Definition

The <u>Issachar Factor</u> refers to that special needed leadership aspect—clarity as to what is happening in the complex situation currently facing a leader and options for addressing the situation.

Now Habakkuk got that needed perspective from his direct interaction with God. Habakkuk was overwhelmed with the local situation. He wanted a *tactical perspective*—that is, what was going on in his local situation and what should be done about it—especially by God. God broadened his perspective to include a *strategic perspective*. God was not only concerned with Habakkuk's tactical situation but also was concerned about the longer range

31. Needed, Sons of Issachar

aims—His working out of history so that His justice and character would be known worldwide. So God let Habakkuk in on a portion of that future working.

And Habakkuk's basic approach is always worth pursuing. Habakkuk had an intimate relationship with God. He spent time with God to hear from God. This is always a healthy approach both for getting tactical perspective but also for strategic perspective.

But can there be some functional equivalent of the Issachar men in our leadership today? Are there ways that we can recognize strategic thinkers and set them aside to do strategic thinking? And can we position them so as to have the ear of top leadership so that analysis and possible scenarios have a hearing?

Mintzberg's 5 Major Elements of Organizations

Henry Mintzberg[89] has impacted my own thinking on organizations and organizational development. He has done grounded theory research on many, many organizations in order to understand the structural aspects of an organization. Mintzberg identifies five major structural elements that make up an organization in terms of necessary and distinct major functions needed. He suggests that there are five structural elements needed in all organizations. I believe these five structural elements apply just as well to Christian organizations and Christian churches. Table Hab 31-1 lists these five elements. One of these structural elements is tailored to focus on the Issachar factor.

Table Hab 31-1. Mintzberg's Five Structural Elements

Element	What it is	What It Does
1. Strategic Apex	The strategic apex refers to the top leader(s) in the organization who have final authority for decision making for the organization as a whole and who insure that the organization serves its mission in an effective way.	The *strategic apex* is charged with the overall responsibility for the organization. In most Christian organizations this responsibility rests with a few top leaders (1-5).
2. Middle Line	The middle line refers to those leaders in the organization who have line responsibility, that is, have formal authority to supervise others in the middle line and operating core and have accountability for this supervision to the *strategic apex*.	A formal line of authority exists in the three inner organizational elements, the *strategic apex*, the *middle line*, and the *operating core*. That is, the *strategic apex* exercises direct supervision over the *middle line* and the middle line exercises direct supervision over the *operating core*. This is in contrast to the *technostructure* and *support staff* elements (the outer organizational elements) which only indirectly influence the *strategic apex*, *middle line*, and *operating core* by doing helpful support functions for them (labeled as staff functions over against line functions). The *middle line* people operate in the organization in line authority coordinating organizational activity between the *strategic apex* and the *operating core*.

---

[89]See Mintzberg's **Structure in Fives – Designing Effective Organizations**. NJ: Prentice-Hall, 1983.

3. Operating Core	The <u>operating core</u> of an organization encompasses those members--the *operators*--who perform the basic work related directly to the production of products or services.	The operating core is the heart of every organization, the part that produces the essential outputs that keep it alive.
4. Support Staff	The <u>support staff</u> refers to those workers in an organization that exist to provide support to the organization outside its operating work flow.	Most organizations have many people whose work aids others in some sort of support capacity. These people do not do the basic work involved in producing the output of the organization, like the *operating core* does. They are specialists who have distinct work to be done. They operate in a staff support capacity quite different from the *technostructure*.
5. Technostructure (Issachar factor can be included here)	The <u>technostructure</u> refers to the analysts and basic clerical support people who serve to provide back-up analytical work for the *strategic apex*, *middle line*, and *operating core* as well as standardization in terms of work, planning, and personnel practices, strategic thinking, forecasting, planning.	In the *technostructure* is found the analysts (and their supporting clerical staff) and the strategic thinkers who serve the organization by affecting the work of others. These analysts are removed from the operating work flow--they may design it, plan it, change it, or train the people who do it, but they usually do not do it themselves. Strategic thinking—forecasting, understanding what is happening and the like require analytically and systemically adept people. The *technostructure* is effective only when it can use its an analytical techniques to make the work of others more effective and to influence the strategic direction of the organization. Since it is out of line authority it must constantly battle with the need to be heard by the strategic apex.

Table Hab 31-2 gives comparatively, examples of Mintzberg's structural elements. Mintzberg's research was dominantly in the manufacturing arena. But his concepts apply across to parachurch and church situations.

Table Hab 31-2. Examples: Mintzberg's Structural Elements

Element	Manufacturing	Parachurch	Church
Strategic Apex	Board of Directors, President, President's Staff, Executive Committee	General Director, Board of Directors, Executive Committee	Senior Pastor Executive Pastor
Middle Line	VPs of Operations; VPs of Marketing; Plant Managers; Regional Sales Managers; District Sales Managers; Foremen	Regional Directors; Area Directors; Field Leaders; Team Leaders;	Associate Pastors; Usually done by committees; Lay Leaders

Operating Core	Purchasing Agents; Machine Operators; Assemblers; Salespersons; Shippers;	Individual Missionaries; Church Planting Teams; Inner-city teams; Various other incarnational communities; Trainers; Teachers; Traveling Evangelistic Teams	Senior Pastor in Public Ministry; Some associate pastors; Lay leaders; Interns; Apprentices;
Techno-structure	Strategic Planning; Controller; Personnel Training; Operations Research; Production Scheduling; Work Study; Technocratic Clerical Staff;	Trainers who do seminars and workshops to upgrade skills of members; Member care providers; Usually missing is training for *middle line* and developmental tracking and provision for members. Usually missing is strategic planning and strategic development of potential *strategic apex* leaders.	Missing Function usually
Support Staff	Legal Counsel; Public Relations; Industrial Relations; Research and Development; Pricing; Payroll; Reception; Mailroom; Cafeteria	Financial support people to track individual members accounts and do receipting functions and some donor work. Secretarial and other administrative back-up for strategic apex and higher level middle line.	Financial Administrators; Various secretarial support functions;

As seen in Tables Hab 31-1,2 the technocratic structural element should be the structural element to perform the Issachar Factor. And its major functions are often missing.

Summarizing Mintzberg in Terms of the Issachar Factor

In short, the technostructure should provide needed PERSPECTIVES that help people understand and function better. Unfortunately, this organizational element is generally the weakest in most Christian organizations. Missing are the Issachars, who can understand the situations and know what ought to be done.

In Christian organizations three major problems arise that impede good technostructure effectiveness.

1. **Lack of Authority**
   Usually the technostructure, if recognized as a division on its own, lacks authority to implement needed organizational solutions seen in analysis;

2. **Lack of Resources**
   Frequently the technostructure is not a formally recognized division and lacks resources to do adequate analytical jobs. Most folks doing technostructure functions usually do *double hatting* and hence only do technostructure functions on the side in addition to other things, frequently more in demand.

3. **Giftedness Not Recognized**
   Often analytical types in an organization are on the periphery of the leadership and are perceived as renegades (trouble makers) rocking the boat. They are not in line authority so as to be heard and see decisions made that can bring about the needed changes they see. People so gifted to do this kind of thinking are not allowed to minister out of being. That is, do the job they were meant to do.

Closure

I am not trying to downplay the need for Habakkuk solutions to strategic thinking. My concern is always that leaders maintain intimacy with God—including getting crucial leadership information. But rather I am trying to stress the importance of resources that the body of Christ usually does not take advantage of.

In my organizational dynamics classes I stress the importance of the technostructure element. I find that most Christian organizations perform the Issachar Factor on the back burner if done at all. And churches do little or none of this.[90]

> **1 Chronicles 12:32**
> 32 And of the children of Issachar, which were **men that had understanding of the times, to know what Israel ought to do**; the heads of them were two hundred; and all their brethren were at their commandment.

Where are those sons of Issachar today? And if we found them, would we actually use them? What is your methodology for recognizing the Issachar types? What is your structural strategy for using them? Who already in the strategic apex, middle line, or operating core are folks that should be freed up to become technostructure people?

---

[90] Sometimes in church plant situations there is thorough research done, which applies the Issachar Factor to those narrowly focused endeavors.

Article 32

32. Paradigms And Paradigm Shifts

Introduction

Missionaries, pastors and other students of missiology[91] use the word paradigm and paradigm shifts like they were common words. But imagine my surprise when on a jet from Singapore to Hawaii I heard those words, in casual conversation from the person sitting next to me, a Chinese executive with IBM. I was so startled that I had to ask him where he had been introduced to them. Again I was surprised when he mentioned that IBM was showing Joel Barker's *Discovering the Future* video to all its employers in a training program. Thousands of IBM employees around the world are suddenly adding paradigm and paradigm shift to their vocabulary. We both exchanged comments on the power of that video. So the word *paradigm* and *paradigm shifts* have come a long way since Thomas Kuhn[92] first introduced them to an esoteric audience interested in philosophy and epistemology.[93]

The meaning of paradigms and paradigm shifts has also become less technical that Kuhn's use of the words. And though many of us, who have learned them sort of second hand, can generally use them in a context which roughly supports them we probably don't have a good grasp of the words. And we most certainly have not connected them with God's developmental processes in the shaping of a leader. My comparative study of many leaders has shown that paradigm shifts are a major way that *God breaks through to expand a leader*. And that is the purpose of this article. I want to define, explain, and clarify the use of the terms paradigm and paradigm shift in connection with its use in shaping leaders—For I am convinced that the *paradigm shift* is God's breakthrough processing that opens new leadership vistas.

Let me first suggest some examples of paradigm shifts in the Bible then I will define paradigm and paradigm shifts and suggest five paradigm shifts that are needed if the church is to make an impact in the post-modern world that is upon us now. Table Hab 32-1 lists some Biblical illustrations of paradigm shifts.

---

[91] Missiology is the science involved in studying the propagation of the Gospel across cultures.
[92] Kuhn's breakthrough 1974 work, **The Structure of Scientific Revolutions**, was studying paradigms at the higher level of the continuum. He was interested in how a whole scientific community viewed a given science.
[93] Epistemology refers to the science dealing with how we know things.

32. Paradigms and Paradigm Shifts

Table Hab 32-1. 10 Examples of Biblical Paradigm shifts.

Who	Where in	Paradigm Before	Paradigm After
1. Job	Whole book of Job	Suffering is the result of sin and is deserved. Righteous people should not suffer.	A righteous person can suffer as a part of God's plan for him/her
2. Jonah	Jonah 1-4	God exclusively deals only with Israel in order to bless. God is basically against non-Israelites.	God is not exclusively Israel. He has concerns for all nations—to show His mercy and grace to all who repent.
3. Habakkuk	Habakkuk 1-3	God is unjust and unfaithful in His dealing with groups of people in history. He does not keep His promises.	God is just. He is complex in His dealings with nations. Ultimately His purposes and justice will be seen by all.
4. Elisha's servant	2 Kings 6:8-23; Note vs 16	Sees only natural situation. Fear of the physical warfare to come.	Sees the supernatural; sees the unseen Angelic Band protecting. Now believes in unseen world.
5. Nicodemus	John 3	Kingdom of God is external and has expected political ramifications.	Must have an inner transformation by the Spirit in order to perceive God's Kingdom (God's rule).
6. Apostles	Acts 2	No church. No one is sure of what will happen next.	Coming of Holy Spirit. Church is born. Message of salvation is for others.
7. Whole Church (example of Ananias and Sapphira)	Acts 5	Moral issues are relative; can follow cultural ethics.	Dishonesty is against God whether inward or outwardly known; integrity is a thing of the heart. God wants whole hearted obedience.
8. Saul	Acts 9	Persecuted Christians; saw Christ as a leader of a cult opposing Judaism.	Saw Christ as the resurrected Lord; loved Christians; propagated Christianity.
9. Peter	Acts 10	Gentiles not acceptable to God; Jews should not fellowship with them.	Gentiles accepted by God. All Christians are one.
10. Woman at the well	John 4	Believed Smaritans had religious views comparable with Jews. Lived an unsatisfied life. Religion not satisfying.	Saw Jesus as one sent from God who had access to supernatural revelation. Christ's religious views brought hope.

Probably the most famous paradigm shift is that of the Apostle Paul whose conversion radically turned him around from opposing Christ to serving Christ. Paradigm shifts can bring about major breakthroughs in a life or ministry.

Definition   A <u>paradigm</u> is a controlling perspective (symbolized by r) which allows one to perceive and understand **REALITY** ((symbolized by R).

32. Paradigms and Paradigm Shifts

Definition — A <u>paradigm shift</u> is the change of a controlling perspective and the perceptive result of that change (little **r**) so that one perceives (new little **r'**) and understands **REALITY** in a different way.

Essentially, then as we have described it a paradigm shift occurs by a changed little **r**, one's perception of reality, which in effect allows us to see more of **R** (absolute reality) or at least some different aspect of it.

A change of little **r** could be simple one like a single idea. Or it could be a change of an idea that ramifies throughout a whole group of related ideas. Not all changes of little **r** have the same impact upon our mental models.

Three Categories of Paradigm Shifts

Comparative study of real life paradigm shifts in case studies of leaders has led to the following three categories. These categories include:

1. **Cognitive**—which dominantly deals with the concept of new ideas or frameworks of thinking as the basis for a paradigm shift. These new Ideas (information, categories, etc.) allow for seeing new things. The heart of the shift has to do with a new idea for seeing things, a possibility not considered before. The cognition may also be accompanied by a volitional to use it but the heart of it is the discovery of the validity of the idea. Examples include: a mono-cultural to cross-cultural perspective; getting church growth eyes; getting new leadership style insights; learning a stewardship philosophical leadership model; learning about change dynamics theory; seeing women as fully qualified leaders in ministry.

2. **Volitional**—which dominantly focuses on the fact of committing oneself to something whether understood cognitively or not. There is a committal by an act of a will to use some idea even though it may not be fully understood or experienced. The heart of the shift is a recognition of the importance of letting go and following the new perspective whether or not it is understood. Usually there is a surrender of the will involved and an acknowledgment to God of this. Examples: radical adult conversion; leadership committal; call to ministry

3. **Experiential**—which dominantly focuses on experiences of something and an affective shift which may ramify toward a volitional and eventually a cognitive shift. These have to do with experiencing the effects of something or wanting to experience it. After the experience there may be a growing awareness of its meaning. Usually these have to do with life power or gifted power or personal experiences with the supernatural-—that is, unusual experience with the Holy Spirit and supernatural power breakthroughs. Life power (the appropriation of the Holy Spirit to enable victorious living) examples include: entire sanctification—Brengle's experience; baptism of Holy Spirit—Torrey's experience; deeper life experience—McQuilkin's experience; Union life shift—Taylor's experience of the exchanged life; infilling of Holy Spirit—Luke's description of several in Acts. Gifted Power (the appropriation of God's power via the Holy Spirit to use giftedness with effective power) in ministry examples include: a major healing experience; experiences with prophetic; confirmed experiences with word of knowledge or word of wisdom or discernings of spirits; miracles; tongues or interpretation of tongues verified; anointing of Holy Spirit for a ministry; experience of unusual effectiveness with giving, helps, mercy, teaching, evangelism, apostleship, pastoral, or any of the normally considered non-supernatural gifts. Power encounters, spiritual warfare, spiritual authority, prayer power, and unusual intercessory experiences involving divine initiative praying are other miscellaneous power type experiential paradigm shifts. Some experiential paradigm shifts have to

do with personhood and include such things as: personality shifts through brokenness or deep processing; isolation and other maturity cluster processes.

Some General Suggestions for Follow-Up

Let me offer four rather simplistic suggestions. They seem almost anticlimactic after offering so much information on paradigm shifts. But they can make a difference.

Suggestion 1. Study Paradigms and Paradigm Shifts Thoroughly

Step 1 for having these ideas impact you is to study them thoroughly so that you understand them and can recognize in real life situations around. Study carefully each of the Biblical examples of paradigm shifts that were given. Study especially the leadership commentary notes in John. John is a *major paradigm shift book*. Study the other paradigm shift books with a view toward identifying paradigm concepts. These include: Job, Jonah, Habakkuk, Acts, and Galatians. Thorough understanding of paradigmatic concepts is a preliminary to actual positive use of them in ministry.

Suggestion 2. Be Open To Them

Recognize that most leaders are usually somewhat inflexible. That's one reason they have convictions and are willing to lead. Also recognize that God uses paradigm shifts to move an inflexible leader. So be open to paradigm shifts to help you become more flexible. Remember, one of your goals is to finish well. One means of doing that is to respond to processing by God which will break unneeded flexibility and develop your potential.

Suggestion 3. Needed Paradigm Shifts in Our Day

Table Hab 32-3 lists some paradigm shifts I believe will be necessary if we are to minister, to lead, and to see lives changed in the post-modern era facing the church.

Table Hab 32-3. Needed Paradigm Shifts;
If Leaders Are to Impact the Post-Modern Era

Paradigm Shift	Explanation
Authentication: Power shift.	Leaders must be able to demonstrate the power of God in ministry in order to break through to post-modern people.
Ministry Base: Shift from doing to being.	Leaders must minister out of being which involves giftedness, character, intimacy with God, inner values, destiny. Success and achievement must not be the driving force. They will be by-products of the essential issue which is to minister out of being.
Social base: Demonstrate God's enablement for this.	Living victoriously as singles and marrieds must be demonstrated. Our world around us is falling apart in terms of social base issues.
Relational Empowerment: Developmental bias	Leaders must develop emerging leaders with mentoring relationships. Developing others must be a major priority.
Future Perfect Thinking: Leading with hope.	Leaders who lead with a future perfect perspective can impart hope. Hope will desperately be needed in a post-modern culture which has at best only hopelessness.

Suggestion 4. Expect Them

Paradigm shifts will come unless you are deliberately fixed in your views and perspectives for viewing things. Especially is this true for some of the needed ones I have listed under suggestion 3. We need these if we are to minister to the post-modern generation. Therefore be expecting God to challenge you with them. Be on the look out for them. Desire them. Ask for them.

32. Paradigms and Paradigm Shifts

Remember, God is full of surprises. When we get to heaven we will find out that things were not always the way we thought them to be. Be open for those surprises, which often come wrapped up in paradigm shift wrappings.

See *Powershift, mentoring definitions, future perfect paradigm,* **Glossary**. See **Article, 7.** *Future Perfect Paradigm.*

Article 33

33. Promises of God

Introduction

Paul makes the following wonderful statement in the midst of a challenge to the Corinthians to give to a relief fund to help out Jerusalem Christians.

> 8 And God is able to provide more than you need. You will have what you need with some left over for giving. 2Co 9:8

I believe this to be a **promise** from God that is broader than just the Corinthians. When believers give cheerfully and generously and to meet God-directed needs, I believe they can expect God to enrich them to give. The right kind of attitude is crucial however. They don't give to get. They give because God gives them grace to give and gives them liberal and joyous hearts to give. And they surrender themselves to God for this giving ministry through them. When this is done, I believe this promise is as good as gold.

I also believe the equalizing principle is in effect.

> 13 I don't intend that you should give so much that you suffer for it. But there is an equalizing principle here. Right now you have more than you need and can help them out. Later you may have need and they may help you out.

If they give out of their surplus they can expect help when they have need. A Pauline leadership value occurs here.

> **Financial Equality Principle: Christian leadership must teach that Christian giving is a reciprocal balancing between needs and surplus.**

This equalizing principle, giving when we have abundance and others have need, and in turn receiving when we have needs and others have abundance, must be recognized, embraced, and then applied very carefully so as to not create dependencies.[94]

---

[94] This principle is difficult for western Christians to see. For the most part western Christians don't realize just how wealthy they are when in comparison with many other non-western Christians. With no exposure to missions and churches around the world, Christians will rarely ever really embrace this principle. Leaders must raise awareness levels about needs around the world as well as teach this principle (and model it in their own lives).

33. Promises of God

What I have just done is introduce you to the notion of a promise from God, but one that has conditions. God will supply. But we must generously give. We can give out of our surplus. Later there will be times when we don't have enough. Others will give to us. Some promises are unconditional and are for all who want to appropriate them. Others promises are for a special group or person. Other promises have conditions. A leader must be able to discern promises of God, both for himself/herself, for the leadership situation, and for followers within his/her influence. This article defines a promise and gives some general guidelines about promises and introduces the image of God as *The Promise Keeper*.

Promises of God

When I was a little boy my friends and I would often say, "I promise." And the other person would say, "Cross your heart and hope to die?" The meaning was, "Do you really mean it?" Now little boys make and break promises about as fast as can be. But with God it is not so. One, He does not promise helter skelter like. And when He does promise He can be trusted. Our problem is learning to hear Him promise and being sure what we heard was a promise from Him, for us.

Definition A <u>promise from God</u> is an assertion from God, specific or general or a truth in harmony with God's character, which is perceived in one's heart or mind concerning what He will do or not do for that one and which is sealed in our inner most being by a quickening action of the Holy Spirit and on which that one then counts.

There are three parts to the promise:

1. the cognitive part which refers to the assertion and its understanding, and
2. the affective part which is the inner most testimony to the promise, and
3. the volitional act of faith on our part which believes the assertion and feelings and thereafter counts upon it.

A leader can err in three ways, concerning promises. One, the leader may misread the assertion. That is, misinterpret what he/she thinks God will do or not do. Or two, the leader may wrongly apply some assertion to himself/herself which is does not apply. It may even be a true assertion but not for that leader or that time. Or the leader may misread the inner witness. It may not be God's Spirit quickening of the leader.

Sometimes the assertion comes from a command, or a principle, or even a direct statement of a promise God makes. The promise may be made generally to all who follow God or specifically to some. It may be for all time or for a limited time. Commands or principles are not in themselves promises. But it is when the Holy Spirit brings some truth out of them that He wants to apply to our lives that they may become promises. Such truths almost always bear on the character of God.

One thing we can know for certain, if indeed we do have a promise from God, then He will fulfill it. For Titus 1:2 asserts an important truth about God.

God can not lie.

He is the promise keeper. This is an image of God that all leaders need. God keeps his promises. He is the Promise Keeper. Table Hab 33-1 gives some examples to shore up our faith in **The Promise Keeper**. I could have chosen 100s of promises.[95]

---

[95] Over the years I have kept a listing of promises I felt God has made to me and my wife. Many of these have been fulfilled. In December of 1997 I reviewed all of these—an encouraging faith building exercise.

33. Promises of God

Table Hab 33-1. God The Promise Keeper—Examples

To Whom	Vs	Basic Promise/ Results
Abraham	Gen 12:1,2	Bless the world through Abraham. Give descendants. Spawn nations. Give a land. / This has happened and continues to happen.
Nahum	Whole book	Judgment on Nineveh/ Assyria. Promises fulfilled.
Obadiah	Whole book	Judgment on Edom. Promises fulfilled.
Habakkuk	Ch 2	Judgment on Babylon. Promises fulfilled. See Da 5.
Zechariah	Lk 1:13	Birth of John the Baptist. Promise fulfilled.
Mary	Lk 1:35	Birth of Jesus. Promise fulfilled.
Hezekiah	Isa 39:1ff, especially vs 5-7	Babylonian captivity. Royal hostages taken (Daniel was one of these). Promise fulfilled.
Daniel	Ch 2	The broad outlines of history/ nations and God's purposes. Promise fulfilled in part with more to come.
Daniel	Ch 9	Messiah and work of cross. Promise fulfilled.
Daniel	Ch 10-11:35	Again the broad outline of history particularly with reference to Israel. Everything up to 11:35 has taken place in detail as promises. The rest is yet to come.

Conclusion

The dictionary defines a promise as giving a pledge, committing oneself to do something, to make a declaration assuring that something will or will not be done or to afford a basis for expectation. Synonyms for promise include: covenant, engage, pledge, plight, swear, vow. The central meaning shared by these verbs is *to declare solemnly that one will perform or refrain from a particular course of action.* God is **The Promise Keeper**. As children of His we should learn to hear His promises and to receive them for our lives. As a leader you most likely will not make it over the long haul if you do not know God **as The Promise Keeper.**

One of the six characteristics[96] of a leader who finishes well is described as,

> **Truth is lived out in their lives so that convictions and promises of God are seen to be real.**

A leader who has God's promises and lives by them will exemplify this characteristic. Paul did. Paul, the model N.T. church leader knew God as **The Promise Keeper**. Do you?

See cognitive, affective, volitional; **Glossary**. See **Article**, *Principles of Truth*

---

[96] The six characteristics include: 1. They maintain a personal vibrant relationship with God right up to the end. 2. They maintain a learning posture and can learn from various kinds of sources—life especially. 3. They manifest Christ-likeness in character as evidenced by the fruit of the Spirit in their lives. 4. Truth is lived out in their lives so that convictions and promises of God are seen to be real. 5. They leave behind one or more ultimate contributions. 6. They walk with a growing awareness of a sense of destiny and see some or all of it fulfilled.

Article 34

34. Prophecy Overview

Introduction

Much of the Bible has prophetic overtones. Prophecy is very important for a Bible student who would grasp the whole Bible. The N.T. comments on why prophecy is so important. It gives two main reasons none of which is to satisfy our curiosity about things to come:

Reason 1. According to John 13:19, the study of fulfilled prophecy should confirm our faith.

Reason 2. According to Revelation 15:15 and 1 John 3:3 the study of unfulfilled prophecy should influence our conduct. It should exhort us and encourage us to get ready, be ready and always be looking for the return of Christ.

Excluding the book of Revelation, which is entirely prophetic, in the N.T., there are 164 prophetic passages. Of these, 141 are directly related to conduct and apparently given to affect conduct not merely to increase our knowledge. There are many O.T. passages.

Definition   *Prophecy* refers to the genre of Scripture in which the thrust of the passage is an authoritative revelation from God usually through a spokesperson, called a prophet or prophetess, to correct a given historical situation or to warn of a future situation.

Example
Genesis 3:15 predicts a long-term conflict between Satan and God's people, which will be culminated by the defeat of Satan by Christ.

Example
Many corrective prophetic passages occur in the book of Amos. For example: Amos 1:3-5; 6-8; 9-10; 11-12; 13-15.

Example
Jeremiah contains both warnings to the present situation and future predictions of the fall of the southern kingdom.

Example
Ezekiel contains both warnings of the on-coming fall of the southern kingdom. Once it fell the remainder of his book contains encouraging prophecies of the future in which God will again bring hope and restoration to His people.

34. Prophecy Overview

Corrective Prophecy

Usually corrective prophecy is straightforward and can be directly applied to the situation. However, futuristic prophecy is more difficult and has the following four characteristics. And occasionally corrective prophecy will also show these characteristics.

4 Characteristics of Futuristic Prophecy

1. Prophecy whenever given was contemporary in nature. Its form was conditioned by the views and ideas at the time of utterance. The prophets felt compelled to speak with a view toward their listeners (true of both corrective and futuristic).

2. Prophecy was often partial in nature. Individual prophetical utterance is often of a partial nature dealing with only one side of the coin (it is written; Yes, but it is written again; e.g. Isa 11:14 and Zec 9:13 Kingdom of God taken by arms or force. But this picture must be balanced by others. Isa 9:6 and Zec 9:9 show that these warlike expressions are to be understood figuratively since the Messiah king is more than all others a Prince of Peace (true especially of futuristic).

3. Jammed perspective. Often the prophet sees together and at once upon the surface of the picture things which are to be fulfilled only successively and gradually. Isa 40-66 shows the near future of the return from captivity and glorification of the City of God—return was near but glorification was to take place in the future (true mainly of futuristic).

4. Progressive. Prophecy is progressive in the following senses.

    a. Later revelation is based upon earlier revelation.
    b. Later revelation is climactic.
    c. Later revelation is more full—it discloses elements omitted from earlier revelation.

Eight Guidelines for Interpreting Prophecy

Prophecy, like Hebrew Poetry, covers a great mass of material. There is a lot of prophetic Scripture both in the Old Testament and New Testaments. It is deeply imbedded in New Testament literature. It is also a subject that is fascinating everyone today. And for that reason, we as Bible teachers should be aware of our need to teach prophetic literature in order to build up faith and get people to change their lives in preparation for Christ's return. Our goal should not be to satisfy curiosity. And we must remember that prophecy is perhaps the least understood Biblical genre. Table Hab 34-1 gives some guidelines, which I am using in my study of prophetic literature.

Table Hab 34-1 Eight Guidelines for Interpreting Prophecy—Basic Hermeneutics

Guideline	Statement/ Explanation
1.	Apply the rules of general hermeneutics.
2.	State to whom and about whom the prophecy is given.
3.	Interpret all figures of speech and all symbols.
4.	Apply the procedure for cultural equivalents where necessary.

34. Prophecy Overview

5.	State concisely the central idea of the prophecy to which the smaller details relate. Here is a good place to observe whether a passage is predictive or didactic and corrective. If it is predictive, note any conditions. If the prediction was fulfilled, study all the materials that illuminate the fulfillment. If unfulfilled, seek to determine the time and nature of the fulfillment.
6.	Where fulfillment of prophecy is found in the New Testament, differentiate between (for the sake of clarity) **direct** and **typological prediction**. (Direct prediction consists of Old Testament prophetical statements which refer to nothing prior to New Testament times—e.g. Birth of Christ at Bethlehem—Micah 5:2 and Matthew 2:5,6)(A typological prediction is an Old Testament prophetic statement that does refer to something prior to New Testament times, although it finds its highest application of meaning in the events, people, or message of the New Testament).
7.	Apply the laws of time element and double fulfillment where the prophecy fits the conditions of these special language prophecy laws.
8.	Let the finality of God's revelation in Christ color all earlier revelations (see Hebrews 1:1ff).

O.T. Prophecy About Christ

One function of prophecy in the O.T. is to predict truth about Jesus Christ. Christ speaks of himself in the New Testament as being seen in the Old Testament. Three such ways that this occurs are shown in Figure Hab 34-1.

3 Types of Prophecy About Christ

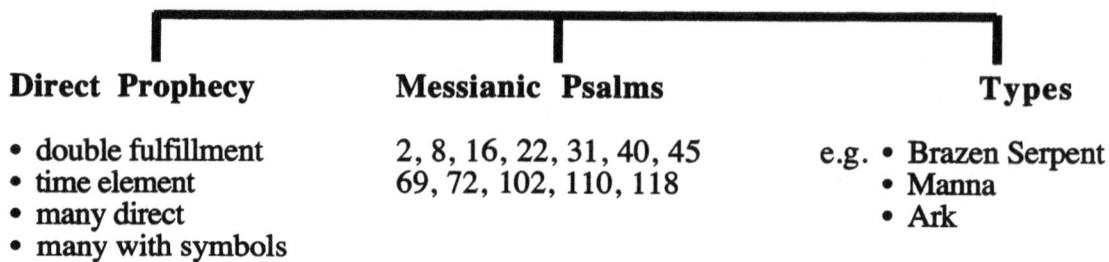

Figure Hab 34-1. 3 Types of Prophetic Genre Concerning Jesus Christ

Commentary on Prophecy—4 Warnings

Prophecy is a very complex genre. Some practical warnings are needed. Here are four such warnings.

1. Be God-centered, not event centered in your study of prophecy.
2. Remember, in prophecy, the total picture is incomplete. Old Testament people sure thought some of these prophecies different than they turned out.
3. Prophecy does not always have to be fulfilled.
4. It is not necessarily wrong not to know and to seek out for understanding. The Old Testament prophets sure did this (2 Peter 1:10).

4 Descriptions of Prophecy

We learn what something is when we contrast it—by showing what it is not as well as what it is. Two things prophecy is not include the first two descriptions below.

34. Prophecy Overview

1. What it is not! Prophecy is not a more vivid way of writing history.

The entire predictive aspect of prophecy came under attack when naturalistic rationalism argued that real prediction is impossible in a universe governed wholly by cause and effect...The rationalists had to do something with the Biblical claims to predictive prophecy, and with the large amount of material which appears to the average prudent person to be predictive prophecy. This was their answer. Most of the apparently predictive materials were written after the events that they predict. Since history is rather dull to many readers, the prophetic style livens up the narrative and makes it more readable. Earlier interpreters who did not perceive the method were either naive or *unenlightened*. If a certain passage could not be dismissed by this strategy, its message was generalized and called brilliant insight by one whose mind refused to be shut up within the confines of Hebrew daily life. (Mickelsen 1963:289)

2. What it is not! Prophecy is not history written beforehand.

Prophecy never gives a complete picture of an event, as does a historian's account. The historian must provide some account of the antecedents to an event, of the event itself, and of its consequences. He must, in other words, supply many particulars...Prophecy cannot be history written beforehand because God does not disclose major and minor elements that are essential for even an incomplete historical picture. What God makes known as well as what he withholds are both a part of the total plan of redemption. As history moves on, the full-orbed picture emerges.

3. What it does!

Earlier intimations of what is to come serve to remind the people that the totality of history is in God's sovereign control.

4. What it is!

Prophecy, simply speaking, is that which someone moving in a prophetic gifting writes or says. The prophet is a spokesperson for God who declares God's will to the people. In declaring God's will to the people, the prophet may touch upon the past, present, or future.

3 Possible Approaches

The following different approaches to the particular language used in prophecy have been noted in the literature.

1. **Literalistic View**—This view expects a literal fulfillment of all details. If the prophet mentions horses and bridles, there will be horses and bridles. If the prophet mentions shields, bucklers, bows and arrows, handstaves, spears (Eze 39:9) these exact weapons will be utilized.

2. **Entire Symbolical View**—in contrast to the literalist, this view may insist on the symbolic meaning of an entire prophecy. Finding elements that belong to a past epoch, the interpreter proceeds to make every aspect of the prophecy simply a picture of ideal hopes, etc. or He/she may apply it as a prophetic picture of the present Christian church (this view is sometimes called *spiritualizing*.)

3. **Analogical Equivalents**—A third way of approaching prophecy is in terms of equivalents, analogy, or correspondence. The transportation (chariot—for example) of the prophet's day will have a corresponding equivalence in the time of its fulfillment (like an armored car). Likewise the weapons mentioned by the prophet will have the counter parts at the time of the fulfillment. The enemies of the people of God in one period will be replaced by later enemies. The details of worship of

34. Prophecy Overview

God's people at an earlier period will be replaced by the means laid down by God during the period of fulfillment (see Mickelsen p. 296 for Eze 40-48 for example).

Two Important Observations

From observation of prophecy both in the Old and New Testaments and comparative study two basic guidelines have emerged. These are the law of double fulfillment and the law of the time element. Table Hab 34-2 gives these observations.

Table Hab 34-2. Two Special Prophecy Observations About Fulfillment

Law	Explanation
Double Fulfillment	The law of double fulfillment means that the prophecy is fulfilled at two different times. Either the fulfillments occur in the day of the prophecy and at the first coming of Christ or the fulfillments occur at the first coming of Christ and will occur again at the second coming in perhaps some fuller way. But it may sound when the prophecy is given that it will occur once. This comes very close to violating our basic axiom of only one meaning generally to a language communication.
Time Element	The law of the time element means that although the prophet states two things apparently as if the were to occur together yet the New Testament shows that they will be fulfilled a different times. It is as if the prophet is looking telescopically at two mountains way down in front of him. They appear together. But as you near the mountains you can see that there is actually much distance between them.

Conclusion

In the Biblical leadership commentaries, O.T. books of Deuteronomy, Daniel, Jonah, Habakkuk, Haggai, Micah, and Malachi all contain various prophetical passages. The information in this article gives a general overview of prophecy. These prophetic passages of these books should first be studied to identify the intent as to corrective, futuristic, or both. Then they should be interpreted using the general hermeneutical guidelines. Of special help is the notion of double fulfillment and the telescoping time element. At the conclusion of this article I give a study sheet for prophecy passages that flows from the information given in this article.

Bibliography

Mickelsen, A. Berkley
    1963   **Interpreting The Bible**. Grand Rapids: Eerdmans Publishing Company.

34. Prophecy Overview

Prophecy Study Sheet

John 13:19...that when it comes to pass our faith will be strengthened.
1 John 3:3...Everyone that has this future expectation will change his behavior.

Name _____ Passage _____ Date _____

A. The Passage in Its Historical Setting

1. What is the occasion for this prophetic passage? State what you believe to be the intent of the one giving the prophetic utterance to the hearers of his day.

2. State explicitly to whom or to what the statement or passage refers. Is the passage addressed to the hearers or readers while also being about them? Or is it proclaimed to them about someone else?

3. Put yourself in the place of the first hearers or readers of the passage. What would it have meant to you in that day?

B. Analyzing the Prophecy

1. Identify any imagery or figurative language involved in the passage. If unidentifiable, state that also. Use the general rules for symbols where apocalyptic imagery is involved.

2. Is the passage primarily predictive or didactic? Identify the didactic purpose. Identify the predictive element.

3. What conditions if any are attached to the predictive prophecy? Has this prophecy been fulfilled? If so, describe its fulfillment. Does the law of double fulfillment apply? Does the law of the time element apply?

4. Are there parallel passages which limit, reveal, or explain further this passage?

C. Drawing Conclusions

1. See if you can rewrite the passage in your own words using modern equivalents, analogies, or correspondences existing in the time of the fulfillment.

2. Since prophecy is given to confirm our faith and to change our conduct you should derive some practical help from this study. List here any practical applications seen in this study.

Helpful Statements in the study of prophecy:

1. Be God centered not event centered or time centered as you study prophecy. God is longing to change lives not to satisfy the curious.
2. Remember the total picture is incomplete.
3. A fulfillment of any prophecy is application not interpretation.
4. The law of double fulfillment means that the prophecy is fulfilled at two different times. Either the fulfillments occur in the day of the prophecy and at the first coming of Christ or the fulfillments occur at the first and second coming.
5. The law of the time element means that although the prophet states two things apparently as if the were to occur together yet the New Testament shows that they will be fulfilled a different times.

Article 35

35. Prophetic Crises—Three Major Biblical Times

Introduction
Years ago, when I took the class on prophets by James (Buck) Hatch, each of us was assigned a major project—do a chart on the prophets. Professor Hatch knew that the historical background was crucial to understanding the writing prophets. I still have that chart today and use it whenever I introduce any of the prophetic books. I am thankful to Professor Hatch for that project and his course that introduced me to each of the prophetic books. Getting perspective, on the times these books address, was a great leap forward in understanding them. Most of the writing prophets cluster around three major crises in the life of God's people. It is these prophetic crises, which prompted the rise of the prophetic ministry as reflected in the writing prophets.

1. The Assyrian Crisis
2. The Babylonian Crisis
3. The Restoration Crisis

Let me briefly describe each of these and identify the books, which speak to them.

General Background And Some Basic Definitions
Samuel's leadership ministry transitioned the commonwealth into a kingdom that Saul ruled over. This was followed by David's rule and then his son Solomon's rule. This sets the stage for God's disciplinary work among His people.

The Assyrian and the Babylonian Crises
The story line leading to the Assyrian crisis and the Babylonian crisis hinges around the following major events:
1. Solomon goes away from the Lord providing a great warning to all leaders—He had the best start of any king yet did not finish well. A good start does not insure a good finish.
2. Rehoboam (1 Kings 12) makes an unwise decision to increase taxes and demands on people—kingdom splits as prophecy said. 10 tribes go with the northern kingdom, Judah with the southern. A poor start might not be overcome.
3. The northern kingdom under Jereboam quickly departs from God. Jereboam is used as the model of an evil king to whom all evil kings are likened; He had a good start also—God would have blessed him. Abuse of power is a major barrier to finishing well.
4. The southern kingdom generally is bad with occasional good Kings and partially good kings: Asa, Jehoshaphat, Joash, Amaziah, Uzziah, Jotham, Hezekiah, Josiah. But the trend was always downward. The extended length

35. Prophetic Crises—Three Major Biblical Times

of life of the southern kingdom more than the northern kingdom is directly attributed to the spiritual life of the better kings. Spiritual leadership does make a difference. Lack of spiritual leadership speeds up deterioration and leads to God's bypassing of the leadership structures and even destruction of the wayward people.

5. During both the northern and southern kingdoms God sent prophets to try and correct them—first the oral prophets (many—but the two most noted were Elijah and Elisha) and then the prophets who wrote.

Now in order to understand this long period of history you should know several things:
1. The History books that give background information about the times.
2. The Bible Time-Line, need to know when the books were written.
3. Need to know the writing prophets: northern or southern kingdom, which crisis, direct or special.

The History Books

The history books covering the time of the destruction of a nation include 1, 2 Samuel, 1,2 Kings, and 1,2 Chronicles. The following chart helps identify the focus of each of these books as to major content.

Chart Hab 35-1 The History Books—Major Content

1 Samuel	2 Samuel 1 Chronicles	1,2 Kings 2 Chronicles
Samuel, Saul, David	David	1,2 Kings: Solomon to Zedekiah (gives time oriented details on northern and southern kingdoms) 2 Chronicles exclusively on line of Judah (southern kingdom)

There are four categories of prophetical books. Prophetical books deal with three major crises: the Assyrian crisis which wiped out the northern kingdom; the Bablonian crisis which wiped out the southern kingdom; the return to the land after being exiled. There are also prophetical books not specifically dealing with these crises but associated with the time of them. The prophetical books dealing with these issues are:

Category 1. Northern—Assyrian Crisis
Jonah, Amos, Hosea, Nahum, Micah

Category 2. Southern—Babylonian Crisis
Joel, Isaiah, Micah, Zephaniah, Jeremiah, Lamentations, Habakkuk, Obadiah

Category 3. In Exile
Ezekiel, Daniel, Esther

Category 4. Return From Exile—The Restoration Crisis
Nehemiah, Ezra, Haggai, Zechariah, Malachi

35. Prophetic Crises—Three Major Biblical Times

In addition, to knowing the crises you must know the prophets that wrote:

A. Direct to the Issue of the Crisis either Assyrian, Babylonian, or Return To The Land—The Restoration Crisis. These were:
Amos, Hosea, Joel, Micah, Isaiah, Jeremiah, Ezekiel, Haggai, Zechariah, Malachi

B. Special-These were:
Jonah, Nahum, Habakkuk, Obadiah, Zephaniah, Daniel.

The special prophets, though usually associated with one of the crisis times, wrote to deal with unique issues not necessarily related directly to the crisis. The following list gives the special prophets and their main thrust.

1. Jonah—a paradigm shift, pointing out God's desire for the nation to be missionary minded and reach out to surrounding nations.
2. Nahum—vindicate God, judgment on Assyria.
3. Habakkuk—faith crisis for Habakkuk, vindicate God, judgment on Babylon.
4. Obadiah—vindicate God, judgment on Edom for treatment of Judah.
5. Zephaniah—show about judgment, the Day of the Lord.
6. Daniel—give hope, show that God is indeed ruling even in the times of the exile and beyond, gives God's plan for the ages.

Having overviewed the story line that threads through the *Assyrian Crisis* and the *Babylonian Crisis* and briefly listed the Biblical books (both history and prophetical) that apply to these crises, we can move on to the *Restoration Crisis*.

The Restoration Crisis Overviewed

Several Bible books are associated with the return to the land from the exile. After a period of about 70 years (during which time Daniel ministered) Cyrus made a decree, which allowed some Jews (those that wanted to) to return to the land. Some went back under Zerubbabel, a political ruler like a governor. A priest, Joshua, also provided religious leadership to the first group that went back. This group of people started to rebuild the temple but became discouraged due to opposition and lack of resources. They stopped building the temple. Two prophets, after several years, 10-15, addressed the situation. These two, Haggai and Zechariah, were able to encourage the leadership and the people to finish the temple.

Another thirty or forty years goes by and then we have the events of the book of Esther, back in the land. Her book describes the attempt to eradicate the Jewish exiles—a plot which failed due to God's sovereign intervention via Esther, the queen of the land and a Jewish descendant going incognito, and her relative Mordecai.

Still another period of time passes, 20 or so years and a priest, Ezra, directs another group to return to the land. The spiritual situation has deteriorated. He brings renewal.

Another kind of leader arrives on the scene some 10-15 years later. Nehemiah, a lay leader, and one adept at organizing and moving to accomplish a task, rebuilds the wall around Jerusalem. He too has to instigate renewal.

Finally, after another period of 30 or so years we have the book of Malachi which again speaks to renewal of the people. The Old Testament closes with this final book.

A recurring emphasis occurs during the period of the return. People are motivated to accomplish a task for God. They start out, become discouraged, and stop. They must be renewed. God raises up leadership to bring renewal.

35. Prophetic Crises—Three Major Biblical Times

Let me now introduce some important definitions before giving further detail on the *Restoration Crisis*.

Some Definitions

In my leadership literature I define two restoration terms that are important. They have some overlap but also need to be seen as distinct.

Definition   *Restoration* (individual leader) is the process whereby a fallen leader is transitioned back into leadership. It usually involves repentance, restitution where appropriate, correction of the aberrant leadership dysfunctionalities, and recognition by other leaders of the restoration process and their stamp of approval for the leader to renew ministry.

Definition   *Corporate restoration* refers to God's attempts to restore the people of God as a viable channel through whom He can work to carry out His Biblical purposes.

It is this latter definition that is important to the third major crisis—the *Restoration Crisis*.

Description   The *restoration crisis* refers to the period of time from 539 B.C. to 430 B.C. and which covers the activity of God in bringing His people back into the land and establishing a testimony there. His providential care of His people (both in the land and outside it) is also shown.

The Restoration Crisis—Further Details

While it is true that God attempts restoration efforts throughout almost all the leadership eras in both the O.T. and N.T., I define the *Restoration Crisis* as the time specifically dealing with the return of the exiles to the land and the aftermath activities that occurred. This means the time from 539 B.C. when Daniel initiated the time with his great intercessory prayer in Daniel 9 to around 430 B.C. when Malachi made a major thrust at restoration. Table Hab 35-1 gives a brief overview of this time. The major Biblical books dealing with the *Restoration Crisis* include: Ezra, Haggai, Zechariah, Ezra, Nehemiah, Esther, and Malachi.

Table Hab 35-1. The Restoration Era Crises And Related Biblical Material

Item	539 B.C.	536 B.C.	520-516 B.C.	486-465 B.C.	465-424 B.C.	430 B.C.
Restoration Activity	Daniel Prays	Work on Temple Begun	Work on Temple begun again and Completed	Israelites Preserved due to Esther and Mordecai's activities	Wall is constructed around Jerusalem—Ezra and Nehemiah bring about restoration movement	Malachi again engenders restoration movement
Biblical Material	Daniel 9	Ez 3:12	Ez 6:13-15 Haggai Zechariah	Esther	Nehemiah; latter part of Ezra	Malachi
Crises	1. God's Timing and Faith	2. Public Testimony Needed Back in the Land	3. Public Testimony Needed—Work Stopped	4. People of God Outside of Land—Danger of being Destroyed	5. Protection of Jerusalem/ Public Testimony of People	6. Leadership Nominality; follower nominality

35. Prophetic Crises—Three Major Biblical Times

The themes of each of the biblical books dealing with the restoration crises should be seen in terms of the crises given above in Table Hab 35-1.

Table Hab 35-2 gives the theme of the relevant books along with the crisis that most likely prompted the activity of the book.

Table Hab 35-2. The Restoration Era Crises And Related Biblical Material

Crisis	Book	Theme/ Brief Explanation Relating to Corporate Restoration
1. God's Timing and Faith	Daniel	**THE MOST HIGH** (sovereign God) **RULES** in the affairs of individuals, nations, and history. **Brief Explanation:** Daniel shows how God is sovereignly working out his purposes and lays out a time table for God's future work. Included in that book is the crucial identification of the 70 years in captivity and the time to begin the restoration effort in Jerusalem.
2. Public Testimony Needed Back in the Land	Ezra	See below for explanation of Ezra theme.
3. Public Testimony Needed—Work Stopped	Ezra	See below for Ezra Theme
	Haggai	**God's Work in Rebuilding the Temple** (Under Haggai's Prophetic Impact) began when His people back in the land were renewed and reprioritized their lives in response to God's Word, initially brought discouragement and was counteracted by God's promise of His presence and blessing as the rebuilders obeyed God's Word, continued to be fueled by a God-given vision of what it could be, not what it was, and carried with it God affirmation and promise of power to the leadership inspiring this work, in an overwhelming time.
	Zechariah	**THE WORKING OF THE LORD ALMIGHTY** involves encouragement in the present to leaders, brings correction and hope to sincere followers, and reveals His future plans so as to cause anticipation and encouragement. **Brief Explanation:** Corporate restoration is an on-going process. Hope along with restoration comes when we get perspective on what God is doing and will do in the future.
4. People of God Outside of Land—Danger of being Destroyed	Esther	**THE PROVIDENTIAL WORKING OF GOD** involves foresight which includes His use of apparently natural events and responses behind the scenes in *anticipation* of later events, will test leadership in the crisis, will have timely intervention in unusual yet natural events to protect, and will accomplish His purposes in the end. **Brief Explanation:** This shows that God is still working both outside the land as well as in the land. The left hand of God is seen in the affairs of preservation that Mordecai and Esther take part in. The Left Hand of God is an important concept in the whole restoration era.
5. Protection of Jerusalem/ Public Testimony of People	Ezra	**EFFECTIVE LEADERSHIP IN JERUSALEM UNDER EZRA** built on a foundation of that done by Haggai, Zechariah, Zerubbabel, and Joshua, and involved a call back to Biblical standards for the people in Jerusalem. **Brief Explanation:** The heart of corporate restoration is to have people understand God's revelation for them and to obey it. Ezra's ministry did this.

35. Prophetic Crises—Three Major Biblical Times

	Nehemiah	**NEHEMIAH'S ORGANIZATIONAL LEADERSHIP** made itself felt in the face of obstacles to rebuild the wall, was inspirational in bringing about reform and a covenant in Jerusalem, and included drastic steps of separation in order to insure an on-going meaningful religious atmosphere. **Brief Explanation:** This book emphasizes the importance of civil leadership working with religious leadership in bringing about corporate restoration.
6. Leadership Nominality; follower nominality	Malachi	**NOMINALITY**, religious form without power and meaning, reflects a lack of understanding of God's love, is manifested by half-hearted obedience which hinders God's purposes, is perpetuated by nominal leadership, and ultimately will be corrected by God. **Brief Explanation:** The heart of corporate restoration is to have people understand God's revelation for them and to obey it. Malachi, like Ezra's ministry, did this. Both Ezra and Malachi's ministries show that the people of God will tend toward nominality over time and need intervention ministries that will call them back to God.

The important macro lessons that are illustrated in the restoration crisis era include the following (numbers refer to a list of 41 macro lessons seen in the Bible):

19.	**Stability**	**Preserving a ministry of God with life and vigor over time is as much if not more of a challenge to leadership than creating one.**
20.	**Spiritual Leadership**	**Spiritual leadership can make a difference even in the midst of difficult times.**
21.	**Recrudescence**	**Kingdom God will attempt to bring renewal to His people until they no longer respond to Him.**
22.	By-pass	God will by-pass leadership and structures that do not respond to Him and will institute new leadership and structures.
23.	Future Perfect	A primary function of all leadership is to walk by faith with a future perfect paradigm so as to inspire followers with certainty of God's accomplishment of ultimate purposes.
24.	**Perspective**	**Leaders must know the value of perspective and interpret present happenings in terms of God's broader purposes.**
25.	Modeling	Leaders can most powerfully influence by modeling godly lives, the sufficiency and sovereignty of God at all times, and gifted power.
26.	Ultimate	Leaders must remember that the ultimate goal of their lives and ministry is to manifest the glory of God.
27.	Perseverance	**Once known, leaders must persevere with the vision God has given.**

35. Prophetic Crises—Three Major Biblical Times

Of these, macro lessons 19, 20, 21, 24 and 27 directly relate to corporate restoration.

General Lessons Learned From Perspective on The There Major Crises

In observing the length of time of the northern kingdom leading to the Assyrian Crisis as compared to the length of time of the southern kingdom leading to the Babylonian Crisis, a much longer time, one can emphasize strongly the spiritual leadership macro lesson.

20. Spiritual Leadership
Spiritual leadership can make a difference even in the midst of difficult times.

In observing the intervention times in all three prophetic crises, one cannot but help notice the crucial sense of timing involved in God's activity through the prophets.

3. Timing Macro-Lesson
God's Timing Is Crucial To Accomplishment Of God's Purposes.

We should also be warned. God has by-passed leadership and structures in the past, which did not respond to His warnings. This can happen again to us in our church leadership eras. We should be warned.

22. By-pass
God will by-pass leadership and structures that do not respond to Him and will institute new leadership and structures.

In general, we note that if we are to be Bible Centered leaders who apply O.T. scriptures appropriately in our N.T. Church leadership era, we must study carefully the details of the historical background surrounding these O.T. writing. We must adhere carefully to the General Hermeneutical principle involved with historical background.

Historical Background Hermeneutical Principle
In The Spirit, Prayerfully Study The Historical Background Of The Book Which Includes Such Information As:
    a. the author of the book and the *historical perspective* from which he/she wrote.
    b. the *occasion* for the book
    c. the *purpose* for the book including where pertinent the people for whom it was intended and their situation.
    d. any geographical or cultural factors bearing on the communication of the material.

Closure
Perspective makes a difference. The difference between leaders and followers is perspective. The difference between leaders and more effective leaders is better perspective. Leaders today need perspective on how God has worked. To understand the writing prophets, the three major crises detailed in this article become very significant. Bible centered leaders who want to apply concepts from the writing prophets to today's ministry must understand the historical background associated with these major crises.

See **Article**, *Haggai—Calendar and Dating; Restoration Leaders; Civil Leadership, The Missing Ingredient; 28. Left Hand of God; 4. Redemptive Drama, The Biblical Framework; 36. Six Biblical Leadership Eras—Seeing the Bible With Leadership Eyes; 29. Macro Lesson, Defined; 30. Macro Lessons, List of 41 Across Six Leadership Eras.*

Article 36

36. Six Biblical Leadership Eras
Approaching the Bible with Leadership Eyes

Introduction

In my opinion, the Bible provides one of the richest resources that Christian leaders have on leadership. The Bible is full of leadership insights, lessons, values and principles about leaders and leadership. It is filled with influential people and the results of their influence... both good and bad.

Three assumptions undergird what I will say in this article.

1. I have a strong **conviction** that the Bible can give valuable leadership insights.
2. I have made a **willful decision** to study the Bible and use it as a source of leadership insights.[97]
3. To study the Bible for leadership insights, you need **leadership eyes** to see leadership findings in the Bible. That is, there are many leadership perspectives, i.e. paradigms, that help stimulate one to see leadership findings. I have been discovering and using these in my own study.

I want to do three things in this keynote overview. I want to introduce two most helpful perspectives for studying the Bible for leadership findings: 1. Seeing Leadership Eras; 2. Recognizing Leadership Genre. I will give more space to *the Six Leadership Eras*. These two concepts will help give one *leadership eyes*. And then I want to talk about the impact of the two most important boundary times between leadership eras, Moses desert leadership and Jesus' foundational work instigating a major movement. Both of these were fundamental and foundational times of Biblical leadership. They introduced radical macro lessons that deeply impact our own leadership today.

The Six Leadership Eras

A first step toward having *leadership eyes*, for recognizing leadership findings in the Bible involves seeing the various leadership eras in the Bible. These time periods share common leadership assumptions and expectations. These assumptions and expectations differ markedly from one leadership time period to the next. Though, of course, there are commonalties that bridge across the eras.

Definition — A *leadership era* is a period of time, usually several hundred years long,[98] in which the major focus of leadership, the influence means, basic leadership

---

[97] I have been doing this deliberately for ten years at this writing.
[98] There is one exception. Though technically, the N.T. Pre-Church Era includes the inter-testamental time, I only really focus on Jesus' ministry which lasted a short period of time. But it is so unique and so radically different from what preceded and followed it that I treat it as the essential time in this era.

functions, and followership have much in common and which basically differ with time periods before or after it.

Table Hab 36-1 contains the outline of the six eras I have identified.

Table Hab 36-1. Six Leadership Eras Outlined

Era	Label/ Details
I.	**Patriarchal Era** (Leadership Roots)—Family Base
II.	**Pre-Kingdom Leadership Era**—Tribal Base A. The Desert Years B. The War Years—Conquering the Land, C. The Tribal Years/ Chaotic Years/ Decentralized Years—Conquered by the Land
III.	**Kingdom Leadership Era**—Nation Based A. The United Kingdom B. The Divided Kingdom C. The Single Kingdom—Southern Kingdom Only
IV.	**Post-Kingdom Leadership Era**—Individual/ Remnant Based A. Exile—Individual Leadership Out of the Land B. Post Exilic—Leadership Back in the Land C. Interim—Between Testaments
V.	**New Testament Pre-Church Leadership**—Spiritually Based in the Land A. Pre-Messianic B. Messianic
VI.	**New Testament Church Leadership**—Decentralized Spiritually Based A. Jewish Era B. Gentile Era

The three overarching elements of leadership include: the *leadership basal elements* (leader, follower, situation which make up the **What** of leadership); *leadership influence means* (individual and corporate leadership styles which make up the **How** of leadership); and *leadership value bases* (theological and cultural values which make up the **Why** of leadership).[99] It was this taxonomy which suggested questions that helped me see for the first time the six leadership eras of the Bible. It is these categories that allow comparison of different leadership periods in the Bible. Later I will apply the taxonomy to each of the eras and give my preliminary findings.

Using these leadership characteristics I studied leadership across the Bible and inductively generated the six leadership eras as given above. Table Hab 36-2 adds some descriptive elements of the eras.

---

[99] See the **Article**, *Leadership Tree Diagram*, which explains in details these three elements of leadership.

Table Hab 36-2. Six Leadership Eras in the Bible—Definitive Characteristics

Leadership Era	Example(s) Leader(s)	Definitive Characteristics
1. Foundational (also called Patriarchal)	Abraham, Joseph	Family Leadership/ formally male dominated/ expanding into tribes and clans as families grew/ moves along kinship lines.
2. Pre-Kingdom	Moses, Joshua, Judges	Tribal Leadership/ Moving to National/ Military/ Spiritual Authority/ outside the land moving toward a centralized national leadership.
3. Kingdom	David, Hezekiah	National Leadership/ Kingdom Structure/ Civil, Military/ Spiritual/ a national leadership—Prophetic call for renewal/ inside the land/ breakup of nation.
4. Post-Kingdom	Ezekiel, Daniel, Ezra, Nehemiah	Individual leadership/ Modeling/ Spiritual Authority.
5. Pre-Church	Jesus/ Disciples	Selection/ Training/ spiritual leadership/ preparation for decentralization of Spiritual Authority/ initiation of a movement.
6. Church	Peter/ Paul/ John	decentralized leadership/ cross-cultural structures led by leaders with spiritual authority which institutionalize the movement and spread it around the world.

When we study a leader or a particular leadership issue in the Scripture, we must always do so in light of the leadership context in which it was taking place. We cannot judge past leadership by our present leadership standards. Yet, we will find that major leadership lessons learned by these leaders will usually have broad implications for our leadership.

Second Major Perspective for Getting Leadership Eyes—The Seven Leadership Genre

Further study of each of these leadership eras resulted in the identification of seven leadership genre which served as sources for leadership findings. I then worked out in detail approaches for studying each of these genre.[100] These seven leadership genre are shown in Table 36-3.

Table Hab 36-3. Seven Leadership Genre—Sources for Leadership Findings

Type	General Description/ Example	Approach
1. Biographical	Information about leaders; this is the single largest genre giving leadership information in the Bible/ **Joseph**	Use biographical analysis based on leadership emergence theory concepts.
2. Direct Leadership Contexts[101]	Blocks of Scripture which are giving information directly applicable to leaders/ leadership; relatively few of these in Scripture/ **1 Peter 5:1-4**	Use standard exegetical techniques.
3. Leadership Acts[102]	Mostly narrative vignettes describing a leader influencing followers, usually in some crisis situation; quite a few of	Use three-fold leadership tree diagram as basic source for suggesting what areas of leadership to look for.

---

[100] See **Leadership Perspectives—How To Study the Bible for Leadership Findings.** Altadena: Barnabas Publishers.

[101] I have identified many of the direct leadership texts and exegetically analyzed the important ones.

	these in the Bible/ **Acts 15 Jerusalem Council**	
4. Parabolic Passages[103]	Parables focusing on leadership perspectives: e.g. stewardship parables, futuristic parables; quite a few of these in Matthew and Luke./ **Luke 19 The Pounds**	Use standard parable exegetical techniques but then use leadership perspectives to draw out applicational findings; especially recognize the leadership intent of Jesus in giving these. Most such parables were given with a view to training disciples.
5. Books as a Whole	Each book in the Bible[104]; end result of this is a list of leadership observations or lessons or implications for leadership/ **Deuteronomy**	Consider each of the Bible books in terms of the leadership era in which they occur and for what they contribute to leadership findings; will have to use whatever other leadership genre source occurs in a given book; also use overall synthesis thinking.
6. Indirect Passages	Passages in the Scripture dealing with Biblical values applicable to all; more so to leaders who must model Biblical values/ **Proverbs; Sermon on the Mount**	Use standard exegetical procedures for the type of Scripture containing the applicable Biblical ethical findings or values.
7. Macro Lessons[105]	Generalized high level leadership observations seen in an era and which have potential for leadership absolutes/ **Presence Macro**	Use synthesis techniques utilizing various leadership perspectives to stimulate observations.

The Criteria For Evaluating An Era

What Are the Distinguishing Characteristics We Are Looking For? I have used the following categories:

1. Major Focus—

Here we are looking at the overall purposes of leadership for the period in question. What was God doing or attempting to do through the leader? Sense of destiny? Leadership mandate?

2. Influence means—

Here we are describing any of the power means available and used by the leaders in their leadership. We can use any of Wrong's categories or any of the leadership style categories I define. Note particularly in the Old Testament the use of force and manipulation as power means.

3. Basic leadership functions—

We list here the various achievement responsibilities expected of the leaders: from God's standpoint, from the leader's own perception of leadership, from the followers. Usually

---

[102] Many leadership acts have been identified and more than 20 have been analyzed. There is much work to do on analyzing leadership acts.

[103] I have studied every parable, exegetically, in Matthew, Mark and Luke for its central truth and applicable leadership lessons.

[104] I have done this for each book in the Bible over the past 10 years. My findings are included in **The Bible and Leadership Values** (and in the commentary series). Though I have made a good start, there is much more to be done here. I am intending other Handbooks which include all of the top 25 Bible books on leadership.

[105] This area needs the most research. Several PhD research projects are now focused on this.

they can all be categorized under the three major leadership functions of task, relational, and inspirational functions. But here we are after the specific functions.

4. Followers—
Here we are after sphere of influence. Who are the followers? What are their relationship to leaders? Which of the 10 Commandments of followership are valid for these followers? What other things are helpful in describing followers?

5. Local Leadership—
In the surrounding culture: Biblical leaders will be very much like the leaders in the cultures around them. Leadership styles will flow out of this cultural press. Here we are trying to identify leadership roles in the cultures in contact with our Biblical leaders.

6. Other:
Miscellaneous catch all; such things as centralization or decentralization or hierarchical systems of leadership; joint (civil, political, military, religious) or separate roles.

Thought Questions—
In addition to the above categories, I try to synthesize the questions that I would like answered about leaders and leadership if I could get those answers. With these thought questions I am considering such things as the essence of a leader (being or doing), leadership itself, leadership selection and training, authority (centralized or decentralized), etc.

My preliminary findings for these categories for each leadership era follows.

1st Leadership Era: Patriarchal Leadership
1. **Major Focus**—Pass on the promise and heritage of the Most High God to the family; priestly role (regularity)—intercede, sacrifice, and worship the Most High God;
2. **Influence means**—apostolic style, father-initiator, father-guardian, full range of Wrong's typology: force, manipulation, authority (coercive, inducive, positional—fatherly head, competence, personal), spiritual authority
3. **Five basic leadership functions**—(1) Godly/ priestly functions:- demonstrate absolute loyalty to God; - demonstrate reality of the unseen God; - pass on heritage of what is known (revelatory) of God and His ways and desires, very little revelation, animistic; - pass on sense of destiny; —God's prophetic promises; (2) Primarily performing the inspirational function—largely through modeling; the relational function consisted primarily of keeping the family together and obedience to the patriarch. Inspirational function -Creating hope in God -Creating sense of God's intervention in life; (3) Mediate Blessing of God: - contagious blessing; - heritage blessing; (4) Military head—protection of family; (5) Civil—judge/ justice
4. **Followers**—family members: (1) Age/masculine-oriented; (2) Almost all of 10 Followership Laws in force; (3) Oldest to receive blessing and birthright; (4) The one receiving blessing and birthright passes it on to next generation
5. **Local Leadership**—in the culture around the Patriarchs: - tribal heads; - City States / Regional heads (called kings);
   - local priests (practitioners/ animistic); - local military
6. **Other:** Highly Decentralized; each given family responsible to God

Thought Questions— 1. How did other families relate to God (Melchezidek's, Labin's, etc.)? 2. What were expectations of Patriarchs as leaders? by followers? by God? by

36. Six Biblical Leadership Eras, Using Leadership Eyes

surrounding culture? 3. What was the foundational aspect of character? What was integrity to the Patriarchs? 4. What was the birthright? What was the blessing? 5. If modeling was the primary training methodology, what were the most important positive leadership qualities modeled by Abraham? by Isaac? by Jacob? by Joseph? by Job? 6. Using a modified form of the six characteristics of finishing well, how did the Patriarchs finish? Abraham? Isaac? Jacob? Joseph? Job?

2nd Leadership Era: Pre-Kingdom Leadership

1. **Major Focus**—Uniting of a people, preparing them to follow God, preparing them to invade the promised land, settling them in the land. The Desert leadership is one of discipline, a heavy time of revelation, and supernatural events backing leadership. The Challenge Era is one of stretching of faith to overcome the many obstacles involved in capturing the land. The Judges Era has the major challenge of how to unite disparate peoples, survive attacks, and degeneration of relationship to God. In each there is Charismatic Leadership: You lead because of spiritual authority, personal authority or competence not because of nepotism or birth; a formal priestly role is secondary—there is an inheritance with this role—and this leadership is weak, probably because of that.
2. **Influence means**—apostolic style, father-initiator, father-guardian, full range of Wrong's typology: force, manipulation, authority (coercive, inducive, positional—fatherly head, competence, personal), spiritual authority
3. **7 basic leadership functions** seen include: (1) Centralize Authority/ Develop Authority Structures:- military, political, religious;- tribal/ trans-tribal (elders); (2) Primarily performing the inspirational function: -Creating hope in God; -Creating sense of God's intervention in life. (3) Revelatory (Desert)/Inscribe and pass on the basic revelation of God as given in the law/how to live separated lives; (4) Military head—protection/ mobilize an on-call army distributed over the tribes; (5) Civil—judge/ justice/ set up legal system for interpreting and applying the law; (6) Fulfill Promise of Taking the Land; settling it; (7) Call to renewal; recrudescence; see God work anew.
4. **Followers**—12 large tribes:(1) Age/ masculine-oriented leadership; (2) Almost all of 10 Followership Laws in force; centralization out of balance; leadership more nepotistic than functional; reciprocal commands a legalistic thing carried by enforcement of law.
5. **Local Leadership**—in the surrounding culture:- tribal heads; - City State / Regional heads (called kings); - local priests (practitioners/ animistic); - local military
6. **Other**: Highly centralized during desert and capturing of land; highly decentralized during Judges era/ continuity of leadership a major problem except for the first transition from Moses to Joshua

Thought Questions:
1. How were leaders selected and developed? 2. What did they do at the different levels? 3. What is missing from the Judges Era that was the driving force of the Warfare Era? 4. What has happened to the Abrahamic mandate? Which of the eras, if any, are concerned with that mandate? 5. How does this era compare with the Patriarchal, spiritually?

3rd Leadership Era: Kingdom Leadership

1. **Major Focus**—The Kingdom united the dispersed tribal groups into a more cohesive nation which could provide government and military protection. The Davidic covenant was part of an on-going means to bring about Abraham's promise and to manifest the concept of God's rule on earth as well as provide resources to bring others into relationship with God. It never lived up to its ideals.
2. **Influence means**—the full range of Wrong's typology : **force, manipulation, authority** (coercive, inducive, positional)—fatherly head; competence, personal, spiritual authority.
3. **6 basic leadership functions** seen include:(1) Centralize Authority/ Develop Authority Structures:- military, political, religious; - tribal/ trans-tribal (elders); (2) Revelatory (Particularly in the Divided Kingdom and the Single Kingdom)/ Much of the

corrective revelation done by the prophets was oral. But there was also the Prophetic revelation which was inscribed. Often these writings were a call to repentance, renewal, and a return to kingdom ideals; (3) Military head—protection/ have a standing army that could defend against the attacks that were coming more frequently from the expanding empires or ambitious kings. They would also mobilize an on-call army distributed over the tribes to go along with the standing army in big crises. (4) Civil—judge/justice/set up legal system for interpreting and applying the law; (5) Call to renewal; recrudescence; see God work anew (prophetic function); (6) Persevere as a people of God; maintain a base from which God could work. Major Problems: communication and control; followership scattered over large area; -large empires on the rise

4. Followers—a. United Kingdom-12 large tribes, also the many surrounding small kingdoms that were conquered
b. Divided Kingdom—Northern-10 1/2 Large Tribes c. Southern—About 1 1/2 tribes—mostly Judah; Leadership (1) Age/ masculine oriented; (2) Almost all of 10 Followership Laws in force; centralization out of balance; leadership more nepotistic than functional;

5. Local Leadership—in the surrounding cultures: - tribal heads; - kings of territories with a number of cities; usually one dominated and was walled; - local priests (practitioners/ animistic); - military.

6. Other: Large Empires are vying for world dominion or at least for large influence: Assyria, Egypt, Babylon

Thought Questions: 1. Why were the prophets raised up? 2. According to Deuteronomy what was the place of the law for the Kings? Was it followed? 3. Was the central religious function (the three yearly treks) carried out? 4. Why was the nepotistic approach to leadership selection used? Was it successful? 5. How does this era compare spiritually with the Pre-Kingdom era?

4th Leadership Era: Post-Kingdom Leadership

1. Major Focus—The nation no longer exists. It has been disciplined by God. Leadership during this time must do several things: analyze what happened and why; bring hope during this time; demonstrate the importance of godliness under oppressive conditions; demonstrate the importance of God's sovereignty; point to the future in which God is going to work.

2. Influence means—largely by modeling, spiritual authority, toward latter time in the time of the return, Jewish leaders again take up roles: political, religious, quasi-military for the Jewish people.

3. Basic leadership functions seen include: The inspirational function is dominant. The need for community in little pockets brings out the need for the relational function of leadership. The rise of the synagogues—small communities upholding their Jewish origins and religion bring about the need for scribes, and those who interpret the written scriptures.

4. Followers—Pockets of scattered Jewish people

5. Local Leadership—in the surrounding cultures: - tribal heads; - City States / Regional heads (called kings); - local priests (practitioners/ animistic); - local military; - emperors/ kings/ heads of powerful international groups formed by conquering vast territories and kingdoms/ various administrative leaders under these

6. Other: ?

Thought Questions: 1. Why did Jewish leaders prosper during these oppressive days? 2. What kinds of leadership did they participate in? 3. What has happened to the Abrahamic promise? How did the Jewish people feel about it in these days? 4. How were religious leaders selected (e.g. for the synagogues)?

5th Leadership Era: Pre-Church Leadership

1. Major Focus—Galatians 4:4. This is the acme of charismatic leadership. Jesus models servant leadership and ideal spiritual authority—all aspects of it. The end result of this leadership is revelation, redemption, and a movement to universalize the redemption to all humankind.

2. Influence Means—the entire range of Pauline leadership styles are demonstrated. The whole range of Wrong's Typology is seen.

3. Leadership Functions: (1) Provide the redemptive base reconciling God and humankind and its major ramifications, the revelation and enabling power for human beings to realize their idealized human potential.
(2) Provide a leadership mandate that will utilize all three major leadership functions in its fulfillment. Task, relational, and inspirational functions are essential to the accomplishment of the mandate. (3) Create a movement that will institutionalize the leadership functions for on-going effective leadership. (4) Provide a call for renewal to Israel. (5) Present the Kingdom of God in concept and power. (6) Provide a revelatory base, model, and standards for future revelation.

4. Followers—In the land there were remnants of the tribes, mixed ethnic groups (like Samaritans), religious leadership like the Pharisees, Saducees, and the political leaders of the Roman empire along with garrisons of Roman Military to give authority as well as the Jewish Religious leaders the Sanhedrin.

5. Local Leaders: Sanhedrin, Saducees, Pharisees, Lawyers, Roman Military, Synagogues/ elders, Rabbis.

6. Other: This is a mixed era of centralized and decentralized means and authority. Jerusalem provided some means of religious centralization. There was political centralization in a number of centers. But Jesus leadership was not centralized.

Thought Questions:1. What renewal aims did Christ specifically focus on? 2. What were the leadership selection and development processes in existence in the culture? 3. What were Jesus' leadership selection and development processes? How different? 4. How does Christ leadership compare or contrast with essential characteristics of each of the previous eras?

6th Leadership Era: Church Leadership

1. Major Focus—When Barnabas and Paul give their report to the elders back in Jerusalem at the Jerusalem conference described in Acts 15, there is much discussion. Finally, James summarizes the essence of the major focus of the Church leadership era, "Simon has declared how God at the first did visit the Gentiles, to take out of them a people for his name (Acts 15;14)." The central message of the book of Acts emphasizes this thrust in more detail. THE GROWTH OF THE CHURCH which spreads from Jerusalem to Judea to Samaria and the uttermost parts of the earth is seen to be of God, takes place as Spirit directed people present a salvation centered in Jesus Christ, and occurs among all peoples, Jews and Gentiles. During this leadership era, God is developing an institution that will carry His salvation to all cultures and all peoples. The development of this decentralized institution which can be fitted to any culture and people, the church, with its nature its leadership and its purposes for existing will be at the heart of this leadership era. Paul is a major architect of this leadership era. The book of 2 Corinthians is especially helpful to give us insights into early church leadership.

2. Influence Means—My past leadership studies have identified a number of leadership styles. In particular, I have categorized ten Pauline leadership styles. The entire range of Pauline leadership styles are demonstrated during the Church Leadership Era. The whole range of Wrong's Typology is seen including force, manipulation, authority, and persuasion power forms.

3. Leadership Functions—All three of the generic leadership functions are prominent: task oriented leadership, relationship oriented leadership and inspirational leadership. The major models for this era include Peter, John, and Paul with much more information given about Paul. Paul is dominantly a task-oriented leader with a powerful inspirational focus. He sees the necessity of relationship oriented leadership but that is not his strength. John is more of a relationship-oriented leader who also has a powerful inspirational thrust. Peter is dominantly a task oriented leader with inspirational thrust. As each matures they become more gentle—that is, relational leadership begins to come to the front. But always they are dominantly inspirational. God is creating new forms through which to reveal Himself to the world and followers must be inspired to participate and carry it all over the world in the face of persecution and obstacles.

4. Followers—The beauty of the church lies in its ability as an institutional form to fit into any culture. Since leadership in a given culture is defined in part by the followers expectations of what a leader is, we will have distinctive differences in various cultures as to leadership and followership. Each cultural situation will be different and hence have its unique demands. But there are commonalties in Biblical church leadership across cultures. This is seen especially in the values which determine why leaders operate and the standards by which they are judged. The book of 2 Corinthians helps us understand key leadership values.

5. Local Leaders—Various kinds of models of leadership existed in the various cultures. Paul, the main architect of local church leadership, gives us various descriptions of qualitative characteristics of leaders in his various epistles. The essential trait that flows throughout all of them is integrity. But Paul having described key character traits recognizes that these will manifest themselves differently in different cultures and situations.

6. Other—The church leadership era is a highly decentralized period of time. Churches are to exist in all cultures and peoples. They will be spread far and wide. Because of the decentralized nature of the church it is especially important to ask what unites it? What is common? Particularly is this important for leadership. And one of the answers is leadership values. 2 Corinthians helps us see some of the values that Paul modeled.

The Findings—The Best of Each Era

Table Hab 36-4 summarizes the more important aspects of each of the leadership eras.

Table Hab 36-4. Six Leadership Eras, On-Going Impact Items, Follow-Up

Era	On-Going Impact Items And Areas For Follow-Up Study
1. Patriarchal	Destiny leadership; Introduction of biographical study of leadership (Abraham, Isaac, Jacob, Joseph, Job); God's shaping processes introduced; intercession macro lesson introduced; character strength highlighted (Abraham, Jacob, Joseph); leadership responsibility to God instigated (accountability); leadership responsibility to followers introduced (blessing); leadership intimacy with God introduced (Abraham—friend of God, Job—trusting in deep processing). **Key Macro Lesson**: Destiny—Leaders must have a sense of destiny.
2. Pre-Kingdom	Seven Macro lessons from Moses' desert leadership (Timing; Intimacy; Intercession; Burden; Presence; Hope; Transition); Spiritual authority highlighted in Moses' and Joshua's ministries; pitfalls of centralized leadership seen; pitfalls of decentralized leadership seen; roots of inspirational leadership seen (Moses, Joshua, Caleb, Deborah, Jephthah, Samuel, David); outstanding biographical genre material. **Key Macro Lesson**: Presence—The essential ingredient of leadership is the powerful presence of God in the leader's life and ministry.
3. Kingdom	Five macros carry a warning for all future leadership (Unity; Stability; Spiritual Leadership; Recrudescence; By-Pass). Excellent biographical material both positive and negative examples (Saul, David, Asa, Josiah, Uzziah, Hezekiah, Elijah, Elisha, Jonah, Habakkuk, Ezekiel, Jeremiah and many others). **Key Macro Lesson**: Spiritual leadership can make a difference in the midst of difficult times.
4. Post-Kingdom	All five macros stress revelational perspective (Future Perfect; Perspective; Modeling; Ultimate, Perseverance). Excellent biographical genre available (Ezekiel, Daniel, Ezra, Nehemiah). **Key Macro Lesson**: Future Perfect—A primary function of all leadership

36. Six Biblical Leadership Eras, Using Leadership Eyes

	is to walk by faith with a future perfect paradigm so as to inspire followers with certainty of God's accomplishment of ultimate purposes.
5. Pre-Church	Selection/ Training/ spiritual leadership/ preparation for decentralization of Spiritual Authority/ initiation of a movement. Major Biographical— Jesus' and his movement leadership. **Key Macro Lesson**: Focus—Leaders must increasingly move toward a focus in their ministry which moves toward fulfillment of their calling and their ultimate contribution to God's purposes for them.
6. Church	Decentralized leadership/ cross-cultural structures led by leaders with spiritual authority, which institutionalize the movement and spread it around the world. Excellent biographical (Peter, Barnabas—a bridge leader, Paul, John); numerous leadership acts. **Key Macro Lesson**: Universal—The church structure is universal and can fit any culture. It must be propagated to all peoples.

The Foundational Transitions—Moses' And Jesus' Leadership Eras

Three figures give perspectives on Biblical leadership. Figure Hab 36-1 illustrates the relative time involved in the six leadership eras. Figure Hab 36-2 pinpoints distinctive features of leadership across the time-line. Figure Hab 36-3 focuses on the two major transitions—Moses' Desert Leadership; Jesus' Movement Leadership.

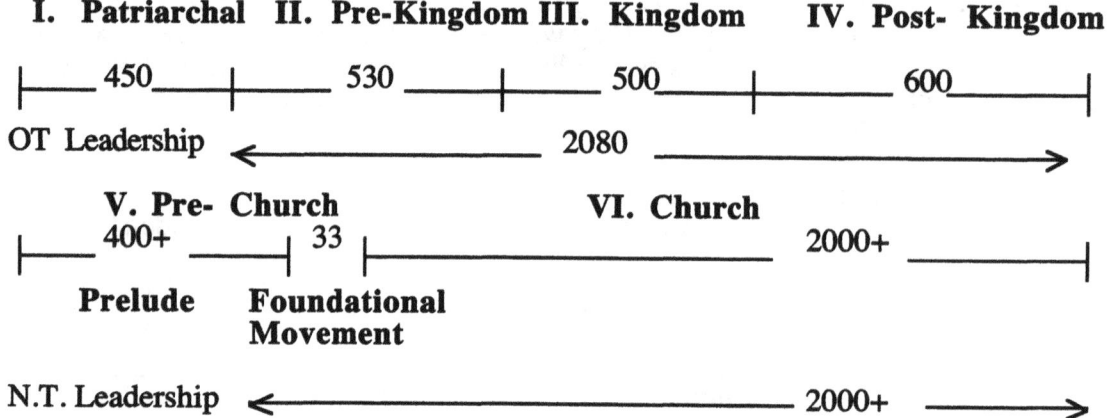

Figure Hab 36-1. Leadership Eras— Rough Chronological Length In Years

36. Six Biblical Leadership Eras, Using Leadership Eyes

I. Patriarchal Leadership Roots	II. Pre-Kingdom Leadership	III. Kingdom Leadership	IV. Post-Kingdom	V. N.T. Pre-Church Leadership	VI. Church Leadership
A. Abraham B. Isaac C. Jacob D. Joseph E. Job	A. Desert B. Conquering The Land C. Conquered By the Land	A. United B. Divided C. Single	A. Exile B. Post Exile C. Interim	A. Pre-Messianic B. Messianic	A. Jewish B. Gentile
Family	Revelatory Task Inspirational	Political Corrective	Modeling Renewal	Cultic Spiritual Movement	Spiritual Institutional
Blessing Shaping Timing Destiny Character Faith Purity	(Timing) Presence Intimacy Burden Hope Challenge Spiritual Authority Transition Weakness Continuity	Unity Stability Spiritual Leadership Recrudescence By-Pass	Hope Perspective Modeling Ultimate Perseverance	Training Focus Spirituality Servant Steward Shepherd Movement	Structure Universal Giftedness Word Centered Harvest

Figure Hab 36-2. Overview Time-Line of Biblical Leadership

In Figure Hab 36-2 above, macro lesson labels occur at the bottom in the six columns. Just above the macro lesson labels are given distinctive characteristics of each of the eras. Finally, above that occurs the outline of the sub-time periods and the major time-line with the six eras.

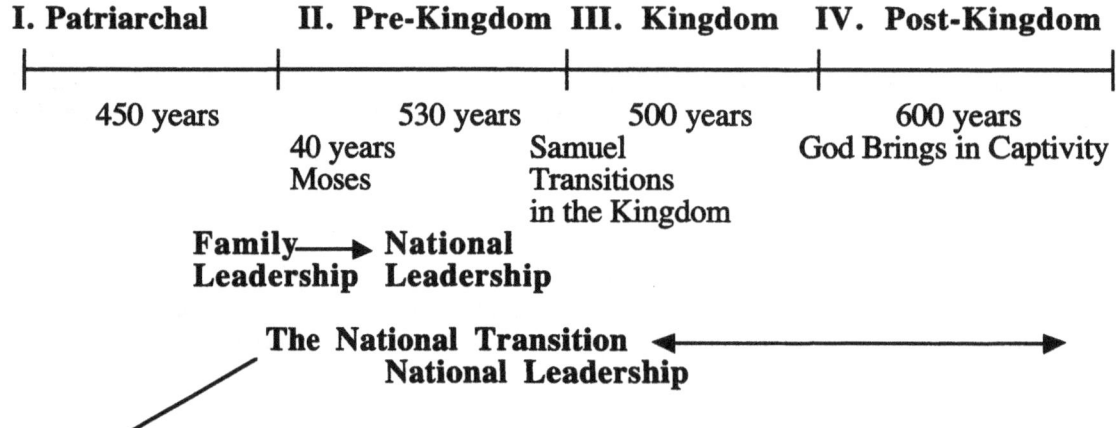

Crucial Macro Lessons: 3. Timing, 8. Intercession, 9. Presence, 10. Intimacy, 11. Burden, 12. Hope, 13. Challenge, 14. Spiritual Authority, 15. Transition.

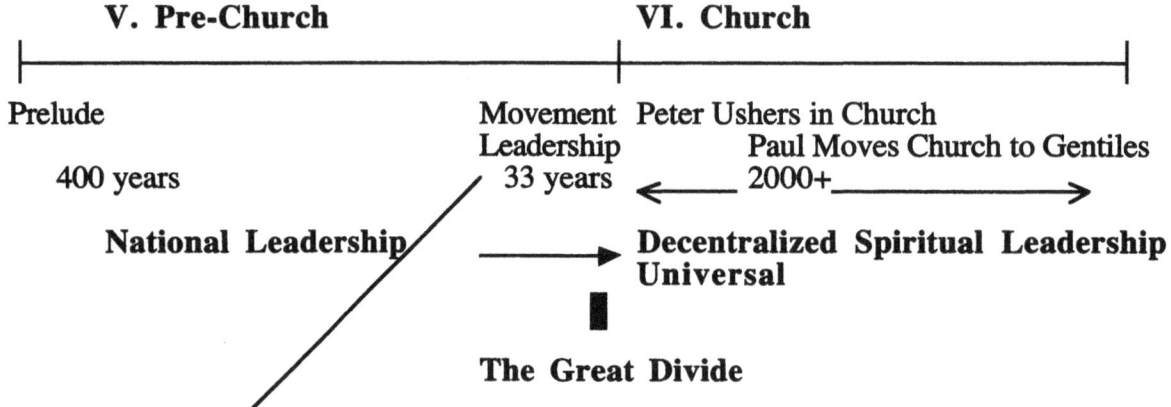

Crucial Macro Lessons: 28. Selection, 29. Training, 30. Focus, 31. Spirituality, 32. Servant, 33. Steward, 34. Harvest, 37. Shepherd, 36. Movement.

Figure Hab 36-3. Two Major Transitions—The National Transition and The Great Divide

Note two things. These major transition times were short. God brought in major changes in a short period of time. Both transition times contain a large number of important macro lessons. For such short periods of time these are relatively large numbers of important leadership lessons.

Table Hab 36-5 lists the transitions and key figures and the result of the transition.

Table Hab 36-5. Transitions Along the Biblical Leadership Time-Line

Transition	Eras Involved	Key Figure/ Results
To God Directed Leadership	Begin Patriarchal Era	Abraham/ a God directed destiny involving an ethnic group and leaders from that group hearing God, getting revelation from Him, and obeying God.
Tribal to National	From the Patriarchal Era to the Pre-Kingdom Era	Moses/ A nation is established. God established concept of influential leader with spiritual authority to direct the nation; God reveals truth about Himself, life, and destiny for this nation. Major leadership guidelines

		(important macro lessons) flow through this transitional leadership.
Federation to Kingdom	Pre-Kingdom to Kingdom	Samuel/ A dispersed geographical/tribal society, each doing its own thing and basically not following God-given truth, is moved toward a centralized, unified national entity directed by one major leader—a king, who is to direct the nation with God's direction.
Babylonian Captivity	From Kingdom to Post-Kingdom	God/ God dismantles the kingdom structure. He disperses the followers. God by-passes the kingdom leadership altogether and begins a long preparation that will eventually emerge in spiritual leadership. In this era, individual spiritual leadership is highlighted in which God's perspective is crucial.
The Great Divide	From Post-Kingdom to Pre-Church. From a defunct national leadership to spiritual leadership which can be decentralized anywhere.	Jesus/ Jesus re-established God-directed leadership—the concept of the Kingdom of God. God by-passes the Jewish national leadership when they reject Him—i.e. His message through Jesus. Jesus at the same time of offering the kingdom also builds the foundational roots of a movement which will eventually contextualize the Kingdom of God in an institutional church form which can move into any culture on earth.
Universal Invitation	From Pre-Church to Church	Peter, Paul/ Peter ushers in the church to the Jewish followers of Jesus. Paul takes the church to the Gentiles. God's invitation of salvation and His truth for living God-directed lives become available (decentralized) to any people on the earth.

Note that that there are transition times between all the eras. Each of these are important in themselves but two stand out: Moses' Desert-Leadership; Jesus' Movement-Leadership. As is sometimes the case crucial transitions in the Bible are foundational. God focuses intently in these times and usually reveals foundational truth. Such is the case with all the transitions.

Tables Hab 36-6 and Hab 36-7 give the macro lessons discovered in these key transition times with suggested implications for today.

Table Hab 36-6. Moses' Transition/ Lessons/ Implications

Timing— God's timing is crucial to accomplishment of God's purposes. **Implication**(s): Leaders today, especially in their complex ministries involving multi-cultural settings, must be more sensitive to the timing of God than ever before.

Intercession— Leaders called to a ministry are called to intercede for that ministry. **Implication**(s): Various prayer movements have gained tremendous momentum in our day testifying to the fact that God sees this as a very important aspect of leadership in our day.

Presence— The essential ingredient of leadership is the powerful presence of God in the leader's life and ministry. **Implication**(s): Much present day leadership misses the balance of this—God both in powerful ministry and in powerful life changing impact in the leader himself/herself.

Intimacy— Leaders develop intimacy with God which in turn overflows into all their ministry since ministry flows out of being. **Implication**(s): Doing and achievement dominate present day leadership. God through the various spirituality movements is calling leaders back to spirituality and beingness as the core of their ministries.

Burden— Leaders feel a responsibility to God for their ministry. **Implication**(s): Accountability is missing altogether in most cultures. This is true of Christian leadership as well. Sensitivity to this needed ingredient would avoid many of the leadership gaffes that are seen.

Hope— A primary function of all leadership is to inspire followers with hope in God and in what God is doing. **Implication**(s): This is especially true for leaders trying to reach Xers—generally without hope. But it is needed in all ministries as complex situations tend to take away hope for most Christians.

Challenge— Leaders receive vision from God which sets before them challenges that inspire their leadership. **Implication**(s): A leader must hear from God if that leader is to influence specific groups of people toward God's purposes—the basic definition of a leader. This is deeply needed especially in the many small churches which are floundering in our day.

Spiritual Authority—Spiritual authority is the dominant power base of a spiritual leader and comes through experiences with God, knowledge of God, godly character and gifted power. **Implication**(s): Abuse of power is one of the five major barriers facing leaders today. There are lots of leaders with all kinds of authority but few who exercise spiritual authority as a primary power base (with all its implications).

Transition—Leaders must transition other leaders into their work in order to maintain continuity and effectiveness. **Implication**(s): Every work of God is just one generation away from failure if it does not transition emerging leaders into its decision-making influential positions.

Table Hab 36-7. Jesus' Transition/ Lessons/ Implications

Selection— The key to good leadership is the selection of good potential leaders which should be a priority of all leaders. **Implication**(s): Leadership selection is desperately needed in church and parachurch organizations. Recruitment is often haphazard at best, especially in local church situations.

Training—Leaders should deliberately train potential leaders in their ministry by available and appropriate means. **Implication**(s): If emerging new leaders are not developed they will exit organizations and go somewhere else, depriving churches and parachurch organizations of on-going leadership. Leading with a developmental bias is the key to seeing on-going recruitment and longevity in organizational life.

Focus— Leaders should increasingly move toward a focus in their ministry which moves toward fulfillment of their calling and their ultimate contribution to God's purposes for them. **Implication**(s): Focused leaders are few and far between. Most leaders are faddish leaders jumping on the bandwagon of other apparently successful leaders. What is needed is leaders, knowing their own focus, and following it. Focused leaders are the need of the hour.

Spirituality— Leaders must develop interiority, spirit sensitivity, and fruitfulness in accord with their uniqueness since ministry flows out of being. **Implication**(s): As previously seen with the intimacy lesson from Moses' era, spirituality is crucial to leadership. And what is true of intimacy, one aspect of spirituality, is true as leaders develop balanced spirituality. Doing and achievement dominate present day leadership. God through the various spirituality movements is calling leaders back to spirituality and beingness as the core of their ministries.

Servant— Leaders must maintain a dynamic tension as they lead by serving and serve by leading. **Implication**(s): Servant leadership is not naturally found in any culture. It requires a paradigm shift for any leader to move into this leadership model—which is what Jesus intended for leaders he developed. Because of accepted leadership patterns in some cultures (great power distance) this is really difficult for emerging leaders to see or

accept.
Steward — Leaders are endowed by God with natural abilities, acquired skills, spiritual gifts, opportunities, experiences, and privileges which must be developed and used for God. **Implication**(s): Accountability is greatly needed in our generation where successful leaders dominantly self-authenticate their own ministries and heed little or nothing from outside resources which could hold them accountable.
Harvest — Leaders must seek to bring people into relationship with God. **Implication**(s): The outward aspect of the Great Commission must be carried out. God is focusing on this as He continues to raise up missionary movements from all over the world. The impetus of the missionary movement has already moved from the western world to the non-western world. We need to support this while at the same time bringing about renewal of missionary thinking in the western world.
Shepherd — Leaders must preserve, protect, and develop God's people. **Implication**(s): God still gets most of the leadership business done at local church level. Leaders who hold to the shepherd model concepts must in fact carry local church ministries — especially as cultures become more radically opposed to Gospel values. This means that more pastoral work will be necessary if we are winning those from deteriorating cultures.
Movement — Leaders recognize that movements are the way to penetrate society though they must be preserved via appropriate on-going institutions. **Implication**(s): New life can be instilled in parachurch organizations and churches when movement ideals are focused on. We see all around us movement leaders being raised up by God who are creating new ministries which God is blessing. This can be done more deliberately and proactively when movement dynamics are heeded.

Conclusion

The Six Leadership Eras and the seven leadership genre provide major perspectives for studying leadership in the Bible. The leadership commentary series analyzes Bible books and applies these perspectives. Of particular importance are two of the leadership genre — the *macro lessons* across each leadership era and the Bible *books as a whole*. The macro lessons flowing from Moses' desert leadership and Jesus' movement foundations are particularly instructive. They apply with great force to today's leadership challenges.

See **Articles**, *Biographical Study in the Bible — How To Do; Bible Centered Leader; Leadership Act; Leadership Eras in the Bible — Six Identified; Leadership Genre — Seven Types; 29. Macro Lessons Defined; 30. Macro Lessons — List of 41 Across Six Leadership Eras; Principle of Truth.*

Article 37

37. Spiritual Disciplines—And On-Going Leadership

Introduction

Comparative study of effective leaders who finished will unearthed five factors[106] which enhanced their perseverance and good finish. One of those was the presence of spiritual disciplines in the life

> **Leaders who have disciplines in their lives are more likely to persevere and finish well than those who do not.**

We do not know whether Habakkuk finished well. Our information on him concerns only one small slice of his life—a crisis moment in his leadership. But we do know that in that crisis moment seven spiritual disciplines are implied. If we had more information about his life we could firm up these tentative identifications. But from a superficial identification we see that Habakkuk probably practiced:

- **4 Disciplines of Engagement:** *Prayer* (the whole book); *Celebration* (see ch 3 especially); *worship* (see 3:1ff); *confession* (the whole book is a confession of a critical time of doubting in his life).
- **2 Abstinence Disciplines:** *silence*, *solitude* (for both see 2:1).
- **1 Miscellaneous Discipline:** *journaling* (we have the book).

Let me suggest that as a practice to remind you of how important spiritual disciplines are for a leader, that when you study any leader in Scripture, seek to identify tentatively any spiritual disciplines that are in the life.

Leaders need discipline of all kinds. Especially is this true of spiritual disciplines.

---

[106] The list of five enhancement factors includes the following. Enhancement 1—Perspective. Leaders need to have a lifetime perspective on ministry. Effective leaders view present ministry in terms of a lifetime perspective. Enhancement 2—Renewal. Special moments of intimacy with God, challenges from God, new vision from God and affirmation from God both for personhood and ministry will occur repeatedly to a growing leader. Enhancement 3—Disciplines. Leaders who have disciplines in their lives are more likely to persevere and finish well than those who do not. Enhancement 4—Learning Posture. The single most important antidote to plateauing is a well developed learning posture Enhancement 5—Mentoring. Leaders who are effective and finish well will have from 10 to 15 significant people who came alongside at one time or another to help them.

37. Spiritual Disciplines—And On-Going Leadership

Definition — <u>Spiritual disciplines</u> are activities of mind and body purposefully undertaken to bring personality and total being into effective cooperation with the Spirit of God so as to reflect Kingdom life.

When Paul was around 50 years of age he wrote to the Corinthian church what appears to be both an exhortation to the Corinthians and an explanation of a major leadership value in his own life. We need to keep in mind that he had been in ministry for about 21 years. He was still advocating strong discipline. I paraphrase it in my own words.

> I am serious about finishing well in my Christian ministry. I discipline myself for fear that after challenging others into the Christian life I myself might become a casualty. 1 Co 9:24-27

Lack of physical discipline is often an indicator of laxity in the spiritual life as well. Toward the end of his life, Paul is probably between 65 and 70, he is still advocating discipline. This time he writes to Timothy, who is probably between 30 and 35 years old.

> 7 But avoid godless legends and old wives' fables. Instead exercise your mind in godly things. 8 For physical exercise is advantageous somewhat but exercising in godliness has long term implications both for today and for that which will come. 1Ti 4:7,8

Certain practices are assumed in the Scriptures as valid for developing spirituality and have been proven empirically in church history to aid development of spirituality. The scriptures do not define most of the disciplines that have come to be accepted but do mention most of them.

37. Spiritual Disciplines—And On-Going Leadership

Three Major Categories of Disciplines

The following two categories have proved helpful in describing spiritual disciplines.

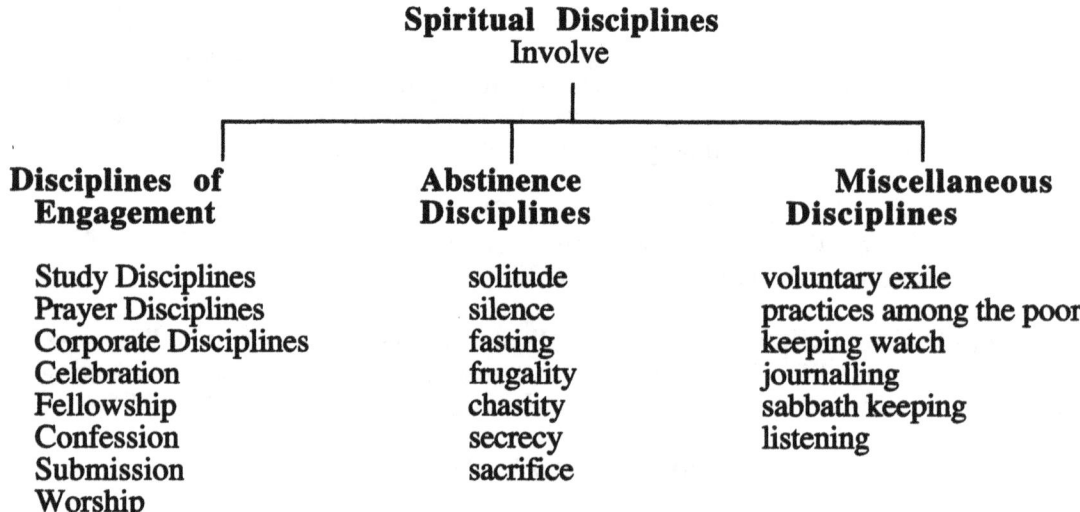

Disciplines of Engagement	Abstinence Disciplines	Miscellaneous Disciplines
Study Disciplines	solitude	voluntary exile
Prayer Disciplines	silence	practices among the poor
Corporate Disciplines	fasting	keeping watch
Celebration	frugality	journalling
Fellowship	chastity	sabbath keeping
Confession	secrecy	listening
Submission	sacrifice	
Worship		

Most leaders are somewhat familiar with the disciplines of engagement. I will define the abstinence disciplines since less is known about them.

Table Hab 37-1 defines the disciplines. Table Hab 37-2 lists purposes/applications of them.

Table Hab 37-1. Abstinence Disciplines Defined

Discipline	Defined
solitude	The discipline of Solitude is a purposeful abstention from interaction with other human beings and the denial of companionship and all that comes from interaction with others with a view toward focussing on spiritual things.
silence	The discipline of silence is the practice of not speaking and closing oneself off from all kinds of sounds.
fasting	The discipline of fasting is the deliberate abstinence from food and possibly drink for a period of time.
frugality	The discipline of frugality is the abstention from using money or goods at our disposal in ways that merely gratify our desires or our hunger for status, glamour, or luxury.
chastity	A chaste person (whether married or single) is one who manifests the qualities of sexual wholeness and integrity in relationship to oneself, to persons of the same sex and to persons of the opposite sex.
secrecy	The practice of secrecy results from disciplined activities in which one seeks to abstain from causing ones good deeds and qualities to be known.
sacrifice	The discipline of sacrifice is the abstention from the possession or enjoyment of what is necessary for our living and involves forsaking the security of meeting our own needs with what is in our possession.

Table Hab 37-2. Abstinence Disciplines—Some purposes

Discipline	Defined
solitude	to free us from routine and controlling behaviors in order to gain God's perspective—to hear better; teach us to live inwardly; teach us to slow down; gain a new freedom to be with people.

37. Spiritual Disciplines—And On-Going Leadership

silence	to cause us to consider our words fully before we say them so as to exercise better control over what we say; to listen to people more attentively; to observe others and other things; to allow life-transforming concentration upon God.
fasting	teaches self-denial; physical well being—cleanse body; releases power; increased sense of the presence of God in intercessory prayer; increased effectiveness; revelation from God; increase of spiritual authority; guidance in decisions; deliverance for those in bondage; increased concentration; brings intensive focus in Bible study.
frugality	frees us from concern and involvement with a multitude of desires; frees from the spiritual bondage caused by debt; teaches us respect for responsible stewardship; lessens the importance of things as essential to life; teaches us empathy for those who do not have resources; can lead toward simplicity as a way of life—the arrangement of life around a few consistent purposes, explicitly excluding what is not necessary to human well-being.
chastity	as an aid to total concentration while having extended times of fasting and praying; in marriage, bring proper focus so that sexual gratification is seen not to be the center of a relationship; recognize the importance of persons as persons; point out the power of lust in a life; teach positive relationships with those of opposite sex.
secrecy	to help us control a desire for fame, justification, or the attention of others; to help us center on God's affirmation; to learn to love to be unknown and even accept misunderstanding without the loss of peace, joy, or purpose; experience a continuing relationship with God independent of the opinions of others; teaches love and humility before God and others; help us see our associates in the best light; to help us see our egocentricity; help us appreciate a breadth of ideas related to competition; teach us to trust God in a deeper way.
sacrifice	learn to trust in God and not our own means of security; enables us to meet others needs; teach us the risk of faith.

Table Hab 37-3. Abstinence Disciplines—Applicational Ideas

Discipline	Defined
solitude	1. Learn to take advantage of little solitudes during the day. 2. Find places that are conducive to solitude and deliberately set out to spend time in them. 3. Have special repetitive times during the year which you set aside to be alone for evaluation and reorientation of life goals. 4. If you go on a retreat for solitude remember the basic outline of such a retreat: entry, listening time, closure. Entry may require an unwinding. Sleeping may well be in order. The actual time of solitude will force inward reflection. Finally, seek to understand what has happened.
silence	1. Arise for a time alone in the middle of the night in order to experience a period of silence. 2. Go away to a retreat center for a day or so of silence. Some retreat centers are set up for silence. 3. Refrain from turning on the radio or TV or CD or whatever at times you usually do so. Instead observe silence. 4. When riding in your car do not turn on the radio but instead meditate. 5. Buy some earplugs or "Jet ears" to use to shut out sound when you study or meditate or read or pray. 6. If you go on a retreat for silence remember the basic outline of such a retreat: entry, listening time, closure. Entry may require an unwinding time--sleeping may well be in order. In your silence learn to listen for God. Seek when you finish to understand what happened in the time of solitude.

37. Spiritual Disciplines—And On-Going Leadership

fasting	<u>Kinds of Abstention in terms of what denied</u>: absolute—without water and food (up to three days); no food, water only—up to 40 days; no food, some liquids other than water (no stimulants)--up to 40 days. <u>Kinds of Abstention in terms of purpose</u>: *Working Fast*—a fast done secretly while maintaining regular working habits. This usually has some goal attached to it. *Isolation fast*--a fast done in which the faster isolates himself/ herself from others concentrating wholly on God and spiritual matters. This usually has some goal. o *Power Fast*—a fast done primarily to increase awareness of spiritual warfare and to release God's power to accomplish victory in power encounters. *Discipline Fast*—a fast done in obedience to conviction from God that it should be done even though there is no apparent goal. *Apostolic ministry Fast*—a fast which has as its major goal the beginning of some new ministry. This can be done solo or in concert with some team.
frugality	1. Learn to eat simply (fewer meat meals). Healthy eating usually leads to less expense for medical and dental care. 2. Learn to opt for leisure activities which do not cost (reading, walking, etc.). 3. Walk instead of riding when feasible. 4. Make knowing choices in buying for home (don't have to choose top of line). 5. Respect the environment (like saving water, preserving plant life, trees, etc.). 6. Pass on clothing to others (that you no longer use). 7. Learn to get by without amassing the latest technological gadgets. 8. Learn to say no to advertising which promotes things you do not need. 9. Learn to budget and stick to it. 10. Recycle whatever you can. 11. Exercise discipline with credit cards (never charge what you can not pay off) or get rid of credit cards altogether. 12. Learn to depend on and utilize fully the resources you do have. 13. Practice "community" thinking (without living in a commune): covenant with one or two other families and/or singles for mutual accountability and encouragement in living responsible life-styles; own jointly some of the more expensive items—lawn tools, shop tools, books, journals; shop in bulk together and share; car pool whenever feasible. 14. Think homegrown: more letters, fewer long distance phone calls; purchase/make inexpensive gifts and then add a home-made personalization to give it a special touch; hand-made or hand-adapted clothing and furniture. 15. Churches and responsible living: our churches can purchase less than "top of the line" organs or other items and use the extra to share generously to the building fund of a 3rd world church. less focus on expensive entertainment and recreation at church outings; learn to get excitement and re-creation from outreach, evangelism, work projects for the needy. Occasionally go without coffee and snacks at group fellowships; use the time to talk about the hungry and give the usual expense money to the hungry. 16. Occasionally fast. 17. Hospitality—invite other to eat at your home rather than eating out; open home to out-of-towners and stay in homes when you are travelling.
chastity	1. Learn to value highly your own personhood and sexuality. 2. Learn to value highly the personhood and sexuality of others--male or female, young or old. 3. Guard thought life. 4. Abstain from any form of entertainment which might indulge improper sexual thoughts. 5. If married, abstain from sexual activity (with consent of partner) for extended times of praying and fasting. 6. Deliberately develop positive relationships with those of opposite sex which are healthy and do not focus on sexuality. 7. Deliberately seek the good of those of the opposite sex that you come in contact with in daily life. 8. Don't allow yourself to be put in potentially compromising situations with an individual of the opposite-sex.
secrecy	1. Refrain in the presence of others of discussing your accomplishments

37. Spiritual Disciplines—And On-Going Leadership   page 212

	or good qualities. 2. Accept compliments graciously without much ado. 3. Recognize inwardly when accomplishments come of God's grace in giving you abilities or opportunities to accomplish. 4. Do not defend when you are attacked. 5. Trust God to both vindicate character if that is needed or to promote character if that is needed.
sacrifice	1. Respond to some other person's need by giving that which you had allocated to meet that same need for yourself. 2. After paying off all your bills at the end of the month give whatever is left over away to some needy cause. 3. Save all your loose change for a month and give it away.

Conclusion

Examples abound in the Scriptures for most of these disciplines. But what do we gain from these disciplines.

Writers on the disciplines often see the discipline of **solitude** as primary and prior to other disciplines. Its lessons are frequently necessary in order to insure profit from them.

We do not realize how much we depend on noise around us to shield out loneliness and to keep us from dealing with the distortions we have of our inner self. **Silence** helps us to separate out the false self from the true self. The practice of silence enables one to deal with loneliness in a constructive way that builds up the interior life. Silence forces evaluation of ones inner self. It helps one learn inward concentration. It will teach us to think before speaking and to choose our words well.

Fasting is a practice which many Christian's are discovering is for today and not relegated to the Bible or historic Christianity. Not to be practices by all, this abstinence almost more than any of the others teaches the value of discipline itself.

Debt is one reason that some Christians are not available to God for service. In II Timothy 2:4 Paul warns Timothy not to become entangled in the things of the world. In Romans 13:8 Paul admonishes Christians at Rome to owe no person anything save love. **Frugality** helps one learn the discipline of wise control of finances and other resources.

Sexuality is one of the most powerful and subtle forces in human nature. Its abuse can be destructive. Discipline in the area of sexuality can be foundational to other disciplines. Some distortions of sexuality are fornication, adultery, lusting, obsessive sexual activities, homosexuality, pornography and sexism. **Chastity** helps one learn about these things.

Proverbs 27:2 cautions a person about praising oneself. "Let other people praise you—even strangers; never do it yourself. The natural tendency of the heart is to be recognized for qualities and good things done. The proverb "tooting ones own horn" occurs in numerous languages and shows the recognition of this desire. **Secrecy** as a discipline counters this natural desire.

Sacrifice goes beyond frugality. Frugality is the careful stewardship of what we have. Sacrifice uses some of what we need for others. It is a discipline which focuses on giving beyond ones means.

Leaders who have disciplines in their lives are more likely to persevere and finish well than those who do not.

Article 38

38. Spiritual Leadership—Prolonging the Life of God in a Work

Introduction

In this article I want to introduce a cluster of four macro lessons needed by leaders today. These macro lessons apply to spiritual leadership today. Many conservative leaders today work in liberal situations that need renewal. Two basic options stand before such leaders. They can get out of the situation and go somewhere more conducive to their conservative leadership. Or they can stay and try to prolong the life of God in their liberal situation. They may never turn the whole situation around. But they may indeed prolong the life of God in their situation—postponing God's Ichabod.

I learned about these macro lessons over a long period of time. But it started years ago at Columbia Bible College when I was assigned a project in my prophets class.[107] I had to produce a prophets' chart. The purpose of the chart was to identify the writing prophets in terms of which kingdom they ministered to and when. This was an excellent project. On my prophets' chart were the northern kingdom, Israel, and the southern kingdom, Judah. Each of the kings were identified and length of reign indicated. There was also a marking for whether the time of the king was spiritually healthy or deteriorating spiritually. And then the prophets were located, also showing length of ministry. Figure Hab 38-1 below gives the basic outline of the prophets' chart, rather simplified, in order to illustrate the major findings I want to mention in this leadership article.

Now this chart is oversimplified. I left off entirely the third crisis, *Return to The Land*, and its cluster of prophets. But this chart has enough on it to draw out some very important observations. I saw several ideas implicitly long ago when I first did my prophets' chart. But it wasn't till I was studying the leadership eras and first began identifying macro lessons from each leadership era that I explicitly identified them. Now I did not know early on of just how important a project the prophets' chart was. As I learned about the prophets, I was also learning about how God works with His people. I did not know it but I was experientially learning about spiritual authority.

---

[107] This was a class taught by Buck Hatch, one of my favorite teachers. This class was foundational for me understanding the prophets. I knew who they were. I knew what situations they were dealing with. And I knew the basic messages they were giving for their times.

213

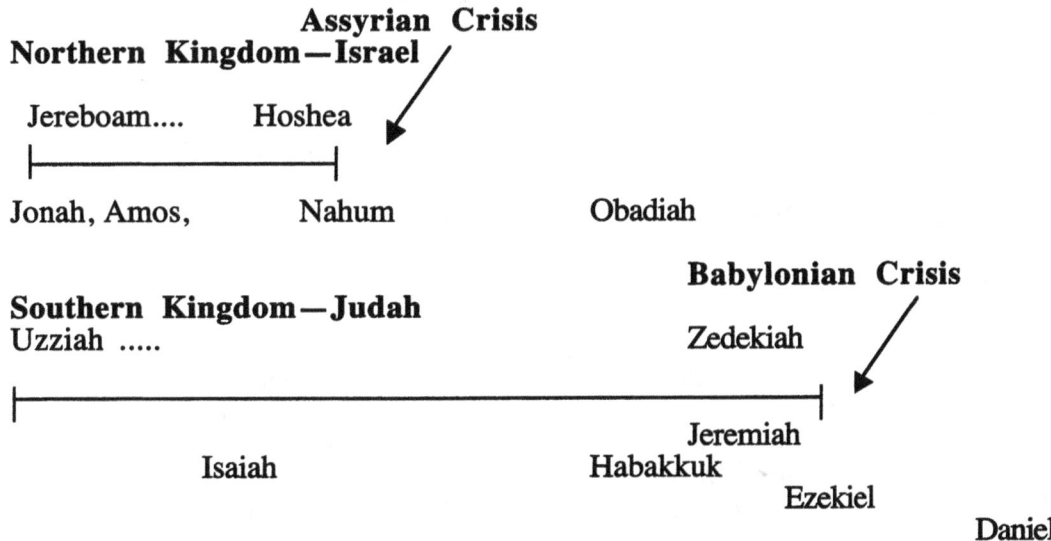

Figure Hab 38-1. Simplified Prophets' Chart

Learning About Spiritual Authority Vicariously

Here is an important leadership lesson I learned as I studied leadership in the Bible. I refer to it in this article, because study of macro lessons such as are given in this article,[108] is one of the processes by which leaders attain spiritual authority.

> **Effective leaders value spiritual authority as a primary power base.**

This is one of seven major leadership lessons that I have identified from comparative study of effective leaders.[109]

Spiritual Authority—What Is It?

Spiritual authority is the ideal power base for a leader to use with mature believers who respect God's authority in a leader. A simplified definition focusing on the notion of maturity of believers follows.

Definition

<u>Spiritual authority</u> is the
- right to influence,
- conferred upon a leader by followers,
- because of their perception of spirituality in that leader.

---

[108] I deal with this subject in depth in another **Article**, *Spiritual Authority—Six Characteristics*.

[109] This is one of seven major leadership lessons that have emerged in my studies of leadership over the past 21 years. They are: (1) Effective Leaders View Present Ministry in Terms Of A Life Time Perspective. (2) Effective Leaders Maintain A Learning Posture Throughout Life. (3) Effective Leaders Value Spiritual Authority As A Primary Power Base. (4) Effective Leaders Who Are Productive Over A Lifetime Have A Dynamic Ministry Philosophy. (5) Effective Leaders View Leadership Selection And Development As A Priority Function In Their Ministry. (6) Effective Leaders See Relational Empowerment As Both A Means And A Goal Of Ministry. (7) Effective Leaders Evince A Growing Awareness Of Their Sense Of Destiny. It is the third one I am referring to in this section. See **Article**, *Leadership Lessons—Seven Major Lessons Identified*.

38. Spiritual Leadership—Prolonging God's Life in a Work

An expanded definition focusing on how a leader gets and uses it is:

Definition

Spiritual Authority is that
- characteristic of a God-anointed leader,
- developed upon an experiential power base (giftedness, character, deep experiences with God),

that enables him/her to influence followers through
- persuasion,
- force of modeling, and
- moral expertise.

Spiritual authority comes to a leader in three major ways. As leaders go through deep experiences with God they experience the sufficiency of God to meet them in those situations. They come to know God. That is, the leader knows God, God's ways, and God's purposes. This *experiential knowledge of God* and the *deep experiences with God* are part of the experiential acquisition of spiritual authority. This first way of acquiring spiritual authority can also be learned vicariously. As we study leaders in the Bible we can come to know God's ways and God's purposes for leadership. We can learn from their lives lessons for our lives. A second way that spiritual authority comes is through a *life which models godliness*. When the Spirit of God is transforming a life into the image of Christ those characteristics of love, joy, peace, long suffering, gentleness, goodness, faith, meekness, temperance carry great weight in giving credibility that the leader is consistent inward and outward. A third way that spiritual authority comes is through *gifted power*. When a leader can demonstrate gifted power in ministry—that is, a clear testimony to divine intervention in the ministry via his/her gifts—there will be spiritual authority. Now while all three of these ways of getting spiritual authority should be a part of a leader, it is frequently the case that one or more of the elements dominates. From the definitions and description of how spiritual authority comes you can readily see that a leader using spiritual authority does not force his/her will on followers.

That first way of learning vicariously leadership lessons that build up a leader's spiritual authority is what I am stressing in this article. And here are four important macro lessons needed by leaders today.

Four Important Macro Lessons

As a leader then, I am conscious of spiritual authority.[110] One way that spiritual authority comes to a leader is through recognition that the leader knows God, God's ways, and God's purposes. When I study a leader's life and learn about God and God's ways, I am building my experiential power base of spiritual authority. Such a knowledge gives a leader credibility with followers.

When I am studying macro lessons, I am learning of God's ways. I am increasing my spiritual authority and my ability to lead God's people. So then, macro lessons are important. The more we know about them and observe them in our own lives the more our leadership will demonstrate spiritual authority.

Let me remind you of my definition of a macro lesson.[111]

---

[110] See **Article**, *Spiritual Authority—Six Characteristics*.
[111] See **Articles**, *29. Macro Lesson Defined; 30. Macro Lessons: List of 41 Across Six Leadership Eras*.

38. Spiritual Leadership—Prolonging God's Life in a Work

Definition

A <u>macro-lesson</u> is a high level generalization
- of a leadership observation (suggestion, guideline, requirement), stated as a lesson,
- which repeatedly occurs throughout different leadership eras,
- and thus has potential as a leadership absolute.

Table Hab 38-1 lists four important macro lessons flowing from the study of kingly leadership, all of which were identified in the Kingdom Leadership Era.[112]

Table Hab 38-1. Three Important Macro Lessons From the Kingdom Era

Lesson	Label	When Seen	Statement
19	Stability	Kingdom Leadership Era	Preserving a ministry of God with life and vigor over time is as much if not more of a challenge to leadership than creating one.
20	Spiritual Leadership	Kingdom Leadership Era	Spiritual leadership can make a difference even in the midst of difficult times.
21	Recrudescence	Kingdom Leadership Era	God will attempt to bring renewal to His people until they no longer respond to Him.
22	By-pass	Kingdom Leadership Era	God will by-pass leadership and structures that do not respond to Him and will institute new leadership and structures.

In my early prophets' chart study, I recognized that the southern kingdom lasted much longer than the northern kingdom. See Figure Hab 38-1. This stands out almost immediately. But it was the tracing of the spiritual health of the various kings that keyed me to the important macro lesson on spiritual leadership. Not one single king in the northern kingdom followed God. All are described as being evil leaders. In fact, Jereboam (who God promised to bless, if he would follow God) was very evil and is used as the standard for describing evil kings. In the southern kingdom beginning with Asa (grandson of Solomon) there appeared every so often kings who followed God and brought renewal. They were interspersed with evil kings. Asa, Uzziah, Jotham, Hezekiah, and Josiah were kings who brought renewal to the southern kingdom. And because of their spiritual leadership, the southern kingdom was prolonged. Macro lesson 20 describes this phenomena.

<u>Spiritual Leadership Macro Lesson</u>
Spiritual leadership can make a difference even in the midst of difficult times.

Table Hab 38-2 Lists some of the Kings who prolonged the life of God in the people of God. That is, they demonstrated that spiritual leadership can make a difference even in the midst of difficult times.

---

[112] From a leadership standpoint the Bible can be analyzed in terms of six leadership eras: 1. Patriarchal Leadership Era; 2. The Pre-Kingdom Leadership Era; 3. The Kingdom Leadership Era; 4. The Post-Kingdom Leadership Era; 5. The Pre-Church Leadership Era; 6. The Church Leadership Era. Habakkuk occurs in the Kingdom Leadership Era. See the short **Article**, 26. *Leadership Eras in the Bible, Six Identified* and the much longer expanded treatment of the subject, 36. *Six Biblical Leadership Eras, Approaching The Bible with Leadership Eyes*.

38. Spiritual Leadership—Prolonging God's Life in a Work

Table Hab 38-2. Spiritual Leaders Who Prolonged God's Work

Leader	Era
Asa	The son of Abijah and grandson of Rehoboam and greatgrandson of Solomon. He was the third king after the two kingdoms split. Solomon did not finish well. Abijah caused the split and was an evil ruler. Rehoboam continued as an evil ruler. Asa turned it around with various kinds of renewal efforts including the deposing of Maacah, his grandmother who essentially ruled from behind the scenes, leading Judah downhill. Asa did not personally finish well but he did turn Judah around toward God.
Uzziah (Azariah)	Uzziah was the son of Amaziah, and 11th king of Judah. He came to the thrown at age 16. He reigned 52 years. His mentor Zechariah was a godly man and had an understanding in visions of God (2 Ch 26:5. Under his influence Uzziah set himself to seek God. This ramified to renewal elements throughout his whole kingdom. When Zechariah died, Uzziah began a downward turn personally. He did not finish well. But during his reign Judah turned to God.
Jotham	Jotham, the 12th King of Judah, was the son of Uzziah. He basically maintained the good his father began. It was during his reign that Isaiah, Hosea and Micah exercised their ministries. So we know that Jotham's reign had plenty of moral problems. He is spoken of as a moderately spiritual king. 2 Ch 27:2 "And he did right in the sight of the lord, according to all that his father Uzziah had done; however he did not enter the temple of the Lord. But the people continued acting corruptly. 3 He built the upper gate of the house of the Lord and he built extensively the wall of Ophel."
Hezekiah	Hezekiah was the 14th King of Judah, the son of Ahaz (a weak king). He is considered one of the greatest kings of Judah. The nation was at a nadir-point, spiritually speaking when Hezekiah came to the throne. Isaiah and Micah were laboring hard to turn it around. Hezekiah from the beginning of his reign instituted religious reforms. He began with the opening and cleansing of the Temple (Ahaz had closed it down and desecrated it). He reorganized the liturgical and choral service. He also began again the Passover observation. He gave a widespread invitation to all to partake of this Passover service. The results of this service began to spread religious fervor for God and folks began to remove the altars in the high places (used to worship other gods). Isaiah was a powerful influence for Hezekiah.
Josiah	Josiah was the 17th King of Judah, the son of Amon. Josiah began to reign at 8 years of age. At 16, he began to seek after the God of David his father. During his reign the Law was discovered when the temple was being repaired. Josiah responded to its revelation by making a covenant with God. Josiah broke up the high places, those numerous centers of evil. His untimely death (perhaps in a venture not ordained by God) brought an end to the depth of his spiritual renewal.

Now a few remarks about these leaders are in order:

1. None were tremendous spiritual leaders. But their efforts to return to God had impact even though they may have had weaknesses. Leaders have influence.

2. Spiritual mentors alongside these leaders had much influence (Zechariah, Isaiah, Jeremiah). Leaders today in similar situations need mentors.

3. Cleaning up the forms of religion (high places, idol worship centers) does not guarantee that inner values are changed in the people. Some of these renewal efforts were surface at

38. Spiritual Leadership—Prolonging God's Life in a Work

best. But they were a call. And some followed that call fundamentally. Others more nominally.

4. Each of these leaders with the exception of Jotham had evil fathers. The wonderful news from this observation is that the behavior of a leader does not have to be determined because of a less than best environment during the growing up years. Emerging leaders out of dysfunctional foundations can move forward spiritually and don't have to have their lives determined by terrible starts in life.

5. Several of these leaders trusted God in dangerous times when foreign powers could have destroyed the southern kingdom. Their trust in God and God's deliverance preserved the nation.

Three other macro lessons can be noted when you look at the big picture represented by the prophets' chart.

Stability Macro Lesson
Preserving a ministry of God with life and vigor over time is as much if not more of a challenge to leadership than creating one.

Recrudescence[113] Macro Lesson
God will attempt to bring renewal to His people until they no longer respond to Him.

By-Pass Macro Lesson
God will by-pass leadership and structures that do not respond to Him and will institute new leadership and structures.

Concerning the stability macro lesson
A spiritual leader who personally turns to God can attempt renewal efforts and see some success as exemplified by Asa, Uzziah, Jotham, Hezekiah and Josiah. It is not easy bringing renewal. None of these kings saw on-going lasting renewal but each of them saw some success. The temptation of a spiritual leader in a situation where folks do not follow God (at least in the way he/she would want) is to pull out[114] and start something new. And for some that is probably the thing to do. But be encouraged if you want to stay. Your renewal efforts may well prolong God's work through that situation.

Concerning the Recrudescence Macro Lesson
The book of Judges exemplifies the recrudescence macro lesson in its repeated cycles of the tribes going away from God and returning under a Judge following God. It is seen in the southern kingdom with the efforts of Asa, Uzziah, Jotham, Hezekiah, and Josiah. Even though these leaders may not have been ideal spiritual leaders, they gave God opportunity to bring renewal. When compared to the northern kingdom, with no spiritual leaders whatsoever the second half of the recrudescence macro lesson is seen. God can no longer work. Such a situation ushers in the fourth macro lesson.

---

[113] *Recrudescence* is a Kenneth Scott Latourette (famous church historian) word. Basically it is a word meaning renewal in a big way. It is one of several repeated themes he identifies throughout church history.
[114] Moses, in Ex 33, exemplifies another leader who stayed in his situation and saw the prolonging of the life of Israel. God tested Moses call by offering to start all over with Moses and destroying the people. Moses pleaded for the people.

38. Spiritual Leadership—Prolonging God's Life in a Work

<u>Concerning the By-Pass Macro Lesson</u>
The northern kingdom illustrates how God gives up on a situation and moves on. It is seen finally in the southern kingdom in Zedekiah's reign. Daniel lives in a time in which the old structure, the kingdom, no longer exists. God moves on and works through Daniel and other godly leaders in an individualistic way, until structures emerge (synagogue, later the movement under Jesus, and the church under the apostles). Romans 9-11 gives a theological backdrop to this macro lesson. What apparently looks like God's giving up might be God's further way of working toward renewal. Long times may be involved in God's dealing with structures, by-passed or newly developed.

Conclusion

Hopefully, this leadership article will encourage some spiritual leaders who are in tough places to stay with it. Knowing that God may prolong the life of the church, denomination or group, because of that small effort to bring renewal may be the incentive to keep on. In my own ministry, I have seen students leave my seminary and go into denominations that apparently are liberal and in decline. And over the years I have seen the efforts of these spiritual leaders bring about pockets of renewal in denominations. Such renewal efforts have brought about change and prolonged the life of the denomination, or at least retarded the decline. Take a final look at the four macro lessons. And see in them both a warning and an encouragement.

<u>Spiritual Leadership Macro</u>
Spiritual leadership can make a difference even in the midst of difficult times.

<u>Stability Macro Lesson</u>
Preserving a ministry of God with life and vigor over time is as much if not more of a challenge to leadership than creating one.

<u>Recrudescence Macro Lesson</u>
God will attempt to bring renewal to His people until they no longer respond to Him.

<u>By-Pass Macro Lesson</u>
God will by-pass leadership and structures that do not respond to Him and will institute new leadership and structures.

And when you read your Bible, look for these lessons as you study leaders.

Article 39

39. Structural Time—Simplified Overview

Introduction

Often God's solution to a perplexed leader is to give that leader a broader perspective, that is, a much larger context in which to evaluate the present perplexing situation. Such is the case with the prophet Habakkuk. The difference in leaders and followers is perspective. Leaders have a broader view on what is happening and what God wants to do. Habakkuk needed this broader view. The difference in leaders and effective leaders is better perspective. Habakkuk gained this better perspective. Sensitivity to God, intimacy with God, and dependence upon God will lead to broader perspective. Habakkuk had this intimacy. Leaders who seek God for broader perspective will find Him (Hab 2:1; 3:1-15). Habakkuk did.

The broader perspective needed by all leaders is how God is working in history over time. A leader must learn to perceive his/her own ministry situation and time in terms of the broader working of God in history. Several macro lessons reflect the importance of understanding perspective and how God is working with His people. Table Hab 39-1 List three such macro lessons.

Table Hab 39-1. List of Macro Lessons Dealing With Important Perspectives A Leader Needs

Number[115]	Label	When Dominantly Seen[116]	Statement
21	Recrudescence	Kingdom	God will attempt to bring renewal to His people until they no longer respond to Him.
22	By-pass	Kingdom	God will by-pass leadership and structures that do not respond to Him and will institute new leadership and structures.
24	Perspective	Post-Kingdom	Leaders must know the value of perspective and interpret present happenings in terms of God's broader purposes.

---

[115] I have identified 41 of these macro lessons. The numbers refer to my list of 41 macro lessons. See **Article, *30. Macro Lessons: List of 41 Across Six Leadership Eras*.**

[116] I have identified six leadership eras in the Scriptures: 1. Patriarchal; 2. Pre-Kingdom; 3. Kingdom; 4. Post-Kingdom; 5. Pre-Church; 6. Church.

In the book of Habakkuk, the prophet is learning first-hand of macro lesson 24. God is breaking through with a paradigm shift that will give Habakkuk an understanding of God's work and His broader purposes. But it is macro lessons 21 and 22 that I wish to focus on in this leadership article. And the concept of structural time helps us understand these two macro lessons. Habakkuk, from his time perspective, would not have been able to understand these two macro lessons. But present day leaders can profit from a reflective look at Habakkuk's situation in terms of structural time.

Structural Time Defined

One way of viewing an organization or movement or other work of God[117] is to expand the time element to include the whole expected life time of that organization or movement or work of God. When so done one sees the work of God not so much in a linear fashion but in terms of cycles or phases or development stages. Present day comparative study of many organizations or movements or works of God has allowed the identification of stages.

Definition

<u>Structural time</u> refers to an overall perspective for analyzing a work of God in terms of built-in cycles of existence by viewing events, states of development, or some discernible stages from initiation of the cycle until completion of the cycle.

Example

For a church there is a BEGINNING, a birth, an early fellowship perhaps in a home. This stage has characteristics, which include a strong sense of fellowship, strong commitment to ideals. All have usually sacrificed to be a part. Much of the behavior is informal. There are strong emotional ties. Leadership, for the most part, is charismatic. FORMALIZATION, the second stage involves expansion and the attraction of outsiders to the group. The church is now too large for ad hoc operation. It needs organization, property, formalization of beliefs. Children become members and are more nominal in their commitment than parents. Emotional levels drop. Newcomers have many characteristics of the early founding members. Some tensions between new members coming in at deep commitment level and increasing level of nominality existing. The next stage, LEADERSHIP involves a change in type of leadership. At first when the church was getting started there was charismatic leadership—a prophet or apostolic type with self-proclaimed authority. The authority lies in the ability to lead. The 2nd generational leadership is more of a priest type. Its power lies in position, institutional structure, not so much ability to lead. The church may continue to expand or may move into a holding cycle or may deteriorate. It will depend on a number of factors and how able the church is to change to meet new contextual situations.

The criterion for identifying the stages or cycles varies depending on whether you are viewing an organization, a church, a parachurch group, a movement or some other kind of structure. For organizations, Greiner sees periods of growth followed by crises repeating in an organization as it expands over a lifetime. Schein sees stages of development of organizational culture over the lifetime of an organization. Mintzberg sees changes of structure over a lifetime or changes of power configurations. Flamholtz sees stages of development in terms of gross financial assets of the organization. Adizes sees stages of

---

[117] I use the broad phrase, organization, movement or work of God to cover all the bases. For our purposes in Habakkuk we are looking specifically at a work of God—via the nation Israel, or more specifically the Southern Kingdom, Judah. I am going to simply say organization or work of God from now on to imply all three.

39. Structural Time—Simplified Overview

corporate growth in terms of four fundamental functions of organizations. I see stages of development in terms of the organization's founding purpose and attempts at renewal.

5 Structural Time Paradigms And Their Importance

Structural time paradigms help us to identify, predictably though not with absolute certainty, the possible next stages an organization will go through. Forewarned is forearmed.

Table Hab 39-2.   5 Structural Time Paradigms Usefulness For Perspective.

Paradigm	How Helpful
1. Clinton Sodality	Points out tendencies of Christian parachurch organizations to lose their purpose over time and suggests possible intervention times by God to renew or change the organization to meet new purposes.
2. Clinton Modality	Points out tendencies of Christian church organizations to lose their purpose over time and suggests possible intervention times. Identifies the degenerative cycle. This structural time paradigm is also useful for looking at a work of God such as was the case with the Kingdom in Habakkuk's time. I will actually use this to discuss the two macro lessons on recrudescence and by-passing of structures.
3. Adizes	Suggests normal patterns of an organization's development in terms of 4 major factors. Points out ten structural stages over the entire lifetime of an organization. At each stage he identifies potential hazards and prescriptive measures to take and shows the normal tendencies of the 4 major factors.
4. Schein	Identifies 3 major stages in the development of organizational culture and points out differing and unique measures that must be taken to change culture at each stage. Very helpful for change agents since many changes will be changing organizational values.
5. Greiner	Identifies 5 phases that organizations go through which expand over their lifetime. Points out the importance of the history of the organization and the necessity for recognizing unwanted ramifications of changes. Essentially changes which solve problems later become problems themselves.

For further study on these structural time paradigms see Clinton's **Bridging Strategies**, chapter 4 Change Climate.   Leaders today in churches or parachurch organizations will profit greatly from Clinton's two paradigms and Adizes' paradigm.

Structural Time: Clinton's Modality Defined

A modality (in terms of structure and dynamics) is usually identified with a local church or a denomination.

Definition

A <u>modality</u> is a structured fellowship, which is a permanent institution reflecting God's work in a given geographical location(s) in which membership is broadly seen as inclusive and makes no distinction between age or sex or whatever.

Examples

• The people of God in the Old Testament, which became a kingdom, aptly illustrates a modality.

39. Structural Time—Simplified Overview

- A given church denomination
- The Roman Catholic Church
- The Greek Orthodox Church
- A given local church

Membership in such a representative group may be almost hereditary. That is, you are born into a group which espouses the form of Christianity (following God). Usually there is much nominality in such modalities. The forms and traditions carry more import than the functions they represent.

Modalities function in the redemptive process by:

1. providing an overall unity,
2. giving continuity and follow-through,
3. maintaining longevity,
4. insuring stability,
5. giving a necessary check and balance to mobile functions,
6. giving authority and authenticity.

Whereas sodalities are task oriented in their mental makeup, modalities are more relationship or community oriented in their mental makeup.

Structural Time: Clinton's 12 Modality Stages

Remember structural time involves determining stages or cycles of time. The linear time between the stages will vary from modality to modality but the stages usually do happen for each modality over time. I will first describe the stages I have identified. Then I will give a diagram which gives an overall flow of how the stages relate to each other. Next, I will give a narrative explanation of the diagram. Finally, I will relate the diagram to Habakkuk's situation commenting on the macro lessons.

Table Hab 39-3. 12 Structural Time Stages Described

Time Label	Symbol	Name	Descriptive Characteristics
1	R	Recrudescence	God's call to some ideals of Gospel.
2	SF	Sodality Function Emerges	Gospel ideals seen in indigenous situation.
3	SS	Sodality Structure Develops	A following committed to the application of these ideals begins to organize.
4	MF	Modality Functions Emerge	Membership becomes more inclusive; the movement stabilizes and becomes a permanent institution in the society, it formalizes and demands conformity.
5	MS	Modality Structure Solidifies	The organizational structure solidifies; it develops leadership with a bent to maintain and preserve the structure.
6	MD	Modality Drift (Degeneration)	As membership becomes more inclusive and representative of the society the process of secularization causes a lessening of commitment; sodality-like function deteriorate and organizational form predominates over functions or ideals.

39. Structural Time—Simplified Overview

7	R	Recrudescence	God will make attempts to deepen commitment levels of membership and return organization to ideals.
8	S/FM-M	Sodality/ Functions Maintained	The organization puts its ideals and functions in proper focus; it will change modality structure to insure proper functions
9	ME	Modality Life Cycle Extended	God uses the modality to continue furthering His purposes.
10	REJ	Recrudescence Rejected	The modality cannot accept the changes to incorporate new life.
11	MDA	Modality Drift Accelerates	The modality becomes increasingly less influential in the Christian movement (God's purposes).
12	DIES		The modality is no longer a part of the Christian core structure (God's plans) furthering God's redemptive purposes.

39. Structural Time—Simplified Overview

Structural Time: Clinton's Modality Cycle

<u>Basic Modality Cycle</u>

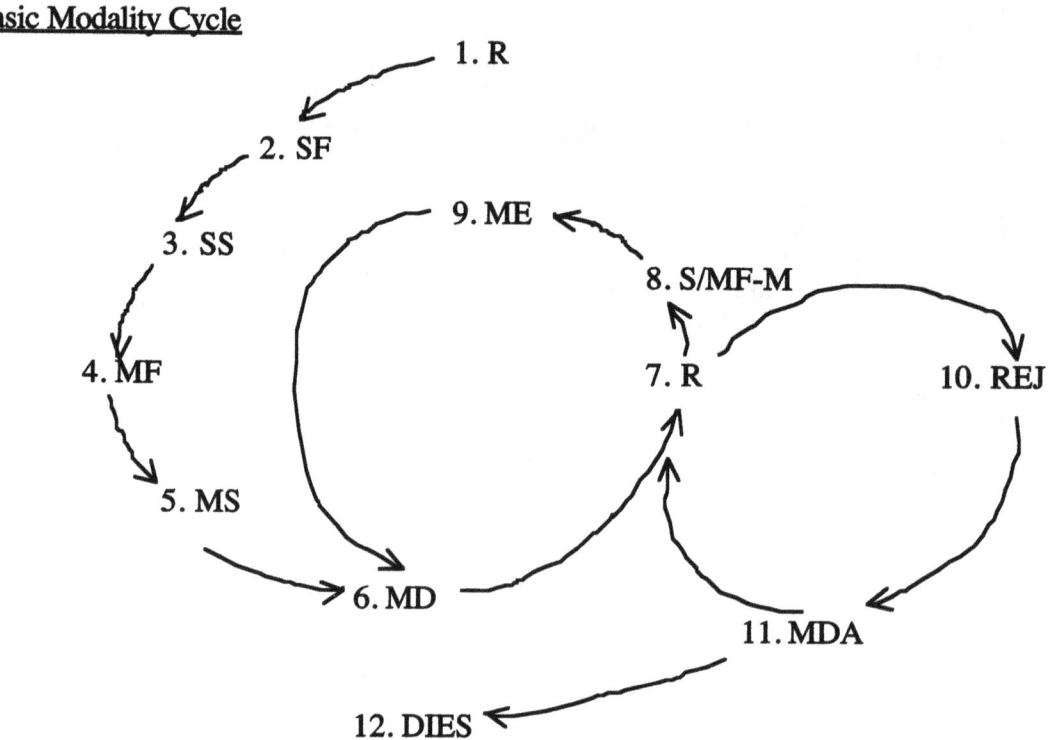

Figure Hab 39-1   Clinton's Basic Modality Cycle

Narrative Description of Modality Cycle

The process of the modality follows basically the same process of the sodality initially. The basic difference is that the modality structure becomes firmly implanted and develops into an organization with broader inclusive membership. It functions to consolidate gains made in the expansion of Christianity and to proliferate the Christian ideals to an entire spectrum of society. Of course there is usually a watering down of the ideals along with the proliferation. However, the proliferation allows for a larger base of resources from which new sodality movements will emerge in response to recrudescence attempts. Because of the stability of the modality there is a longer death cycle. There is usually repeated attempts at recrudescence over a long period of time. Partial inclusion of recrudescence extends this death cycle. Finally after repeated attempts over a long period a modality dies as part of the Christian infra-structure.

Habakkuk

Dates for Habakkuk vary depending on the exegetical commentary and the author's viewpoint. I am assuming that Habakkuk lived and operated after the northern kingdom was taken into captivity and prior to or overlapping with Jeremiah's ministry. His closing remarks seem to indicate he will actually go through the Babylonian invasion and its ramifications. If my timing is fairly accurate then in terms of the modality cycle, the book is dealing with stages 7-12. God is indicating that His attempts at recrudescence have been rejected and stages 8-12 will follow. However, we know from Jeremiah's ministry and Ezekiel's (first part) that God was still trying to reach out to renew His people. So we can view this interlude in Habakkuk's life as another attempt at recrudescence. My guess is that Habakkuk's remaining ministry was an attempt to get God's people to respond to God. So this book, giving its dire prophetic news is actually a desperate attempt to awaken the people of God. Note Habakkuk's interceding cry for mercy in the midst of the judgment.

39. Structural Time—Simplified Overview

Closure

The book of Habakkuk at least partially illustrates these two important macro lessons.[118]

> **God will attempt to bring renewal to His people until they no longer respond to Him.**
>
> God will by-pass leadership and structures that do not respond to Him and will institute new leadership and structures.

These two lessons apply to us today as well. I am reminded of that simple little warning phrase in Romans 11:20, 21

Romans 11:20,21

> 20 Well, because of unbelief they (Israel—northern and southern kingdoms) were broken off, and you stand by faith. Be not high-minded, but fear: 21 For if God spared not the natural branches, **take heed lest He also spare not you.**

We as leaders today must seek to recognize and move with God's recrudescence attempts or we may well find our church and parachurch structures being by-passed.

---

[118] This book must be taken along with Jeremiah's (recrudescence attempts) and Ezekiel's ministry (both recrudescence attempts and structure by-passed and then Daniel's (to see the structure already by-passed).

Article 40

40. Transparency With God

Introduction
In the small three chapter book of Habakkuk, the prophet Habakkuk is facing the crisis of his life. This crisis can make or break Habakkuk. How does he respond in this crisis? It probably no surprise to you. He prays! The entire book records Habakkuk's talking and listening to God—dialoging about his crisis issues. A most interesting observation emerges about this leader. Habakkuk is transparent in his prayer dialog with God. And Habakkuk is transparent with us—sharing it with us. Let me share two observations about transparency seen in Habakkuk.

A leader can be absolutely honest with God in prayer concerning how he/she feels or thinks.

A leader who is transparent, with God and others, can impact lives via his/her modeling of transparency.[119]

Notice the ways that Habakkuk is transparent with God.

<u>Way #1.</u> He attacks God's character—especially holiness and justice. He is accusing God of not intervening in his situation.

2 O Jehovah, how long shall I beg for your help,
    When will you listen?
  I cry out unto you about violence,
    And you will not deliver.

3 **Why do you tolerate the iniquity I see,**
    And cause me to experience such injustice?
  For destruction and violence are before me,
    And there is strife,
    And criminal activity all about.
4 Therefore, the law is not enforced,
    And justice does not happen.
    For evil people outnumber the righteous.
  Therefore justice is distorted.

---

[119] See 2nd Corinthians for the most powerful demonstration of this second observation on transparency. Paul is transparent with others about his dealings, motivation, values, etc.

40. Transparency With God

These are honest words. Habakkuk is accusing God of laxity in holiness; lack of intervention in a situation needing God's touch. He is saying that God is not just. He is saying that evil is not punished.

<u>Way #2.</u> Now having found out that God is indeed doing something about his situation, Habakkuk not only brings God's character traits up trying to use them to convince God not to use the Babylonians, he also challenges God's approach. How can God use the Babylonians, a nation that is as bad as Judah (actually much worse) to bring justice in Judah's situation? Notice the bold faced challenges to God.

Habakkuk Speaks Referring to God's Traits[120]

12 Aren't you from everlasting,
    O Jehovah, my God, my Holy One?
    Surely we must not die.
    O Jehovah, have you ordained them for judgment?
    And you, Rock, have you established them for correction?

13 Your **pure eyes should not behold evil**,
    You cannot look on wrongdoing,
    Why do you look on faithless men, and are silent,
    When the wicked devour a people more righteous than themselves?

<u>Way #3.</u> Now Habakkuk challenges God about his justice—concerning the Babylonians.

16 Therefore he sacrifices to his net.
    And burns incense to his seine,
    For by them he lives in luxury,
    And his food is rich.
17 Is he then to keep on emptying his net,
    And mercilessly slaying nations forever?

Look also at the following from Habakkuk 2. It sums up Habakkuk's accusative words towards God's use of the Babylonians (Hab 2:12-17).

Way #4 And finally Habakkuk flat out rebukes God

2:1 I will doggedly set myself to wait for God's answer,
    And station myself on the watch tower,
    And watch carefully to perceive, what He will communicate to me.
    And then I will have an answer to my **complaint**.

The last two lines seem to indicate that Habakkuk will persistently wait till he can **perceive what God is saying**. Habakkuk is hoping for some **restorative word** (answer SRN 07725) to his **complaint** (SRN 0843) to God. Note, the word complaint connotes **rebuke**—a very honest expression toward God.

---

[120] Habakkuk has gone through a major paradigm shift at this point. He now believes God is doing something. But he does not think it is fair. The Babylonians are more unrighteous as a nation than are the Israelites. So Habakkuk pleads with God to correct this apparent unfairness. Note, however, that Israel has far more revelation for which it is being judged than the Babylonians. This whole prayer illustrates the prayer macro lesson. See *paradigm shift*, **Glossary**. See **Articles**, 29. *Macro Lesson Defined; 30. Macro Lessons— List of 41 Across Six Leadership Eras; Paradigm Shifts; Judgment and Revelation.*

40. Transparency With God

Habakkuk is certainly transparent in his accusations to God.

But Habakkuk is also transparent to us, the readers of this little book. And to those who would be singing its final chapter in their public words. I see Habakkuk as being transparent with us in three ways.

<u>Way #1.</u> We have the book. If Habakkuk were a person who kept his cards close to his chest[121] we would never have gotten the book in the first place. Habakkuk would never have written this for public use, if he was not a transparent person.

<u>Way #2.</u> Habakkuk shares the downer side of his feelings. He is fearful. He knows that trouble is coming his way. He does not look forward to his personal suffering but does look forward to the process of God's justice being worked out. Notice the boldfaced below.

<u>Way #3.</u> Habakkuk also shares the upbeat side of his feelings. Notice the underlined below.

Notice in his final closing testimony, the downer side (boldface words) and the upbeat side (underlined words).

Habakkuk's final fearful and joyful response to God's meeting him.

16 I hear your message, and I am **weak with fear**,
   My lips **quiver fearfully**.
   My bones **feel like they are giving way**.
   I **stumble as I walk**.
   I will quietly wait for the day of judgment,
   When disaster will come upon the people who invade us.

17 Though the **fig tree quits blossoming**,
   There is no **fruit on the vines**,
   The **olive trees do not produce**,
   The **fields yield no food**,
   The **flock be cut off from the fold**,
   And there be **no herd in the stalls**,
18 Yet <u>I will rejoice</u>[122] in Jehovah,
   I will <u>joy in the God of my salvation</u>.
19 <u>Jehovah, the Master, is my strength</u>.
   He makes my feet <u>like hinds' feet</u>.
   He makes me <u>tread upon my high places</u>.

To the choirmaster: with stringed instrument.

Notice the note to the choirmaster. Habakkuk wanted to have this openly sung in public worship. That's being transparent.

---

[121] I am using an idiom here. "Keeping one's cards close to the chest" means not being very open about how one feels about things or not letting people in on one's secrets or thoughts.

[122] *Yet I will rejoice* translates one Hebrew word (SRN 05937). That word carries with it the sense of rejoicing but also of exulting and doing so triumphantly. Note, Habakkuk's triumphant rejoicing is not in the circumstances but in God: Jehovah the eternal one (SRN 3068); Elohim—the God who delivers (SRN 0430; 03468); Jehovah Master (Adonai) (SRN 3068; SRN 0136). A leader's view of God is the most important thing about that leader. Habakkuk now has a good view of God.

40. Transparency With God

Closure

One of the reasons Habakkuk is such a powerful book is that Habakkuk is modeling for us. He deliberately shares with us his experience with God so we can learn from it. The more a leader can be transparent with others about his/her deep relationship with God the more the impact in others lives. Transparency is the hallmark of modeling as a means of powerful influence. Transparency for Habakkuk involved honest sharing in prayer, challenging God personally about his holiness and justice, challenging God about His justice, both in Judah and with the Babylonians (and by extension over the whole world). But once Habakkuk deeply responded to those powerful faith words, "the just shall live by faith," he went through a paradigm shift in recognizing that God's way are right and that God would be vindicated over all the earth.

Transparency for Habakkuk also involved sharing with others. He wrote this book in order that we may learn from his experience. He wrote this closing testimony so that it could be sung in public worship. He shared his bad feelings and his good feelings. Habakkuk's final modeling is his most powerful. He shares his innermost feelings at the hard things to come but rejoices in his trust of God to do things right—to deliver, God of my salvation.

I have noted in my leadership emergence case studies of leaders that there are a few people who are truly free to be transparent. There are also a few who can not be very transparent at all. And then there are the larger majority who have a tendency to become transparent in their leadership, but have a long way to go.

Which one of these three categories are you? (1) Not transparent; (2) a lot to learn about transparency and its place in leadership influence; (3) Very transparent and have seen God use it in leadership influence.

Habakkuk

CLINTON'S BIBLICAL LEADERSHIP COMMENTARY SERIES

Hope for a Leader in Troubled Times

Glossary and Bibliography

Glossary—Leadership Definitions

The following leadership related definitions occur throughout the **Habakkuk Leadership Commentary**. They are listed here alphabetically for convenience in referencing. SRN stands for Strong's Reference Number. These numbers can be used to look up the definitions of these words in the **Strong's Exhaustive Concordance** containing Hebrew and Greek dictionaries. These numbers are now also used by many other Bible study aids.

Item	Definition
Affect	a learning domain, that is, a term describing learning which primarily moves the feelings and emotions.
Aftermath	Aftermath refers to the after effects and ramifications of some past act or event which has continuing influence of the present.
Authority Insights	from leadership emergence theory. One of 51 process items that God uses to shape a leader. Authority insights describe those instances in ministry in which a leader learns important lessons, via positive or negative experiences, with regards to: submission to authority, authority structures, authenticity of power bases underlying authority, authority conflict, how to exercise authority.
Beforemath	Beforemath refers to the effects and implications of some future event or state which has influence reaching back into the present, at least to the eye of the leader holding the future perfect vision by faith.
Brokenness	a state of mind in which a person recognizes that he/she is helpless in a situation or life process unless God alone works. It is a state of mind in which a person acknowledges a deep dependence upon God and is open for God to break through in new ways, thoughts, directions, and revelation of Himself that was not the case before the brokenness experience. Example: Jacob in Genesis 32 faced a life threatening situation in which he was forced to desperately depend upon God.
Capture	a technical term used when talking about figures of speech being interpreted. A figure or idiom is said to be captured when one can display the intended emphatic meaning of it in non-figurative simple words. e.g. not ashamed of the Gospel = captured: completely confident of the Gospel.
Celebration	Celebration refers to a corporate time, a gathering of a group of God's people, who recognize God for who He is and what He does, and worships Him, in such a way as to honor Him and to renew their committal to follow this God.
Cognitive	a learning domain, that is, a term describing learning which primarily focuses on the transmittal and understanding of knowledge and ideas.
Conflict	from leadership emergence theory. One of 51 process items that God uses to shape a leader. The conflict process item refers to those instances in a leader's life-history in which God uses conflict, whether personal or ministry related to develop the leader in dependence upon God, faith, and inner-life.
Connector words	In Hebrew Poetry analysis, a connector word(s) is a word(s) such as *but, and, nevertheless*, which connects two phrases or two couplets or a line

Glossary of Leadership Definitions

	with a couplet and serves to help interpret the relationships between the things connected.
Connector phrase	In Hebrew Poetry analysis, a <u>connector phrase</u> is a phrase placed between reduction statements or lines (inserted by the interpreter) to indicate the flow of thought in the extended parallelism.
Corporate restoration	<u>Corporate restoration</u> refers to God's attempts to restore the people of God as a viable channel through whom He can work to carry out His Biblical purposes.
Crisis Process Item	from leadership emergence theory. One of 51 process items that God uses to shape a leader. <u>Crisis process items</u> refer to those special intense situations of pressure in human situations which are used by God to test and teach dependence.
Different parallelism	*Hebrew Poetry* is said to be <u>different parallelism</u> when one or more members of one phrase is in different correspondence with its related member of the parallel.
Divine Contacts	from leadership emergence theory. One of 51 process items that God uses to shape a leader. A <u>divine contact</u> is a person whom God brings in contact with a leader at a crucial moment in a development phase in order to accomplish one or more of the following to: affirm leadership potential, encourage leadership potential, give guidance on a special issue, give insights which may indirectly lead to guidance, challenge the leader God-ward, open a door to a ministry opportunity, other insights helping the emerging leader to make guidance decisions.
Double Confirmation	from leadership emergence theory. One of 51 process items that God uses to shape a leader. <u>Double confirmation</u> refers to the unusual guidance in which God makes clear His will by giving the guidance directly to a leader and then reinforcing it by some other person totally independent and unaware of the leader's guidance.
Extended parallelism	<u>Extended parallelism</u> describes any unit of *Hebrew Poetry* larger than a couplet in which three or more phrases are placed in parallel. There exits the possibility of thought relationships between any of the phrases in parallel.
Exteriority	One of eight spirituality factors. Describes the outward testimony of a person as perceived by others.
Faith challenge	from leadership emergence theory. One of 51 process items that God uses to shape a leader. A <u>faith challenge</u> refers to those instances in ministry where a leader is challenged to take steps of faith in regards to ministry and sees God meet those steps of faith with divine affirmation and ministry affirmation and often with guidance into on going ministry leading to a focused life.
Figure	A <u>figure</u> is the unusual use of a word or words differing from the normal use in order to draw special attention to some point of interest.
Flesh act	from leadership emergence theory. One of 51 process items that God uses to shape a leader. A <u>flesh act</u> refers to those instances in a leader's life where

Glossary of Leadership Definitions 234

	guidance is presumed and decisions are made either hastily or without proper discernment of God's choice. Such decisions usually involve the working out of guidance by the leader using some human manipulation or other means and which brings ramifications which later negatively affect ministry and life. See Genesis 16 for an example in Abraham's life. See Joshua's treaty with Gibeonites in Jos 9. See Isa 39:4 for Hezekiah's action with Babylonian envoys.
Future perfect paradigm	The future perfect paradigm refers to a way of viewing a future reality as if it were already present which in turn, inspires one's leadership, challenges followers to the vision, affects decision making, and causes one to persevere in faith, which finally results in the future reality coming into being. For leaders who move in revelatory gifts, especially futuristic prophecy and apostolic types, especially with the gift of faith, who must get vision and motivate followers toward it, this is a very necessary paradigm.
Gifted Power	refers to the empowerment of the Holy Spirit when using giftedness; 1Pe 4:11 gives the basic admonition for this to the use of word gifts. It is naturally extended to other areas of giftedness.
Giftedness Discovery	from leadership emergence theory. One of 51 process items that God uses to shape a leader. Giftedness discovery refers to instances in which a leader becomes aware of natural abilities, or acquired skills, or spiritual gifts so as to use them well in ministry. This is a significant advance along the giftedness development pattern.
Giftedness Set	a term describing natural abilities, acquired skills, and spiritual gifts which a leader has as resources to use in ministry. Sometimes shortened to giftedness.
Guidance	from leadership emergence theory. One of 51 process items that God uses to shape a leader. Guidance is the general category which refers to the many ways in which God reveals information that informs a leader about decisions to be made.
Habakkuk's Dilemma	a phrase describing the situation in which Habakkuk's situation seemed to deny the existence and work of God. In general, a situation in which a leader's perspective on a situation he/she faces seems to deny God's existence and working.
Hebrew Poetry	Hebrew Poetry is a way of expressing relationships between parallel thoughts in an emotional language. Usually it is the repetition of phrases in which member of one phrase relate to the members of the other phrase.
Idiom	the use of words to imply something other than their literal meanings. An idiom is a group of words, which have a corporate meaning that cannot be deduced from a compilation of the meanings of the individual words making up the idiom. People in the culture know the idiomatic meaning of the words. Example, I smell a rat. Some idioms are patterned in which case you can reverse the pattern to get the meaning. Others must simply be learned in the culture from contextual usage of them.
Integrity	the top leadership character quality. It is the consistency of inward beliefs and convictions with outward practice. It is an honesty and wholeness of

Glossary of Leadership Definitions

personality in which one operates with a clear conscience in dealings with self and others.

Integrity Check — from leadership emergence theory. One of 51 process items that God uses to shape a leader. The integrity check refers to the special kind of process test which God uses to evaluate heart –intent, consistency between inner convictions and outward actions, and which God uses as a foundation from which to expand the leader's capacity to influence. The word check is used in the sense of test—meaning a check or check-up. See also testing patterns.

Interiority — One of eight spirituality factors. Describes the inward life and relationship with God of a person.

Isolation Processing — from leadership emergence theory. One of 51 process items that God uses to shape a leader. Isolation processing refers to the setting aside of a leader from normal ministry involvement in its natural context usually for an extended time in order to experience God in a new or deeper way.

Issachar Factor — The Issachar Factor refers to that special needed leadership aspect—clarity as to what is happening in the complex situation currently facing a leader and options for addressing the situation.

Leadership Backlash — from leadership emergence theory. One of 51 process items that God uses to shape a leader. The leadership backlash process item refers to the reactions of followers, other leaders within a group, and/or Christians outside the group, to a course of action taken by a leader because of various ramifications that arise due to the action taken. The situation is used in he leader's life to test perseverance, clarity of vision, and faith.

Leadership Challenge — a leadership emergence theory term referring to the shaping process God uses to give a leader an on-going renewal experience about leadership and to direct that leader to some new leadership task.

Leadership Committal — a special shaping activity of God observed in leadership emergence theory which is usually a spiritual benchmark and produces a sense of destiny in a leader. It is the call to leadership by God and the wholehearted response by the leader to accept and abide by that call. Paul's Damascus road experience, the destiny revelation given by Ananias, and Paul's response to it as a life calling provide the New Testament classic example of leadership committal.

Leadership Era — A leadership era is a period of time, usually several hundred years long, in which the major focus of leadership, the influence means, basic leadership functions, and followership have much in common and which basically change with time periods before or after it.

Left hand sensitivity — Left hand sensitivity refers to gaining a perspective on God's use of other nations and groups, apart from those dedicated to His service, to accomplish His purposes.

Macro lesson — A macro-lesson is a high level generalization of a leadership observation (suggestion, guideline, requirement), stated as a lesson, which repeatedly occurs throughout different leadership eras, and thus has potential as a leadership absolute.

Glossary of Leadership Definitions

Mentoring	a relational experience in which one person, the mentor, empowers another person, the mentoree, by sharing God-given resources. See the 9 mentor roles: mentor discipler, mentor spiritual guide, mentor coach, mentor counselor, mentor teacher, mentor sponsor, mentor contemporary model, mentor historical model, mentor divine contact. e.g. The apostle Paul demonstrated many of these roles in his relationships with team members and others in his ministry. See Stanley and Clinton **Connecting** for a popular treatment of mentoring. See Clinton and Clinton **The Mentor Handbook** for a detailed treatment of mentoring.
Mentor Coach	one of nine mentor roles. Coaching is a process of imparting encouragement and skills to succeed in a task via relational training.
Mentor Discipler	one of nine mentor roles. A mentor discipler is one who spends much time, usually one-on-one, with an individual mentoree in order to build into that mentoree the basic habits of the Christian life. It is a relational experience in which a more experienced follower of Christ shares with a less experienced follower of Christ the commitment, understanding, and basic skills necessary to know and obey Jesus Christ as Lord.
Mentor Divine Contact	one of nine mentor roles. A person whose timely intervention is perceived of as from God to give special guidance at an important time in a life. This person may or may not be aware of the intervention and may or may not have any further mentoring connection to the mentoree.
Mentor Spiritual Guide	one of nine mentor roles. A spiritual guide is a godly, mature follower of Christ who shares knowledge, skills, and basic philosophy on what it means to increasingly realize Christlikeness in all areas of life. The primary contributions of a Spiritual guide include accountability, decisions, and insights concerning questions, commitments, and direction affecting spirituality (inner-life motivations) and maturity (integrating truth with life).
Mentor Sponsor	one of nine mentor roles. A mentor sponsor is one who helps promote the ministry (career) of another by using his/her resources, credibility, position, etc. to further the development and acceptance of the mentoree.
Mentor Teacher	one of nine mentor roles. A mentor teacher is one who imparts knowledge and understanding of a particular subject at a time when a mentoree needs it.
Mentor Model (contemporary)	one of nine mentor roles. A mentor contemporary model is a person who models values, methodologies, and other leadership characteristics in such a way as to inspire others to emulate them.
Mentor Model (historical)	one of nine mentor roles. A mentor historical model is a person whose life (autobiographical or biographical input) modeled values, methodologies, and other leadership characteristics in such a way as to inspire others to emulate them.
Metaphor	a figure of speech which involves an implied comparison in which two unlike items (a real item and a picture item) are equated to point out one point of resemblance. e.g. The Lord is my shepherd. These can be simple (all elements present) or complex (verbal metaphor, some element may be

Glossary of Leadership Definitions

	missing and has to be supplied). 2Ti 1:6 stir up the gift is complex, a verbal metaphor. Gift is compared to a flame which has gotten low. Timothy is urged to develop and use with power that gift.
Ministry Task	one of 51 process items that God uses to shape a leader. A ministry task is an assignment from God which primarily tests a person's faithfulness and obedience but often also allows use of ministry gifts in the context of a task which has closure, accountability, and evaluation. e.g. Barnabas trip to Antioch; Titus had 5 ministry tasks.
Modality	a structural time definition. A modality is a structured fellowship, which is a permanent institution reflecting God's work in a given geographical location(s) in which membership is broadly seen as inclusive and makes no distinction between age or sex or whatever.
Negative Preparation	from leadership emergence theory. One of 51 process items that God uses to shape a leader. Negative preparation refers to the special guidance process involving God's use of events, people, conflict, persecution, or experiences, all focusing on the negative, so as to free up a person from the situation in order to enter the next phase of development with a new abandonment and revitalized interest.
Networking Power	a leadership emergence theory term. One of 51 processing items used by God to shape a leader's ministry. It describes how God can connect a leader to resources of all kinds which can come from contacts with people. People provide a bridge, connecting a given leader with other persons or needed resources.
Obedience Check	from leadership emergence theory. One of 51 process items that God uses to shape a leader. An Obedience checks refer to that special category of process items in which God tests personal response to revealed truth in the life of a person.
Other Parallelism	Other parallelism relates to the broad classification of *Hebrew Poetry* not specifically same or different.
Paradigm	a controlling perspective in the mind which allows one to perceive and understand REALITY.
Paradigm Shift	a change of a controlling perspective so that one perceives and understands REALITY in a different way than previously.
Pivotal Point	A pivotal point is a critical time in a leader's life in which processing going on will be responded to in such a way that one of three typical things may happen: The response to this processing can: 1. curtail further use of the leader by God or at least curtail expansion of the leader's potential. 2. limit the eventual use of the leader for ultimate purposes that otherwise could have been accomplished, 3. enhance or open up the leader for expansion or contribution to the ultimate purposes in God's kingdom, that is, it may be a springboard to future expanded use by God of the leader.
Power Encounter	A power encounter identifies a situation in which the power of God is tested over against some other god's power.

Glossary of Leadership Definitions

Power Gifts	a category of spiritual gifts which authenticate the reality of God by demonstrating God's intervention in today's world. These include: tongues, interpretation of tongues, discernings of spirits, kinds of healings, kinds of power (miracles), prophecy, faith, word of wisdom, word of knowledge.
Power Ministry	refers to use of the power gifts to demonstrate God's intervention and often to validate or vindicate a leader's spiritual authority in a situation.
Powershift	a term describing the paradigm shift in which a leader moves from not believing in God's supernatural intervention in ministry to believing it and using it. See Jn 6:1-15; 16-21.
Prayer Power	from leadership emergence theory. One of 51 process items that God uses to shape a leader. Prayer power refers to the specific instance in which God uses the situation to answer prayer and demonstrate the authenticity of the leader's spiritual authority.
Process item	A process item is the technical name in leadership emergence theory describing actual occurrences in a given leader's life including providential events, people, circumstances, special divine interventions, inner-life lessons and other like items which God uses to develop that leader by shaping leadership character, leadership skills, and leadership values.
Progressive calling	the recognition that most leaders will receive on-going leadership challenges from God throughout their lifetimes and not just some initial call; such challenges will bring renewal, divine affirmation, ministry affirmation and will continue to give strategic guidance to a leader's ministry.
Promise from God	A *promise from God* is an assertion from God, specific or general or a truth in harmony with God's character, which is perceived in one's heart or mind concerning what He will do or not do for that one and which is sealed in our inner most being by a quickening action of the Holy Spirit and on which that one then counts.
Prophecy	*Prophecy* refers to the genre of Scripture in which the thrust of the passage is an authoritative revelation from God usually through a spokesperson, called a prophet or prophetess, to correct a given historical situation or to warn of a future situation.
Reduction statement	A reduction statement (sometimes shortened to reduction) is a one line summary statement representing the emphatic meaning of a Hebrew Poetic couplet.
Restoration	Restoration (individual leader) is the process whereby a fallen leader is transitioned back into leadership. It usually involves repentance, restitution where appropriate, correction of the aberrant leadership dysfunctionalities, and recognition by other leaders of the restoration process and their stamp of approval for the leader to renew ministry.
Restoration crisis	The restoration crisis refers to the period of time from 539 B.C. to 430 B.C. and which covers the activity of God in bringing His people back into the land and establishing a testimony there. His providential care of His people (both in the land and outside it) is also shown.

Same parallelism	Same parallelism refers to the type of *Hebrew Poetry* in which members of one phrase relate to members of the parallel phrase in basically the same way.
Simile	a figure of speech, which involves a stated comparison of two unlike items (one called the real item and the other the picture item) in order to display one graphic point of comparison. The words like or so or as or than are used to indicate the stated comparison between the real and picture items. e.g. 1 Pet 2:24 All flesh is as grass.
Sovereign mindset	an attitude demonstrated by the Apostle Paul in which he tended to see God's working in the events and activities that shaped his life, whether or not they were positive and good or negative and bad. He tended to see God's purposes in these shaping activities and to make the best of them.
Spiritual Authority (short)	Spiritual authority is the right to influence, conferred upon a leader by followers, because of their perception of spirituality in that leader.
Spiritual Authority (longer)	Spiritual Authority is that characteristic of a God-anointed leader, developed upon an experiential power base (giftedness, character, deep experiences with God), that enables him/her to influence followers through persuasion, force of modeling, and moral expertise.
Spiritual disciplines	Spiritual disciplines are activities of mind and body purposefully undertaken to bring personality and total being into effective cooperation with the Spirit of God so as to reflect Kingdom life.
Spiritual gifts	a God-given unique capacity which is given to each believer for the purpose of releasing a Holy Spirit empowered ministry either in a situation or to be repeated during the Church Leadership Era. I identify 19 such gifts from a comparative analysis of the 8 major and 16 minor passages about gifts in Scripture. I categorize these 19 in terms of major purposes for the church as Word gifts, Power gifts, and Love gifts. The 19 include: teaching, exhortation, pastoring, evangelism, apostleship, prophecy, ruling, word of wisdom, word of knowledge, faith, miracles, gifts of healings, governments, helps, giving, mercy, tongues, interpretation of tongues, discernings of spirits. All leaders have at least one word gift. See word gifts. See Clinton and Clinton **Unlocking Your Giftedness** for detailed explanation of leadership and spiritual gifts.
Structural time	Structural time refers to an overall perspective for analyzing a work of God in terms of built-in cycles of existence by viewing events, states of development, or some discernible stages from initiation of the cycle until completion of the cycle.
Summary statement	In Hebrew Poetry analysis, a summary statement is a condensed statement of the entire poetic unit. It consists of the subject of the unit and each major idea developed about the subject.
Volitional	also called conative; a learning domain, that is, a term describing learning which primarily focuses on the influencing a person to commit to the things being learned; it wants to bring about volitional compliance—a willingness

	to use what is being learned. Jesus stresses this emphasis in Jn 7:17 and Jn 13-17.
Word Check	from leadership emergence theory. One of 51 process items that God uses to shape a leader. A <u>word</u> <u>check</u> is a process item which tests a leader's ability to understand or receive a word from God personally and to see it worked out in life with a view toward enhancing the authority of God's truth and a desire to know it.

Habakkuk Bibliography

American Bible Society, General Editors
    2001   **The Learning Bible, contemporary English Version.** New York: American Bible Society.

(Bratcher, Robert G. et al)
    n.d.   **Good News Bible—Today's English Version.** New York: American Bible Society.

Clinton, Dr. J. Robert
    1977   **Interpreting The Scriptures: Figures and Idioms.** Altadena, Ca: Barnabas Publishers.

    1986   **Coming to Conclusions On Leadership Styles.** Altadena, Ca: Barnabas Publishers.

    1986   **Short History of Leadership Theory**, 1986, by Dr. J. Robert Clinton. Altadena, CA: Barnabas Publishers.

    1989   *The Ultimate Contribution.* Altadena, Ca: Barnabas Publishers.

    1989   **The Making of A Leader.** Colorado Springs: NavPress.

    1989   **Leadership Emergence Theory.** Altadena, Ca: Barnabas Publishers.

    1993   **The Bible and Leadership Values.** Altadena, Ca: Barnabas Publishers.

    1993   **Leadership Perspectives.** Altadena, Ca: Barnabas Publishers.

    1995   *The Life Cycle of a Leader.* Altadena, Ca: Barnabas Publishers.

    1997   **Having A Ministry That Lasts.** Altadena, Ca: Barnabas Publishers.

Clinton, Dr. J. Robert and Dr. Richard W.
    1993   **Unlocking Your Giftedness—What Leaders Need To Know To Develop Themselves and Others.** Altadena, Ca: Barnabas Publishers.

Davis, Stanley B. Davis,
    1982   *Transforming Organizations: The Key To Strategy Is Context* in **Organizational Dynamics.**

    1987   **Future Perfect.** New York: Addison-Wesley, 1987.

Kuhn, Thomas
    1970   **The Structure of Scientific Revolutions.** Chicago: University of Chicago Press.

Mickelsen, A. Berkley
    1963   **Interpreting The Bible.** Grand Rapids: Eerdmans Publishing Company.

Mintzberg, Henry
    1983   **Structure in Fives – Designing Effective Organizations.** NJ: Prentice-Hall.

Bibliography

Pusey, E. B. D.D.,
    1907   **The Minor Prophets With a Commentary, Vol. VI, Habakkuk and Malachi**, London: James Nisbet and Co.

Strong, James
    1890   **The Exhaustive Concordance of the Bible** (with Dictionaries of the Hebrew and Greek Words). Nashville: Abingdon Press.

(Taylor, Ken did original version; other Bible scholars the new version)
    1996   **Holy Bible—New Living Translation**. Wheaton, Il: Tyndale house Publishers, Inc.

Terry, Milton S. (2nd edition)
    1964   **Biblical Hermeneutics.** Grand Rapids: Zondervan.

Tippett, Alan
    1967   **Solomon Island Christianity**. Pasadena: William Carey Library.

Wrong, Dennis
    1979   **Power—Its Forms, Bases, and Uses**. San Francisco, CA: Harper and Row.

| CLINTON'S BIBLICAL LEADERSHIP COMMENTARY SERIES | Habakkuk Hope For A Leader In Troubled Times |

About the Leadership Commentary Series

Dr. Clinton has studied each of the books of the Bible from a leadership persective. His book, **The Bible and Leadership Values**, contains that initial research on the Bible. From this study he has selected the top 25 books that contribute much to leadership thought. From a leadership standpoint, Dr. Clinton comments on the text. He defines leadership concepts which shed light on the leadership implications in the text. Further, Dr. Clinton writes short leadership articles, which further suggest the importance of Biblical insights for leadership. **Titus—Apostolic Leadership,** is the first of the series to be published in paper back. Thirteen others previously in draft manuscript, are forthcoming as E-books. Nehemiah is the first in E-book form. Habakkuk is the second.

About the Author

Dr. J. Robert (Bobby) Clinton is Professor of Leadership at the School of World Mission of Fuller Theological Seminary. He has coordinated the leadership concentration in the School of World Mssion for more than 20 years. Bobby models and teaches the concepts of lifelong development and of the focused life, as well as the importance of mentoring to develop leaders. Before coming to Fuller, he and his wife, Marilyn, served as missionaries for Worldteam in Jamaica. His writings include numerous biblical examples of leadership development. His publications include: **The Making of A Leader; Leadership Emergence Theory; Connecting—Mentoring Relationships; The Mentor Handbook; Focused Lives; Strategic Concepts— That Clarify a Focused Life;** and **Having a Ministry That Lasts—By Becoming a Bible Centered Leader**. Currently Bobby is writing on 5 other leadership commentaries, part of the top 25 biblical books on leadership.

BARNABAS PUBLISHER'S MINI CATALOG

Approaching the Bible With Leadership Eyes: An Authoratative Source for Leadership Findings — Dr. J. Robert Clinton
Barnabas: Encouraging Exhorter — Dr. J. Robert Clinton & Laura Raab
Boundary Processing: Looking at Critical Transitions Times in Leader's Lives — Dr. J. Robert Clinton
Connecting: The Mentoring Relationships You Need to Succeed in Life — Dr. J. Robert Clinton
The Emerging Leader — Dr. J. Robert Clinton
Fellowship With God — Dr. J. Robert Clinton
Finishing Well — Dr. J. Robert Clinton
Figures and Idioms (Interpreting the Scriptures: Figures and Idioms) — Dr. J. Robert Clinton
Focused Lives Lectures — Dr. J. Robert Clinton
Gender and Leadership — Dr. J. Robert Clinton
Having A Ministry That Lasts: By Becoming a Bible Centered Leader — Dr. J. Robert Clinton
Hebrew Poetry (Interpreting the Scriptures: Hebrew Poetry) — Dr. J. Robert Clinton
A Short **History of Leadership Theory** — Dr. J. Robert Clinton
Isolation: A Place of Transformation in the Life of a Leader — Shelley G. Trebesch
Joseph: Destined to Rule — Dr. J. Robert Clinton
The Joshua Portrait — Dr. J. Robert Clinton and Katherine Haubert
Leadership Emergence Theory: A Self Study Manual For Analyzing the Development of a Christian Leader — Dr. J. Robert Clinton
Leadership Perspectives: How To Study The Bible for Leadership Insights — Dr. J. Robert Clinton
Coming to Some Conclusions on **Leadership Styles** — Dr. J. Robert Clinton
Leadership Training Models — Dr. J. Robert Clinton
The Bible and **Leadership Values:** A Book by Book Analysis— Dr. J. Robert Clinton
The Life Cycle of a Leader: Looking at God's Shaping of A LeaderTowards An Eph. 2:10 Life — Dr. J. Robert Clinton
Listen Up Leaders! — Dr. J. Robert Clinton
The Mantle of the Mentor — Dr. J. Robert Clinton
Mentoring Can Help—Five Leadership Crises You Will Face in the Pastorate For Which You Have Not Been Trained — Dr. J. Robert Clinton
Mentoring: Developing Leaders... Without Adding More Programs — Dr. J. Robert Clinton
The Mentor Handbook: Detailed Guidelines and Helps for Christian Mentors and Mentorees — Dr. J. Robert Clinton
Moses Desert Leadership—7 Macro Lessons
Parables—Puzzles With A Purpose (Interpreting the Scriptures: Puzzles With A Purpose) — Dr. J. Robert Clinton
Paradigm Shift: God's Way of Opening New Vistas To Leaders — Dr. J. Robert Clinton
A Personal Ministry Philosophy: One Key to Effective Leadership — Dr. J. Robert Clinton
Reading on the Run: Continuum Reading Concepts — Dr. J. Robert Clinton
Samuel: Last of the Judges & First of the Prophets–A Model For Transitional Times — Bill Bjoraker
Selecting and Developing Those Emerging Leaders — Dr. Richard W. Clinton
Social Base Processing: The Home Base Environment Out of Which A Leader Works — Dr. J. Robert Clinton
Starting Well: Building A Strong Foundation for a Life Time of Ministry — Dr. J. Robert Clinton
Strategic Concepts: That Clarify A Focused Life – A Self Study Guide — Dr. J. Robert Clinton
The Making of a Leader: Recognizing the Lessons & Stages of Leadership Development — Dr. J. Robert Clinton
Time Line —Small Paper (What it is & How to Construct it) — Dr. J. Robert Clinton
Time Line: Getting Perspective—By Using Your Time-Line, Large Paper — Dr. J. Robert Clinton
Ultimate Contribution — Dr. J. Robert Clinton
Unlocking Your Giftedness: What Leaders Need to Know to Develop Themselves & Others — Dr. J. Robert Clinton
A **Vanishing Breed:** Thoughts About A Bible Centered Leader & A Life Long Bible Mastery Paradigm — Dr. J. Robert Clinton
The Way To Look At Leadership (How To Look at Leadership) — Dr. J. Robert Clinton
Webster-Smith, Irene: An Irish Woman Who Impacted Japan (A Focused Life Study) — Dr. J. Robert Clinton
Word Studies (Interpreting the Scriptures: Word Studies) — Dr. J. Robert Clinton

(Book Titles are in Bold and Paper Titles are in Italics with Sub-Titles and Pre-Titles in Roman)

BARNABAS PUBLISHERS

Unique Leadership Material that will help you answer the question: "What legacy will you as a leader leave behind?"

"The difference between leaders and followers is perspective. The difference between leaders and effective leaders is better perspective."
Barnabas Publishers has the materials that will help you find that better perspective and a closer relationship with God.

BARNABAS PUBLISHERS
Post Office Box 6006 • Altadena, CA 91003-6006
Fax Phone (626)-794-3098

www.ingramcontent.com/pod-product-compliance
Lightning Source LLC
Chambersburg PA
CBHW080448170426
43196CB00016B/2720